AF736806

Leadership for Lawyers

Essential Leadership Strategies
for Law Firm Success
Second Edition

Consulting Editors **Heidi K Gardner** and
Rebecca Normand-Hochman
on behalf of the International Bar Association

Consulting editors
Heidi K Gardner, Rebecca Normand-Hochman

Managing director
Sian O'Neill

***Leadership for Lawyers: Essential Leadership Strategies for Law Firm Success, Second Edition*
is published by**

Globe Law and Business Ltd
3 Mylor Close
Horsell
Woking
Surrey GU21 4DD
United Kingdom
Tel: +44 20 3745 4770
www.globelawandbusiness.com

Leadership for Lawyers: Essential Leadership Strategies for Law Firm Success, Second Edition

ISBN 9781787422865
EPUB ISBN 9781787422872
Adobe PDF ISBN 9781787422889
Mobi ISBN 9781787422896

© 2019 Globe Law and Business Ltd except where otherwise indicated.

All rights reserved. No part of this publication may be reproduced in any material form (including photocopying, storing in any medium by electronic means or transmitting) without the written permission of the copyright owner, except in accordance with the provisions of the Copyright, Designs and Patents Act 1988 or under terms of a licence issued by the Copyright Licensing Agency Ltd, 6–10 Kirby Street, London EC1N 8TS, United Kingdom (www.cla.co.uk, email: licence@cla.co.uk). Applications for the copyright owner's written permission to reproduce any part of this publication should be addressed to the publisher.

DISCLAIMER
This publication is intended as a general guide only. The information and opinions which it contains are not intended to be a comprehensive study, or to provide legal advice, and should not be treated as a substitute for legal advice concerning particular situations. Legal advice should always be sought before taking any action based on the information provided. The publishers bear no responsibility for any errors or omissions contained herein.

FSC www.fsc.org MIX Paper from responsible sources FSC® C013604

Table of contents

Introduction

Heidi K Gardner
Harvard Law School
Rebecca Normand-Hochman
Institute of Legal Talent & Leadership

When our publisher asked us to consider a second edition of this book because the first one had done so well, we accepted this new challenge with great enthusiasm. In our seven years of collaborating on various projects, working on this book has been one of the richest ways to combine our thinking about how the latest research insights can help lawyers address some of their most complex leadership challenges.

Let's face it: lawyers face specific challenges in the area of leadership. The way they are trained, their organisational cultures and firms' systems that affect their day-to-day work, as well as the highly technical nature of their expertise all make dealing with the strategic and human issues more complex (and sometimes less appealing) than in many other sectors. But their sharp cognitive capabilities also present fascinating opportunities to grow leadership potential at every stage of lawyers' careers, in a business context that needs it more than ever before.

These challenges and opportunities are what inspire us in our work, and what we have tried to convey throughout this book – with the insights of many accomplished contributors. We have combined our backgrounds in the law, academia, consulting and coaching, and we also had the privilege to include some of the best experts on the most important and fast-changing aspects of leadership.

To be clear, throughout this book we take the point of view that leadership permeates the firm. Every partner is a *de facto* leader of a law firm. In the best firms that are equipped to handle today's dynamic environment, leadership responsibilities also flow across roles, functions and disciplines. By taking an inclusive view of leadership, we aim to help firms draw on the full range of capabilities and perspectives that are vital in our fast-changing world.

What is new in the second edition? A number of completely new chapters introduce topics that today's law firm leaders are grappling with. For example, "Leading law firms in the digital age" lays out practical, research-based steps for effectively guiding through the technological transformation that is sweeping across the legal arena. The "Succession planning" chapter likewise addresses a burning need in the profession: nearly all firms are facing a partnership with many people approaching retirement age, yet few firms have structured processes in place to address client, leadership and financial transitions. Given the pace of consolidation in the legal industry, many leaders will need to draw on insights from the chapters "Building consensus for a merger" and "Leading merger integration".

In our work, we have clearly heard about the pressures of steering a firm in today's increasingly competitive landscape; we chose to include the new chapter "Leading and creating a rainforest" because it demonstrates a practical approach to building a business development culture, which is more sustainable than relying on individual stars. What characteristics do leaders need? The chapter on "Authentic gravitas" lays out the underlying research and practical steps for developing key components including influence, connection and wisdom. "Leading lawyers in a VUCA world" combines recent findings on the behavioural aspects of leadership with research about lawyers' personalities to shed light on the psychological barriers to leadership in the legal world – and finishes with a practical roadmap for mitigating those obstacles.

Beyond the brand new chapters, all the rest have been updated to include the most advanced thinking on their topics. The "Leadership and decision-making in emerging legal markets" chapter addresses the critical juncture when firms are becoming more institutionalised and transitioning to non-founder leaders. The "Generations in the workplace" and "Successfully hiring leaders" chapters bring fresh perspectives on the essential demands of attracting, retaining and engaging the best talent. "Leading teams of lawyers in an increasingly global and virtual world" helps firms to make the most of their talent that is dispersed in different locations – a trend that has radically increased since the first edition. Finally, the chapters "Leadership, power and politics" and "Learning to lead" help firms navigate these perennially important issues.

We hope that this book will challenge your thinking and inspire you to cultivate a leadership mindset for yourself and for those around you. We also hope that it will help you face the challenges and embrace the opportunities that will cross your path as a leader in the future.

If you have any success stories or particular issues that you would like to share with us, we invite you to contact us (heidi@gardnerandco.co; r.normand-hochman@legaltalentandleadership.org).

Leading lawyers in a VUCA world

Heidi K Gardner
Harvard Law School
Rebecca Normand-Hochman
Institute of Legal Talent & Leadership
Larry Richard
LawyerBrain LLC

1. Introduction

Law firms are under pressure not only to add value to their clients' legal matters, but also to deliver a holistic and contextualised solution to their wider business problems. Clients increasingly describe these business problems – everything from digital disruption to data privacy concerns – with the term 'VUCA': volatile, uncertain, complex, and ambiguous. Their VUCA problems are so complicated that only teams of experts can solve them. Yet, law firms have separated their highly specialised experts into narrowly defined practice groups, and collaborating across these silos is often messy, risky and costly.

In response, sophisticated firms are moving fast to adopt agile methodologies across business units and to increase accountability for budgets and forecasts – among other strategic initiatives. This monumental change in task and responsibility requires lawyers to alter the way they operate. For law firms to deliver on their promise of superior client service, they need to collaborate more and better, adopt innovative technology, and embrace valuable skillsets outside of pure legal ones (eg, operations, data scientists, pricing specialists, marketing and business development professionals and leadership).

Achieving such a revolution requires firms to distinguish leadership from management – and then work on developing both sets of competencies and making sure that people optimally (or even adequately) perform the respective duties. Between the three co-authors, we have about five decades of experience researching, advising and working in law firms, and we have seen first-hand how much impact great leaders can have on both commercial and human outcomes. And to be clear: our strong belief is that all partners are *de facto* leaders, regardless of whether or not they hold a formal title. On the flip side, we have also seen too many cases where lawyers with a strong sense of urgency who, under pressure to deliver short-term results, focus on tactical management tasks and abdicate their leadership responsibilities.

Given the complexity of their clients' VUCA problems, it is more important than ever for law firms to adapt with strong leaders at the helm. This chapter clarifies the core differences lawyers need to understand between leadership and management, defines the specific leadership behaviours (not style) lawyers need to develop, outlines the psychological barriers that prevent many lawyers from naturally acting as leaders and presents practical strategies on how to engage people, set direction and foster collaboration in law firms.

2. Distinguishing leadership from management – and why it matters

The difference between management and leadership has been the subject of much debate since 1977 when Harvard Business School professor Abraham Zaleznik published a Harvard Business Review article titled "Managers and Leaders: Are they Different?".[1] In this piece, Zaleznik argued that leadership – contrary to management – was about inspiration, vision and messy human nature. As Harvard Business School professor John Kotter later argued, management is about responding to complexity: to get a job done, managers must focus on control and predictability and they must organise processes that will produce orderly outcomes. Planning, budgeting and staffing are all management activities.[2]

By contrast, leadership is about responding to change. Leaders see opportunities in the instabilities and they emphasise ideas over process. Setting direction, aligning people and providing motivation are all leadership activities. Kotter argues that management and leadership are complementary modes of being and need not be in conflict. The most successful leaders in today's challenging business environment leverage both management and leadership competencies selectively to benefit their firm.

Unfortunately, the very characteristics that make for great lawyering tend to make for poor leadership, lacklustre collaboration and virtually no true innovation. Partners with true leadership competencies are hard to come by because the skills and tasks are nebulous, discreet, and traditionally not part of lawyers' training or way of thinking. For example, creating a shared vision, building trust and providing recognition are all hard to quantify and difficult – indeed, nearly impossible – to definitively complete. Alternatively, managers cope with complexity in often quantifiable terms and tasks. Making a checklist and then crossing off completed tasks is significantly easier and more instantly gratifying. While both leaders and managers are vital to the sustainability of a firm and provide complementary, interdependent functions that all partners need to be skilled at, the differentiation has dramatic consequences for how effectively a firm is run.

1 Adam Zaleknik, "Managers and Leaders: Are They Different?", *Harvard Business Review*, 1977.
2 John Kotter, "What Leaders Really Do", *Harvard Business Review*, 2001.

3. Leadership behaviours for lawyers in a VUCA world

As leaders, lawyers have to navigate a complex landscape of new behavioural competencies to help others do their best and succeed. By communicating strategy, supporting career development, facilitating collaboration and ensuring that processes are aligned with the firm's goals, senior lawyers are required to demonstrate leadership capabilities that are not easy to develop (for reasons explained in section 5 of this chapter).

When they invest in their growth as leaders, lawyers begin to measure their success by the value and innovation they generate for their firm. They find their reward not only in their own performance or their team's performance but also in the environment that surrounds their firm's success. Like engineers, lawyers hate being micromanaged on the technical side but they thrive when they are closely guided on the career side. By examining data from employee surveys and performance reviews, Google's people analytics team[3] identified eight key behaviours demonstrated by the company's most effective managers and leaders (those managers and leaders were all engineers and had the producer and manager roles in the same way as lawyers have). According to this research, a good leader:

1. Is a good coach;
2. Empowers the team and does not micromanage;
3. Expresses interest in and concern for team members' success and personal well-being;
4. Is productive and results-oriented;
5. Is a good communicator – listens and shares information;
6. Helps with career development;
7. Has a clear vision and strategy for the team; and
8. Has key technical skills that help him or her advise the team.

Do you think most lawyers would formulate the leadership behaviours required from them in this way? From our experience, probably not. But without a doubt, these eight behaviours are essential for senior lawyers to embed in their day-to-day practice of law.

We often think of leadership as requiring a set of innate traits such as self-confidence, vision, or charisma. In the past, people with all of these traits were deemed 'born leaders' or 'natural leaders'. But as science has revealed the plasticity of the human brain, we no longer think about these qualities as inborn or fixed. Instead, leadership is seen as a variety of skills that can be learned and capacities that can be nurtured over time.

---

3 David A Garvin, "How Google Sold Its Engineers on Management", *Harvard Business Review*, 2013.

Try this:

With the questions below, assess which of your leadership traits are most valuable in your role and to your firm's culture.

Then think about your own self-image as a leader and how you want others to see you. This will help you identify what strengths to leverage and where you have an opportunity to improve:

- Are you well informed about your market, your clients' business, and your priorities? (being informed)
- Do you organise short-term tasks according to long-term priorities? (being future-focused)
- Do you make decisions even if all the facts are not available? (being decisive)
- Can you operate in uncertain environments with few dependable guideposts? Do you adapt well to change? (being comfortable with ambiguity)
- Do you pay attention to how your behaviour affects others? (being self-aware)
- Do you maintain a positive, focused perspective and continue to lead during turmoil and confusion? (being steady)
- Are your actions consistent with your values? Do you keep promises? (being trustworthy)
- Do you work well and frequently with your peers and your team members to deliver outstanding collective results? (being collaborative)
- Do you listen closely, find common ground, and express yourself clearly to persuade and influence outcomes in the organisation? (being influential)
- Do you understand your organisation's power structure? Do you grasp how key players think? Do you know where to turn for support and resources? (being politically astute)
- Do you challenge the status quo? Do you convince others to set high standards and stretch goals? (being stimulating)[4]

4. Leadership competencies that lawyers need in practice

Leadership doesn't require formal authority, but rather a number of competencies that need to be developed throughout lawyers' careers. Each requires lifelong practice. The essential leadership skills that lawyers need can all be captured in the following 11 competencies:

1. **Growing a strategic mindset:** As lawyers gain in experience and seniority, they transition from individual contributor to manager and

4 Adapted from Harvard Business Reviews' Manager's Handbook, *The 17 Skills that Leaders Need to Stand Out* (Harvard Business Review Press, 2017).

leader, and start viewing problems and measuring success in new ways. They need to understand how they and their team fit into the bigger picture of their firm and its wider strategic objectives.

2. **Working with emotional intelligence:** Emotional intelligence is the ability to accurately perceive our own and others' emotions, to understand the signals that emotions send about relationships and to manage your own and others' emotions. Since the idea of emotional intelligence was introduced in the 1990s, it's become essential to how we think about leadership.[5]
3. **Building trust:** Trust is a combination of our values and competence and is a crucial element of leadership. It is built by showing that we value others by giving them a voice, recognising them for their achievements, regulating our emotions toward them, and showing respect.[6]
4. **Developing influence:** Influence is the ability to persuade others and have a positive impact on decisions, plans and results. It is a combination of two kinds of power: positional power (which comes from our role) and personal power (which comes from cultivating relationships). Leaders need to convince others to follow and to endorse their ideas; and they also need to be able to advocate effectively for their people in order to both keep their trust and also enhance the work that they can do for the firm.
5. **Communicating effectively:** To succeed, leaders need to be able to capture and keep people's attention. We're accustomed to thinking that great communicators have a special kind of charisma. But charisma isn't a magic trait that some people have and some people don't. Becoming a masterful communicator is possible for anyone who learns the set of behaviours.
6. **Delegating with confidence:** Delegating is about ensuring the right people are doing the right work, at the right time, and in the right way. The most effective leaders spend less time 'doing' and more time organising resources and coaching people to achieve their best possible results. While senior lawyers never get away from 'doing', the goal is to ensure that the work that they do is high priority and high impact for the firm.
7. **Self-development:** For lawyers' careers to be fulfilling, it's important that they actively manage their own growth. Too often, lawyers assume that if they work hard, their career will unfold the way they hope. But because of the fast pace of global innovation and change, professionals

---

5 For the seminal writing on this topic, see Daniel Goleman, *Emotional Intelligence: Why It Can Matter More Than IQ* (Bantam books, 1996).

6 For information on eight 'oxytocin-producing' behaviours that build trust, see Paul Zak, *Trust Factor: The Science of Creating High-Performance Companies* (American Management Association, 2017).

must update their skills and broaden their abilities more frequently than ever before.[7]

8. **Giving effective feedback:** Leaders need to give regular feedback to their constituents. Doing so is critical to the success of both. Positive feedback reinforces good work. Praise and coaching can create trust and create powerful connections that build respect. Corrective feedback urges the recipient to change course or adjust practices that aren't working. Lawyers, even experienced supervisors, often dread these conversations. But when handled well, these conversations produce real change in people's behaviours, skills and outcomes.
9. **Developing talent:** The role of leaders is to develop talent that meets the needs of the business. It is fundamentally future-oriented, ensuring the teams can deliver exceptional performance both today and tomorrow. Feedback aims to improve performance now, but talent development expands people's capacities for the future. The best leaders know how to balance the needs of the organisation with the interests of their people.
10. **Recruiting and retaining the best lawyers:** Leaders' role is to bring the best and most promising lawyers into the firm, to actively help these lawyers find their place, create opportunities for them to develop and to maintain their motivation over time.
11. **Fostering collaboration:** Collaborating is vital to a firm's success, requiring lawyers to actively generate trust and credibility across sectors and jurisdictions. Clients want their lawyers to understand their issues deeply enough to offer sophisticated advice and to line up the right legal team to deliver it – no matter where in the firm the needed experts reside. Collaborative leaders strengthen clients' loyalty to the firm and provide juniors with an increased opportunity to learn and demonstrate new capabilities. Each of these aspects, in turn, enhances the retention of high-performing associates, young partners and clients.

4.1 How leadership competencies develop

For most of us, leadership competencies develop in three stages of our experience and career:

Leadership foundation[8] is built during the first part of a lawyer's career. It is measured by the degree to which associates are able to manage their careers, are rewarding to deal with and have good organisational sensitivity. It requires them to follow process, think broadly and to get along.

---

7 Antonin Besse, *The Lawyer as a Leader: How to own your career and lead in law firms* (Globe Law and Business, 2019).

8 Adapted from Hogan's High Potential Assessment Talent Report.

Figure 1: Stages of leadership development

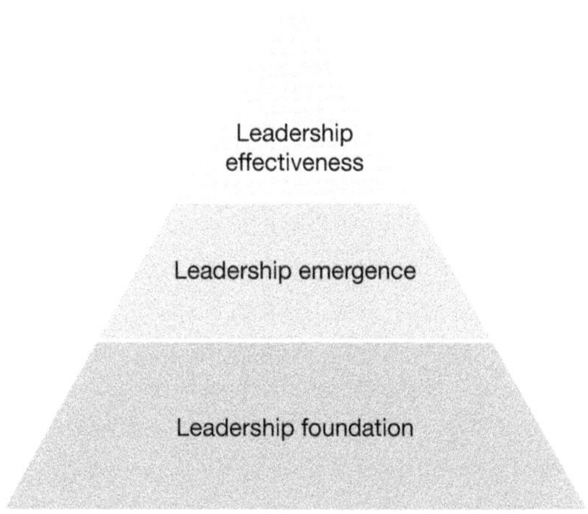

Leadership emergence starts to appear after a few years of practice; it is measured by the likelihood that someone will stand out, emerge and be labelled as a "high potential or emerging leader" in their firm.

Lawyers having developed these behaviours: stand out, influence others, build strategic networks and relationships.

Leadership effectiveness is only reached by a small number of lawyers in practice. It is measured by the ability to successfully guide teams and lead a department or a firm towards productive outcomes. Truly effective leaders are life-long learners; they engage in formal leadership development programmes such as training and individual coaching, they practise their competencies day in and day out, proactively seek regular feedback from multiple sources, and use those inputs to modify and improve their leadership competencies. Lawyers who become effective leaders lead the business, manage the firm's resources and lead large teams.

5. Psychological barriers

Given that the core elements of leadership are quite basic – set a direction and mobilise others to follow in that direction – and given that lawyers are generally highly intelligent, why is it so hard for lawyer-leaders to adopt effective leadership practices?

There may be many reasons, but based on the research of one of our co-authors, individuals who become lawyers have certain atypical, 'outlier' personality traits, and these traits mostly help those individuals practice high-quality law. However, those very same advantageous traits can become significant disadvantages when a lawyer shifts from the 'lawyer' role to the 'leadership' or 'collaboration' roles.

This research shows that there are seven distinct outlier traits that characterise most lawyers and set them apart from other members of the general public. Let's look at each one and the impact it has on leadership effectiveness, and then we'll review several tips on what lawyer-leaders can do about this dilemma.

Personality traits are represented as percentiles on a zero-to-100% scale. For example, a common trait like 'extroversion' might be reported as follows: "Individual X has a 75% extroversion score." That means that individual X is more extroverted than 75% of the base population.[9] In a typical sample of any occupational group, the scores for any personality trait are distributed in a bell curve, with any given trait averaging at the 50th percentile for the group. On average, two-thirds of such a group will score within the middle of the bell curve. But every now and then, an occupational group will have one or two personality traits that are so distinctive for that occupation that the average for those traits falls outside the middle area – either below average or above average.

When it comes to lawyers, however, the data shows a dramatic departure from the bell curve distribution that we see in the general public. In the assessment tool that we use,[10] lawyers have seven outlier traits out of a total of the 18 traits measured by the tool. We've been unable to find any other occupation that shows such a departure. What are these traits, and how do they impact leadership and collaboration?

High scepticism: Scepticism is defined as a high level of vigilance, even suspicion, about data, assertions, and people's motives. A person scoring high on this trait questions suggestions or assertions by others, is reluctant to give the benefit of the doubt, may focus more on what's wrong or what could go wrong than on what's working, and may hunt for possible ulterior motives when dealing with others. A low-scoring individual is generally trusting, accepting of others, gives the benefit of the doubt, and is open and approachable.

As you might imagine, lawyers tend to score very high on this trait. It's the central cognitive tool in the practice of high-quality law. Lawyers are professional sceptics, and they exercise that trait in order to protect their clients. Many of the very best lawyers are highly sceptical.

9 More precisely, it means that individual X is more extroverted than 75% of the 'norm group' – the reference group that psychologists use to make these kinds of comparisons. Norm groups are used for these kinds of comparisons because they're easier to work with than an entire population, and they can be more precisely measured in ways that account for and reduce possible sources of distortion.

10 The Caliper Profile.

While that makes perfect sense within the context of practising law, the roles of leadership and collaboration require just the opposite. Leadership is an inherently interpersonal role. In a world of unprecedented change, leaders can never fully reassure their constituents that a chosen direction is guaranteed to be the right one. Hence, all leaders must build trust among their constituents in order to gain their followership. This calls for the very opposite of scepticism – a trusting, accepting, open-minded approach. While it's theoretically possible for the highly sceptical lawyer to dial it back when shifting into a leadership role, in our experience this type of agility is quite rare.

High autonomy: Most people don't like to be told what to do. But our data shows that lawyers take this to an art form. Lawyers have a preternaturally high need for autonomy – to not have others telling them what to do. In the days when the amount of legal specialisation was minimal, and a lawyer could easily practise as a generalist, this highly independent quality worked well. But in today's complex world, where, as noted above, the problems are more complex, and yet most lawyers have become so specialised that they function in silos, collaboration is becoming increasingly essential. The high levels of autonomy seen in most lawyers act as an inhibitor to collaboration.

In subtle ways, it can also stifle effective leadership. Leadership experts Jim Kouzes and Barry Posner tell us that based on their 30 years of research, they've concluded that leadership is fundamentally based on relationships.[11] Autonomy, when practised to an extreme, can be isolating, not relationship-building. To this point, Harvard Business Review published a study by Shawn Achor *et al* in April 2018 that found that practising law ranks as the occupation with the greatest level of loneliness that they studied.[12]

High urgency: Lawyers are dispositionally more impatient ('high urgency') than the public in general. They may finish other people's sentences, or push towards artificial deadlines. While this serves them well in their 'lawyer' role – it helps them be responsive to clients, which clients clearly want – this very same urgency undercuts both effective leadership and collaboration. Leaders need to build buy-in for their initiatives, a task that's much more readily accomplished by a leader who patiently listens to the ideas of others and engages in a give-and-take, and less likely when a 'cut to the chase' motif is employed.

Likewise, collaboration is built on cultivating relationships. Urgency is not on anyone's list as a relationship builder.

---

11 Jim Kouzes and Barry Posner, *The Truth about Leadership: The No-fads, Heart-of-the-Matter Facts You Need to Know* (Jossey-Bass, New York, 2010).

12 Shawn Achor, Gabriella Rosen Kellerman, Andrew Reece and Alexi Robichaux, "America's Loneliest Workers, According to Research", *Harvard Business Review*, March 2018.

High abstract reasoning: Lawyers enjoy intellectual challenge. They like solving difficult problems, thinking abstractly, being mentally stimulated. The law provides ample opportunity to meet this need. However, the same type of analytical thinking can be a turn-off when trying to build collaborative relationships. The same thing holds true when highly analytical lawyers try to gain buy-in with their constituents using an analytical style. This is best illustrated by the old axiom, "I want to know how much you care before I care how much you know."

Low sociability: Sociability measures the inclination that an individual has to initiate intimate, authentic connections with another human being. High sociability individuals are willing to be self-disclosing and vulnerable in order to deepen a new relationship. They're interested in the human details of another's life, and tend to track and remember those details. They share their own private details. Low sociability individuals are much more private and even guarded. They may be reluctant to initiate authentic connections, preferring to stick with those for which they've already done the hard work of building the relationship. At the extreme, low sociability individuals see anything having to do with 'relationships' as automatically suspect, as soft, or as 'touchy-feely' and readily dismissed. Our data shows that lawyers are remarkably low on this trait.

While low sociability does not confer any obvious advantages on lawyers, it certainly doesn't impede the effective practice of law for most practitioners. Yes, it may inhibit the ability to develop business, but there are other ways to do so besides building relationships.

However, when it comes to leadership and collaboration, both absolutely depend on relationship skills, and those dispositionally uncomfortable with using those skills need to figure out how to do so anyway.

Low resilience: Resilience, as a personality trait, is a measure of how thick- or thin-skinned a person is in the face of criticism, rejection or other setbacks. High resilience individuals are durable. They tolerate life's bumps well, and when they hit one, they generally take it in their stride and recover quickly. Low resilience individuals are more sensitive and easily hurt, wounded, or set back. They readily become defensive, and often try to explain their criticised behaviour. They feel bad. They sulk and ruminate. And it takes them a long time to recover from a perceived criticism or rejection. Lawyers are remarkably low in resilience. Consistently, over the past 25 years, 90% of the lawyers we measure score in the bottom half of the scale for this trait! Research suggests that both an optimistic attitude and a strong, ongoing set of authentic relationships can build resilience. Lawyers generally have neither. Most lawyers are more sceptical and pessimistic than trusting and optimistic. And, as noted above, most lawyers are awkward and uncomfortable around intimacy and connecting, eschewing the formation of new relationships.

Low resilience doesn't really help one to be a better lawyer. Unlike high scepticism, urgency, or abstract reasoning, which help one practice high-quality law, low resilience is a common lawyer trait not because it serves a positive purpose, but rather more likely because it's simply a negative by-product of the high scepticism and low sociability that characterise most lawyers.

More importantly, low resilience plays havoc with both leadership and collaboration. As a general rule, leaders tend to be targets of criticism far more than other people. Good leaders stick their necks out, they take risks. And sometimes they pay the price by drawing fire from others. If a leader is low in resilience and they react defensively to this very predictable criticism, they will lose followership.

Low resilience also undermines collaboration. The low resilience individual (as well as the highly sceptical individual) sees the downside of collaborating. To the low resilience lawyer, bringing other lawyers into a matter is always fraught with social risk – low resilience lawyers often generate negative thoughts, such as "they might poach my client"; or "they might discover that I'm not as competent as I appear". And low resilience lawyers may become jealous of any contact that another lawyer has with their client.

Low empathy: We noted earlier the importance of "taking the client perspective". When an individual is low in empathy, that's exactly the skill that's missing or diminished. Low empathy lawyers (and lawyers are, on average, about 12 to 15% less empathic than the average score of the general public) are less likely to see the advantages of collaboration, are less likely to understand how to motivate other lawyers and are less likely to build and sustain rapport with others.

So what are lawyers to do about the dilemma outlined above? Specifically, because many of the individuals who are drawn to the legal profession also possess outlier personality traits that equip them to be effective as lawyers, but those very same traits inhibit them from effectively leading or collaborating. Therefore, the better they are as lawyers, the harder it is for them to be effective as leaders, and thus the harder it is to get others to collaborate.

Our experience, and some research, suggests that among the seven traits described above, both empathy and resilience represent the 'low-hanging fruit' of performance improvement. While both are traits, they both also can be seen as learnable behaviours. There is an ample and growing body of scientific literature on how to build psychological resilience through the repetitive rehearsal of several simple cognitive strategies.[13]

Empathy can be increased through the simple expedient of training yourself to pay more attention to the needs, interests and likely reactions of others

13 We recommend the excellent book *The Resilience Factor* by Karen Reivich and Andrew Shatte as a self-help guide to building psychological resilience.

before you act yourself. There are a number of more formal empathy training methods, most of which involve inviting an individual to consider a number of scenarios and to work at guessing what the protagonist needs in order to accomplish a stated goal. Practice over time, coupled with high-quality feedback, can increase one's empathy capacity. Perhaps the most interesting technique for building empathy was reported in the journal Science in 2013.[14] The researchers found that individuals who read high-quality literary novels were more empathic.

Finally, leaders are well advised to consider taking a high-quality, reliable and valid personality assessment and obtaining feedback about their own personality traits. Self-awareness is the first step in being able to manage and adjust your traits so that they serve you best across the various roles you play in today's increasingly complex world.

6. Practical roadmap

6.1 What potential do we have to develop leadership competencies?

Technical expertise is relatively easy to assess and measure: professional standards and increased clients' expectations make lawyers adapt the way they technically practise law so that they can keep at the top of their art. But as a leader or partner, do you know what other competencies you are capable of growing for the benefit of yourself, your clients, your firm?

6.2 Developing leadership requires an individual approach

We are all different in what motivates us, rewards us and in the needs that we have. Today, the most advanced organisations take a tailored approach to develop human potential. They see the benefit of that approach in a number of ways, from the ability to attract the best talent, innovate, adapt to change and be ahead of the competition. We frequently advise the law firm leaders who we work with to recognise, build and reward individual strengths and contributions rather than make all lawyers fit in the same criteria for partnership evolution and progression. Some firms have started this journey but significantly more effort could be deployed to assess and support the development of individual behavioural competencies throughout lawyers' careers.

Are you wondering:

1. How can behavioural competencies such as influence or social empathy be learned?
2. How to build these new areas when you've been practising law for a number of years without them?

14 See the article in the *New York Times* summarising the study: https://well.blogs.nytimes.com/2013/10/03/i-know-how-youre-feeling-i-read-chekhov/.

6.3 Keys that enable leaders to learn and change

It all starts with commitment and self-awareness. The most important question to ask yourself as a starting point is: "Do I really need and/or want to change the way I do things?" Until about 15 years ago, the assumption was that either someone had the natural talent and abilities to be a good leader or business developer (or any other behavioural competencies) or didn't, in which case it was not really worth trying because the room for developing new behavioural competencies was small.

The rapid development of neuroscience has shown that new neural connections are created in the brain throughout life and that new skills and behaviours can be learned at any stage.

New neural connections enabling us to learn and change are created upon two conditions:

- that one makes a decision and commitment to learn or change;
- that the new skill or behaviour is repeated and practised often and consistently over a period of time.

Once the decision and commitment to change have been made, then the second ingredient to learn or change is to increase the level of self-awareness about how we do things.

Self-awareness can be described as the ability to understand our own behaviours, emotions, needs and motivations and how they impact on others around us. It gives us the ability to grow and adjust to situations and to go through change with the agility and resources that we need.

6.4 A straightforward way to raise self-awareness at senior level

Today's most common way to start to build self-awareness at a senior level in organisations is through the use of psychometric tools that assess competencies, potential, motivations and needs. Some tools also measure leadership styles and analyse the impact of these styles on teams. This is a powerful way to start thinking and reflecting about oneself and what drives individual and collective behaviours.

Some assessments measure over 40 different talents and competencies. They also assess the degree to which someone has a strong natural ability to develop a specific behavioural competency (potential). Combined with coaching, they help leaders and their teams become aware of where they are and what are their motivations and potential for building themselves and their firms further.

The ability for formal leaders (who in many firms also retain deep involvement in client work) and for partners to balance their 'producing' and their 'managing' roles is a particularly vexing challenge in law firms.

Leadership is at the heart of today's practice of law. Lawyers undoubtedly could achieve a significant upside – both personally and professionally – by becoming more aware of their competencies, motivations, needs and potential to embrace leadership challenges.

7. Conclusion

Every partner in a law firm is a *de facto* leader, and the demands of today's profession require each one to step up their ability to lead effectively. It is tempting for any time-stretched, client-focused professionals to focus on concrete managerial tasks rather than their more nebulous, never-ending leadership responsibilities. For lawyers in particular, this temptation may be especially vexing given the lack of leadership training in most law schools, the 'outlier' personality profiles (compared to other professionals) that make most lawyers averse to core leadership behaviours and the relative paucity of both constructive feedback and role models inside many firms.

For too long, 'good lawyering' has focused on client service as distinct from leadership, as if the former was an external, value-creating, intellectual pursuit whereas the latter was an internal responsibility reserved for times when the real work was finished. Today, leadership skills are vital to cope with clients' business problems that are evermore 'VUCA': volatile, uncertain, complex and ambiguous. These VUCA problems are so complicated that only teams of experts can solve them. As a minimum, lawyers need the ability to lead these teams effectively. As leaders, lawyers have to navigate a complex landscape of new behavioural competencies to help others optimise their performance and succeed in delivering superior client service.

Beyond direct client service, developing leadership skills and embedding those behaviours across the partnership is essential for law firms' survival. Firms that will win in today's competitive legal arena are moving fast to adopt innovative methodologies and technology, to increase accountability through the use of data analytics and behavioural science, and to collaborate more effectively throughout the firm, with their clients and with other kinds of service providers. The leadership behaviours and competencies that we outline in this chapter are directly linked to firms' ability to make these required changes.

It is an exciting time to work in the world of law, and lawyers who become great leaders will have the ability to shape the future in untold ways.

Leading law firms in the digital age

Heidi K Gardner
Harvard Law School
Herminia Ibarra
London Business School

Artificial intelligence and other emerging digital technologies are undoubtedly poised to disrupt the business models of both law firms and their clients. Legal tech is shifting the competitive landscape by creating a whole new set of alternative legal service providers, from online gig-economy players to niche start-ups to in-house legal departments and established players like the Big Four firms. At the same time, client needs have become more complex and more interdisciplinary, and a technology-enabled gig economy combined with a generational shift have produced a talent pool that wants a different career proposition. These developments mean that law firms need leaders to navigate the transformation from their historically successful business strategies, structures and cultures to new, emerging models and the different ways of operating they require.

A primary role of law firm leaders over the decade will be to lead their firms through the process of digital transformation. A 2015 PwC report showed that improving the use of technology was the top priority (94%) in law firms in the following year. But, putting technology in place to do the same things faster and cheaper is only a starting point. Decades of research on technological innovation show that technology itself is rarely a source of sustained performance improvements; benefits invariably depend on the firm's ability to reinvent its core business models and internal operating processes and procedures. Getting the productivity and innovation benefits of any new technology inevitably requires organisational change – and change is precisely the work of leadership. To be clear, this effort requires collaboration across a range of leaders inside law firms, including both lawyers and business professionals, such as the management committee, practice group leaders, office managing partners, and functional leaders in marketing, human resources, business development, technology and other support areas.

Moreover, digital technologies are inherently iterative and experimental, learning from data and adjusting along the way. This is a radical departure from the traditional 'plan and implement' approach to organisational change, one that places a premium on experimenting and learning. But most law firms' people processes and organisational cultures are geared towards flawless performance, leaving little room for error. Instead, a learning mindset is required to embed the new forms of collaboration that are essential for meeting clients' needs. Thus, law firm leaders throughout the organisation will need to guide not only business model and structural change but also the 'softer' process of cultural and mindset transformation.

This chapter lays out a practical, research-based approach to help law firm leaders become more effective in guiding their organisations through the complexities and vagaries of the digital age. The chapter starts with a brief exposition of what it truly means to be a leader in the digital age, and makes the case that leaders need to undertake three core actions: (1) set a future course; (2) lead transformation processes to reinvent outdated systems and cultures; and (3) instil a 'growth mindset' culture that inspires people to experiment and learn outside their current strengths. The subsequent sections take each action in turn, laying out what those actions mean, providing examples from firms that have adopted them and recommending concrete steps for leaders.

1. What do leaders do – and, is it different in the digital age?

To answer this question, first consider the age-old distinction between management work and leadership work.[1] At its essence, management work entails doing today's work as efficiently and competently as possible within established goals, procedures and organisational systems. Leadership work, in contrast, is aimed at creating change in what we do and how we do it, which is why it requires working outside established goals, procedures and structures and explaining to others why it is important to change – even when it may be blatantly obvious to you.

When we are going about our routine work, we're asking, "How can we do the work better (ie, faster, in a less-costly way, with higher quality)?" We spend our time with our teams and current clients, or on our individual contributions, executing plans and goals to which we have committed. We usually know what we'll get for the time, effort and resources we invest. We have faith that we'll meet our goals because we are using the skills, processes and procedures which have worked for us in the past. The time horizon is the near-term: achieving goals for the quarter or the year and solving immediate problems.

When we go about our leadership work, we're asking, "What should we be doing instead?" We spend our time on tasks that might not have any immediate payoff and may never pay off. For example, when connecting with experts outside the firm in order to understand future trends that might affect firm strategy, you have no guarantee either that you're listening to the right person

1 The classic distinction was first developed by Abraham Zelesnik (HBR) and popularised by John Kotter in his book *A Force for Change.*

or that the world will evolve as they predict. Similarly, when investing in developing the next generation of partners, you have to admit that some of those individuals may leave the firm or even the profession; your returns may be limited to the satisfaction of building stronger relationships and fostering talent, rather than commercial or quantifiable ROI. Ultimately, leadership is about creating change towards a better future, and that inevitably involves strategy, organisation and talent. The time horizon is the longer-term-making strategic, architectural and talent choices that will nurture innovation and sustain performance over the longer term.

The importance of these leadership capacities is only growing in the wake of the technological changes affecting the legal profession. In a world in which intelligent technologies will increasingly do more and more of the routine legal and administrative work, leadership is needed to set a future course, lead transformation processes to reinvent outdated systems and cultures, and instil a 'growth mindset' culture that inspires people to experiment and learn outside their current strengths.

2. Set a future course by leveraging outside networks

As new technologies alter the delivery of legal services, law firms need leaders to be able to set a future course in which digital technologies are not only a tool for efficiency but also a driver of innovation to meet emerging client needs. The ideas and knowledge that often prove most relevant for innovation, however, typically reside outside the firm and even outside its established network of relationships with clients and other parties. Often ideas and knowledge come from very unlikely sources. That's why setting a future course requires first and foremost an external focus. But when most lawyers in large firms consider leadership, they think only about internal processes, influence and relationships.

In study after study, over a time span of more than 20 years, MIT professor Deborah Ancona and her colleagues have debunked consistently this conventional wisdom about what makes for effective team leadership.[2] These ideas translate directly to practice group leaders, office managing partners, partners running client relationship teams and to business professionals across functional areas. The researchers found that the leaders who delivered the best results did not spend the bulk of their time playing internal roles. Instead, the best leaders worked as bridges and boundary-spanners between the team and its external environment. They spent much of their time outside, not inside the team: going out on reconnaissance; making sure the right information and resources were getting to the team; broadcasting accomplishments selectively;

2 Internal versus Integrated Approach in Deborah Ancona and Henrik Bresman's, "Why Good Teams Fail" in *X-teams: How to build Teams that Lead, Innovate and Succeed* (Harvard Business School Press, 2007).

getting buy-in higher up when things got controversial; and monitoring what other teams – potential competitors, potential teams from whom they could learn and not reinvent the wheel – were doing.

Strategic leaders, therefore, need a network of well-placed contacts outside the firm who will help them understand the bigger context in which they operate.

Key questions to consider when soliciting outside views

If you put this idea into practice in your own firm, remember that it's not enough to bring in just any outside views. Think carefully about which examples are both analogous and will resonate with partners – for example, using high status companies or leaders whose reputation will bring credibility to the ideas.

Beyond this, consider these key questions:

1. Which parts of the firm are most ready to engage in experiments? Once you identify willing partners, think about how to structure a pilot so that you capture data on what works and what doesn't.
2. How can you create a process to identify outside exemplars on a regular basis? Consider using associates or business development staff who might find it energising to take on this role of seeking external ideas. Make sure to give them due credit for their efforts, and then keep them involved in the firm's efforts to build on these new ideas.
3. What is the best way to overcome the 'not invented here' problem – that is, convince partners to adopt ideas from external sources like tech companies? Think about drawing in a couple of the firm's key influencers: partners who may not have a formal title, but actually play an outsize role in shaping how their colleagues think about issues. Once you personally engage them in a change effort and address their concerns, they can be critical resources for helping to drive internal changes.

David Benton, head of capital markets at Allen & Overy, is a good example of the value of bringing the outside in to help chart the firm's direction. His own experience led him to conclude that the firm's annual, rankings-based performance appraisal process was no longer fit for purpose. Wanting something that encouraged more frequent, and more developmental conversations between associates and partners, he looked at what other organisations like Adobe and PwC were doing, and then asked his firm to help him create a new, tech-enabled continuous feedback approach. The new system, Compass, is already producing returns in terms of enhancing engagement and boosting the firm's ability to retain the very best talent.

Finding such innovative ideas requires leaders to reach beyond the boundaries of their own firm – and often well beyond the bounds of the legal arena. Part of the secret of their success is that all their bridging activity gives them the perspective they need to develop a point of view on their business overall, see the big picture organisationally and set direction accordingly. Here are two concrete actions that help to harness external ideas to become more adaptive and innovative:

- *Start with your colleagues to scout for innovative external ideas.* Hold internal focus groups to seek ideas about clients who excel in tackling problems with interesting technologies or using digital solutions in new ways. This approach starts to build awareness and buy-in from partners about the topic; consider including associates who are often *au fait* with outside trends and excited by the chance to contribute. Also involve your business development team to leverage their knowledge of competitors and clients.
- *Organise forums or special events that convene key players from across the ecosystem.* Your clients are also wrestling with the challenges of digital transformation. Demonstrate leadership by bringing together key players from across your client organisations; for example, invite general counsels to bring along their company's chief technology officer or chief strategy officer. Keep the meetings intimate enough to build trust and encourage genuine knowledge sharing. This approach helps to create more people in your organisation who are capable of functioning as bridges to external parties, and it provides insights on pain points and opportunities in the ecosystem.

Setting a future course for the firm to cope with digital shifts – both disruption and possible upside – demands that leaders across the firm develop, nurture, and use their external networks across the ecosystem for soliciting ideas and generating insights.

3. Lead change to reinvent outdated internal processes

The last decade has witnessed an unprecedented acceleration of technology diffusion and adoption in top law firms. This technology sets the stage for firms to more directly and quickly reach their clients, transforming how, when, and where work gets done, as well as by whom and for whom, leading to the creation of new business models (eg, new employment arrangements via platforms whose algorithms enable the short-term contractual engagement of independent workers).

Gaining sustainable competitive advantage from these transformative technologies depends crucially on the ability of leaders in adapting firms to confront, and ultimately reinvent, an often outdated system of interlocking processes, behaviours and mindsets. That's why a second key set of skills for law firm leaders is the capacity to lead change, from an old, highly successful but increasingly outdated model, to new and different ways of serving clients and developing their people.

To return to our example above, at Allen & Overy, the new performance management system's champions wanted partners to spend their time focusing on helping people develop and giving regular, meaningful feedback – not on 'pushing paper' to create dozens of backward-looking written assessments. But the idea couldn't simply be rolled out to the rest of the firm. The highly opinionated experts and rainmakers who populate the ranks of law firm partnerships don't easily follow along, unless they are persuaded of the value of changing. So, the process of leading change is not simply the product of one individual's vision but a collective endeavour, created through conversation and interaction among powerful peers.

At Allen & Overy, colleagues who were intrigued enough to experiment with the new idea set up pilots – in Singapore and in the Middle East, alongside the original pilot in capital markets. Each group was interested in different facets of what it was designed to do, so they implemented it differently; one was much more interested in the technology, for example. The experiences of the pilot groups and the data analytics generated provided food for debate among the partners. Learning how to make the case for change, knowing who to enlist in developing and testing the ideas, iterating on the basis of what has been learned in experimental pilots, and most importantly, constantly engaging in crucial conversations with an ever-expanding subset of the partner group about "what are we trying to do and why", is part of the key work of today's law firm leaders. Here are a few more specific suggestions:

- *Monitor the shifting winds within the firm.* One of the biggest risks in using an outside-in approach is ideas will get rejected by the organisation because they lack buy-in from the users or other critical stakeholders. Influential colleagues with a not-invented-here mentality can stamp out innovation, and so it is essential to understand their concerns and bring them into the discussions in productive ways. The best leaders will persuade influencers through specificity: by appealing to their particular concerns and articulating concrete benefits that they especially care about, not by using general arguments or evidence.
- *Manage up and across to get support and resources from top leaders and peers.* One of the most crucial resources is time: make sure the institution signs on to a timeline that gives you the opportunity to properly plan, pilot, and prove an idea's worth before the firm gives up on it. Especially for ideas that come from outside the firm, implementation requires time for adaptation. Commitment from the executive committee is essential, but you also need strong buy-in from formal leaders of practice groups and functions.

- *Exercise patience yourself: Leaders with a strong vision and a high sense of urgency are often in a hurry to implement change.* Resist the temptation to jump ahead without strong alignment of interests. The work of convincing peers, listening respectfully to objections and compromising all take more time than you would like. If you've done the hard work of getting top leaders' and others' support for a clear process, then stick to it.

4. Instil a learning culture

With technology – and the business models it enables – evolving in unpredictable ways, leaders cannot simply set a future course and restructure accordingly. They must stay abreast of the constant changes in their clients' needs and in the marketplace, and adopt a flexible mindset about changing their course when necessary. A third critical skillset for leaders, therefore, is instilling a learning culture that allows the firm to detect changes and to react nimbly and decisively.

Learning processes, individual mindsets, and cultural norms are all critical underpinnings to a culture that promotes experimentation. Why? Because initial trials are inevitably replete with disappointments, and eventual success is not guaranteed. For example, many law firms are using technology to analyse pricing data, manage caseloads, forecast legal or transactional outcomes, and even decide whether or not to take on a new client. But getting real insights from such analytics is a learning process. The first attempts to build a system for scrutinising any of those decisions nearly always reveal problems with the way a firm's data has been entered and coded. Rather than point fingers, add up costs, and turn to the next shiny idea, firms need the discipline to learn how to improve from their findings.

That's why many of the firms that are most effectively adopting such technologies are also investing heavily in training their partners to be better coaches facilitating the development, learning and performance of one another. In essence, they are using coaching as a tool for their transformation.

At Allen & Overy, the firm's leaders had also observed that younger associates were demanding deeper and more meaningful support to help them develop professionally, as well as open conversations about development and the opportunity to explore career paths. Former Global Managing Partner David Morley put it like this: "The average adult has around 10,000 conversations a year (do the math). As a senior leader, roughly 100 of those a year in your professional life will be particularly high value. High value in the sense they will change your life or the life of the person you're talking to. We want to help you acquire the skills to maximise value from those 100 conversations, unlock previously hidden issues, uncover new options and reveal fresh insights. That resonated. When we introduced the coaching skills training to partners, almost all of them realised they struggled with those uncharted or 'difficult' conversations and could readily see they lacked skills."

At another professional services firm, partners were pleasantly surprised to see that the coaching training the senior team embarked on had a significant bottom line impact on their relations with their clients. As one of the partners put it, people used to dread the inevitable moment when clients would ask for help on big messy problems totally outside their area of expertise: "Before we really knew how to structure an open conversation, my heart would sink – we're experts, people hire us for our answers. But now that we've added an expertise on coaching, we have confidence that we can help on any topic they throw at us – because our task is to dig the answer out of them. So we say, 'Pull up a chair.'" So often these conversations, which we all used to dread, have led to us winning the most interesting kinds of new work."

In one research study we conducted, a law firm reaped an incredible financial return on its investment in this kind of training. For several years in a row, the firm selected between 16 to 20 partners to undergo intensive training to learn how to change the nature of their dialogue by asking open ended questions and developing "honest and informed curiosity". We used an experimental design to analyse the impact of the training; in essence, we treated the participants as if they were subjects in an experiment, and statistically examined their outcomes relative to a matched[3] set of partners who hadn't been trained (ie, the control group). In the few years following training, the subjects significantly and reliably out-performed their peers – often by very large margins. These pilots clearly showed the value of these coaching-style conversations in client settings, which we studied because the outcomes were clear and measurable. Beyond that, we have strong anecdotal evidence that partners trained in those coaching-style skills became far more effective leaders inside the firm. They were also more willing to take and tolerate risks – an essential element of a learning culture.

Here are some concrete steps that leaders can take to foster a learning culture in their law firm:

- *Train partners in the core skills of coaching.* A critical part of developing a learning culture, because coaching is about asking good questions instead of telling people what to do. Many lawyers mistakenly believe that their questioning skills, such as in a deposition, already equip them with coaching competencies, so you will need to help them understand the major differences between the approaches and outcomes.

---

3 A 'matched set' means that we paired each trained partner with a set of colleagues who were identical (or highly similar) on a range of demographic and professional characteristics. Most importantly, the subjects and control group had nearly identical levels of business development at the outset of the pilot. In subsequent years, business development levels were used as the performance outcome. For more information, contact Dr Gardner.

- *Destigmatise failure.* Lawyers tend to be perfectionists, so law firm leaders need to consistently emphasise that mistakes are learning opportunities rather than a cause for embarrassment or punishment. Leaders' own behaviour will be closely watched, so they must act in ways that reinforce their message.
- *Use a data-driven approach to identify what caused success or failure.* Although many leaders believe that data is important for uncovering the root causes of different outcomes, they don't always insist on collecting and analysing the necessary information. And don't just focus on 'post-mortem' analyses of failed initiatives: understanding the reasons behind successes allows you to replicate them more readily.

5. From know-it-alls to learn-it-alls

Across industries and sectors, practitioners and academics seem to agree on one thing: successfully piloting new technologies requires shifting from a traditional plan-and-implement approach to change to an experiment-and-learn approach. But experiment-and-learn approaches are by definition rife with opportunities for failure, embarrassment and turf wars. Without parallel work by senior management to shift corporate cultures toward a learning mindset, change will inch along slowly, if at all.

When Microsoft CEO Satya Nadella took charge, for example, he saw that fear – and the corporate politics that resulted from it – was the biggest barrier to capturing leadership in cloud computing and mobility solutions. A convert to Carol Dweck's idea of a growth mindset[4] – the belief that talent is malleable and expandable with effort, practice, and input from others – he prioritised a shift from a 'know it all' to a 'learn it all' culture as a means to achieving business goals. Today, not only does Microsoft rank among the top firms in cloud computing, but the company is also 'cool' again in the minds of the top engineering talent it needs to compete.

As smart technologies and rapid growth transform law firms' services, internal operations and even business models, they also enable – and demand – new ways of leading. Of course, specialised expertise and rainmaking prowess still matters a great deal but so do innovative thinking, collaboration across practice areas and the ability to engage peers and associates in open and effective conversations centred on their development and growth.

4 Carol Dweck, "What having a growth mindset actually means" (2016) *Harvard Business Review.*

Succession planning

Susan Saltonstall Duncan
RainMaking Oasis LLC

One of the greatest challenges for law firm leaders is the number of partners nearing retirement age with relatively few structured processes in place to address client, leadership and financial transitions. A recent survey by Major, Lindsay & Africa estimates that over the next 10 years 38% of baby boomer partners (those born between 1946 and 1964) in law firms will retire. While some firms are using early retirement and de-equitisation as ways to reduce high compensation to underperforming senior partners, other firms are nervous since many of their most productive rainmakers also fit into the category of those nearing traditional retirement age.

The demographic trends are daunting. Seven adults per minute turn 65 and by 2030, more than 20% of the workforce will be 65 or older (according to the US Census Bureau). In law firms, the problem is exacerbated because senior rainmakers aged 55 or older often control 50% or more of key client relationships and revenue, and often serve in key leadership positions. Given how tentative many relationships are today between law firms and their clients, the threat of losing clients, that is, revenue, when partners retire is significant.

In my nearly 40 years working with over 150 law firms, I have found a number of contributing factors as to why most law firms have not put sound client succession policies into place:

- The majority of law firms have no mandatory retirement age; firms believe this allows them the flexibility to make decisions on an individual-by-individual basis but lacking a framework also makes it difficult to establish uniform approaches to succession planning;
- As better health habits and improved medical care have resulted in longer life expectancy, firms and vibrant partners are reluctant to establish a date for retirement at;
- The focus on short-term profits results in compensation systems that reward both origination and working hours, both of which act as disincentives to senior partners who otherwise might start cutting back but who aren't ready to reduce their compensation; and
- Those same compensation systems that reward individual originations and matter credits make partners develop and hold on to 'my client'

relationships, resulting in client relationships as belonging to a single partner rather than to the firm.

Having a good client transition plan in place will be critical for firms as large numbers of baby boomers near retirement. Firms can be de-stabilised easily if they lose client revenue so the goal is to ensure that both clients and the firm are well served during and at the conclusion of a transition period.

In this chapter, we consider succession management as a natural aspect of a talent management life cycle. We will provide a roadmap that covers all aspects of succession that firms should attend to including:

- revenue, finance and compensation;
- managing the transition of client relationships;
- transitioning knowledge;
- transitioning to the next generation of leaders;
- senior partner transitions and next career support.

1. Consider succession planning as part of a continuum

An effective approach to retirement and succession is to evaluate and address them as part of a continuous talent life cycle, not a one-time event. At present, many law firms approach succession the way they do other aspects of their business: on a reactive or *ad hoc* basis and with an internal focus that often leaves clients out of the conversation. Firms often do not have a strategic plan in place, much less succession and transition plans.

Figure 1: Succession management continuum checklist

- ✔ Define leadership/client relationship/rainmaker roles and core competencies for each key partner role and management area.
- ✔ Conduct a gap inventory of present and future skills, competency and role gaps.
- ✔ Define your criteria for 'high potentials', whether that be as leaders, rainmakers or managers.
- ✔ Review your current talent pipeline using something like the 'Nine-Box' method.
- ✔ Devise a strategy that incorporates recruiting, training and development, promotion, retention, and evaluation for filling key positions.
- ✔ Provide leadership and other skills development and coaching.
- ✔ Develop and implement succession/knowledge transfer plans for each person; build these into practice groups and departmental plans.
- ✔ Appoint new leaders and rainmaker successors, evaluate and support.

There are three stages on the succession planning continuum: replacement planning, succession planning and succession management. All three of these reflect different levels of talent management and all three represent more formal planning than most law firms do now.

Figure 2: Succession planning continuum stages

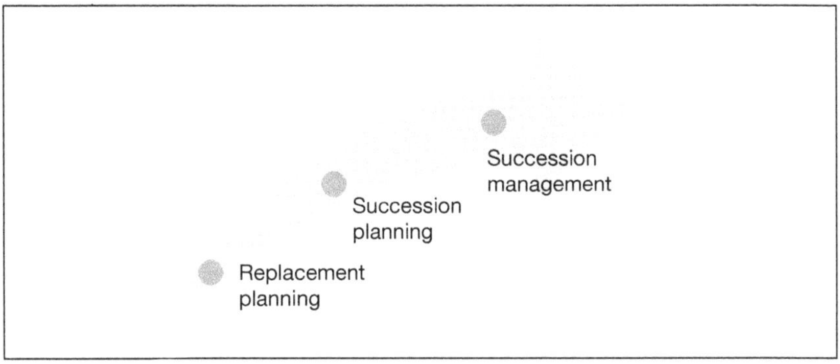

Replacement planning is the process by which the firm identifies the top two or three founders, leaders and/or rainmakers that the firm risks losing to pending retirements. Possible replacements for those individuals are identified but other than this, nothing else is done.

Succession planning is more systematic than replacement planning in that once individuals are identified as successors, there is some development, support and transition planning that takes place from the individuals to the identified successors. It still, however, focuses only on the top positions and roles where imminent departures exist.

Succession management is the most robust and effective approach as it seeks to achieve talent continuity throughout the firm at multiple levels. It is a strategy that occurs throughout the talent life cycle that considers the skills your firm needs now and in the future. These needs are translated into an analysis of core competencies needed for high-performing professionals, the talent you currently have to fill important roles in management, leadership and rainmaking and the type of recruiting, professional development, and experiential support you will need to develop and retain that talent.

Embracing succession management helps protect firms from unexpected or unwanted departures or turnover, build stronger and broader talent pools from which to select and creates a nimbler and more stable organisation. If your goal is to build a resilient law firm that withstands the inevitable challenges of running a law firm today and that results in a legacy that can be passed down to the next generation, you will want to begin a more systematic and ongoing approach to succession management.

Figure 3: Making the case for a succession planning checklist

- ✔ Produce a demographic analysis of the firm's lawyer 'talent' and identify those likely to retire in 5–10 years.
- ✔ Do an analysis of the firm's revenue by partner/age (for all partners 60+).
- ✔ Educate partners of dangers and risks and resulting instability to the firm.
- ✔ Talk to partners about leaving a legacy.
- ✔ Set goals and timelines; develop a plan and budget for execution.
- ✔ Show hard facts and numbers, revenue by demographics; provide examples of the firms that have collapsed.
- ✔ Bring associates into the discussion – see what they think about their future and the firm's future, then share with partners.

2. Use a succession roadmap to put a process in place

Even in the absence of a strategic plan, a succession management programme should be aligned with the firm's goals and its culture. Every firm's succession management programme will be customised but should encompass some fundamental components:

- Retirement age guidelines/policies: For example, when every partner turns 55 or 60, the managing partner meets with individuals to talk about their plans for the later stage of their careers, both at the firm and elsewhere.
- Mutual goals and expectations: For every partner aged 60 or older, the managing partner (or department chair) should explore each partner's expectations regarding annual compensation, client transition credit, capital paybacks and whether they expect a 'tail' (this represents continuing payment for work that the retiring partner originated that is still being billed and collected on after retirement). This dialogue helps prevent misunderstandings and should encourage more productive transitions.
- Annual partner business plans/timelines: Firms that require annual business/practice plans for all partners have an easier time with the onset of client and practice transition discussion. In some firms, by the age of 55, 57 or certainly by the age of 60, they add a modified set of questions that must be answered concerning clients, identified successors, progress made on transitions, practice expertise gaps and transitions, etc.
- Phase down options: Different partners will want or need different timetables for phasing out of the practice or the firm. In some firms, partners are invited to stay as long as they want and are provided an office. In other firms, partners aged 65 and older must request an annual extension of their transition out of equity partnership to be reviewed and approved each year by the management committee.

Figure 4: Succession roadmap

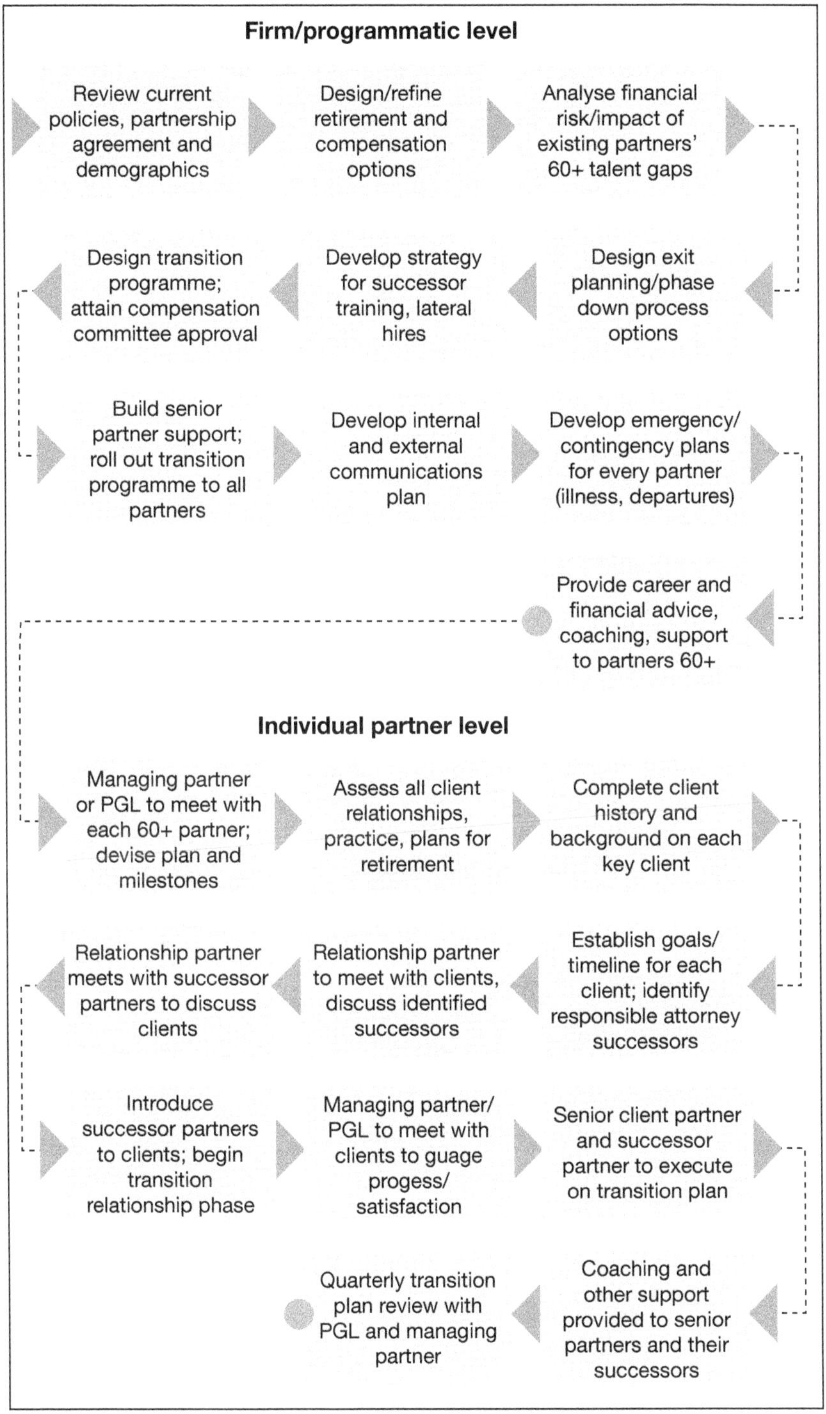

- Internal and external communications: Succession, retirement and client relationship transitions should become a natural sequence in a firm's talent and client life cycle. Clients want transparency and clear communication about how and by whom their needs will be met in the future. The firm should also promote honest and open communication internally, assuming senior partners have agreed to the timeline of transition.

The roadmap above can be used to execute both firm level and individual partner steps as shown in Figure 4.

3. Revenue, finance and compensation

Much of the baby boomer/retirement/succession dilemma revolves around money: the firm's revenues, senior partners' contribution to and control of client revenue, partner compensation and incentives to transition and other financial aspects of retiring partners.

Figure 5: Compensation and incentives checklist

- ✔ Introduce a 'transfer credit' partner report to go along with origination, responsible and working attorney credit columns.
- ✔ Use a sliding scale reducing origination credit over five years; for example, after five years, become a 'firm' client.
- ✔ Create a team of partners to develop origination percentages.
- ✔ Incentivise beyond retirement, eg, senior partners keep % of revenue beyond retirement.
- ✔ Develop a policy and formula to measure and reward originating attorneys for bringing additional partner(s) into client relationships and growing that business.
- ✔ Modify billing reports to better reflect and measure, and review billing records regularly to determine whether senior partners are working with/transferring work to mentees/successors.
- ✔ Establish criteria to identify partners eligible to continue employment; review this periodically.
- ✔ Provide reduced salary and benefits for minimum required billing.
- ✔ Consider whole life key man policies to help finance buy-outs.

According to several surveys, nearly three-quarters of partners don't want to forfeit their current compensation and anecdotally, many partners say they cannot afford to retire. Whether this is due to unplanned expenses later in life, poor financial planning or management, children still in college, and/or unfunded retirements, this challenge is real for many partners. This is an important reason why many firms are now offering their partners financial planning and retirement planning services early in a partner's career.

Firms should take a number of steps to better understand and manage the financial aspects of retirement and succession.

3.1 Analyse client/partner revenue

First produce a report on the firm's top clients, those that produce 80% of the revenue. Secondly, associate each client with the partner that 'controls' or is responsible for that relationship and establish the age of each partner. Thirdly, identify additional partners that have significant relationships with each client and the associated age of each partner.

3.2 Establish financial goals and expectations

The managing partner or department chair should meet with each partner of a certain age (this varies from firm to firm from 55 to 62). Once a partner's timeline for retirement has been established, there must be a conversation pertaining to the timeline, the successors, billable contributions and scaling back, compensation expected, etc.

3.3 Incentivise client transitions

In order for client transitions to occur, firms may have to double up on credit for a few years, that is, the partner handing off the client gets credit for doing so, and the successor gets credit for becoming the responsible/originating partner.[1] Both parties must feel incentivised.

3.4 Create compensation plans with phase down options

An important consideration for retiring partners is how compensation is scaled and accounted for. For example, is it tied to a scaled down number of billable hours and over what time period? How is a retiring partner compensated for sending new business? Will the retiring partner be paid a 'tail' for A/R and/or for business that continues to be generated from his or her originated accounts for a period of time (eg, three years or five years?)

3.5 Determine the impact of capital buy-outs; unfunded or underfunded retirement programmes

Every firm has a different structure to their partnership agreement in terms of the amount in capital accounts, how soon and in what increments this can be withdrawn by partners when they retire and whether the firm has funded

1 This does not mean that compensation for each partner is doubled. It means that the metrics used to measure contribution to firm profits are added to the compensation formula for both the partner handing off the origination and billing responsibility and the successor who will now be responsible for overseeing and growing the relationship.

retirement plans. Firms with funded retirement plans faced a crisis in recent years with the onslaught of retiring partners (many in firms with mandatory retirement) and the payouts that required. Most firms do not fund retirement any more.

4. Managing the transition of client relationships

The subject of succession planning often is limited to internal firm or management discussions and consideration. This is a mistake. Clients know and worry that senior partners may be nearing retirement, and in the absence of any proactive outreach, may begin to make assumptions and start transitioning work to other firms. Clients also must have a say in who their relationship successor will be. In a recent client feedback interview I conducted, a client shared with me, "I don't know exactly when John plans to retire but he must be in his mid-sixties. I don't really know other partners at the firm as he is my main contact. I hope John discusses this with me soon as I'd like to have a say in who we work with going forward. We have relationships with other firms and I might be inclined to begin giving more work to them as I know many of the people there." Again, firms often identify someone and announce this to clients. This assumes clients will agree to and like the choice, which is a risky assumption.

Firms that are most successful with institutionalising clients are the ones where succession is less of an issue because numerous capable lawyers have been introduced to clients throughout the lifetime of the relationship. In these firms, no client relies on a single partner. In many firms, however, compensation models encourage client relationship control by those who are the top partners on client accounts.

In most firms, there is significant competition among partners for origination credit. In some instances, partners prevent other partners from freely contacting or entertaining 'their' clients. Firms will have to consider their compensation policies in order to effectuate smooth client transitions. There are a number of steps and components to address in this pillar of succession management:

4.1 Analyse client portfolio

Do a three-year trend analysis of clients that generate 80% of the revenue broken out by service specialty. (This exercise is important to do at all times, not just for succession purposes, since it helps firms assess how broadly the firm is cross-servicing/cross-selling clients.) Investigate which partners, practices and offices have been engaged with clients and develop a relationship map for each client that includes key members of the client's team matched to the firm's partners and associates.

4.2 Identify successor(s) for client relationships

Too often, a partner has retained such close control over a client relationship that once retirement nears, there is no one in the next generation that is a good fit to become the successor. Ideally, client successors should be identified five to 10 years before a partner retires, but certainly no later than three years. In some instances, two partners will have to serve as successors – one who is more of a trusted adviser and the other who might be a top subject matter expert in the client's industry. Firms may have to hire laterally for a successor.

4.3 Collect information about the client

For each client whose relationship partner may transition in three to five years, someone who serves the client should develop a central repository of important information about the client and the firm's relationship with the client. This will include financial data for history of the client to assess trends and services utilised, a relationship matrix, an organisational chart, the client's panel of law firms and procurement policies, the client's annual plan, competitive intelligence, litigation and deals report and market research on client industry and competitors.

Figure 6: Client transition checklist

- ✔ Run a report on partners who are 55+ and associate with key client relationships.
- ✔ Analyse highest revenue clients to identify all partners that they have relationships with and have worked on their matters.
- ✔ With each partner indicated, identify other partners who can continue to service these clients.
- ✔ Give a financial incentive to begin the transfer of client relationships.
- ✔ Meet with clients to gauge their needs, any concerns they have and identify skills/traits which are what the clients want and need in their successor.
- ✔ Ask senior rainmakers what characteristics they are looking for in the right successors.
- ✔ Identify more potential candidates to be successors; mentor and provide skills development.
- ✔ Bring potential successors to client meetings; foster familiarity for client so transition is seamless.
- ✔ Conduct client interviews throughout client life cycle.
- ✔ Cross-sell clients to other practice areas to expand loyalty.
- ✔ Implement a more intentional recruitment effort to improve gender and ethnicity representation to break the cycle of unconscious bias in selecting successors.

4.4 Engage with client about succession plan

Once the successor(s) has been identified and the internal team has met to discuss the client, the relationship partner should meet in person with the client to discuss the proposed successor. Shortly thereafter, the successor should be introduced to the client decision-maker as well as others at the client's business that interact with the law firm. Ideally, the client will have already met and worked with the chosen successor and has a familiarity and comfort level with the partner, but this is not always the case. Asking the client for input on the successor selection is critical.

4.5 Gauge and enhance the successor's progress

The senior partner and the successor should be implementing a plan for gradual transition of the relationship. This will include having the successor begin scheduling and leading meetings, sending the bills and soliciting feedback on the firm's servicing of the client. The managing partner should also meet with the client several times during the transition period to gauge how well the transition is going so that any issues or concerns can be addressed. This is a critical phase of the transition as the client may be assessing whether or not this is the time to make a change in outside law firms. It is best to encourage open and honest dialogue in order to make any course corrections necessary, which in some cases might even include changing the successor.

4.6 Monitor transition of client responsibility

Once a formal succession process has been put in place, firm management should begin to assess actual transition metrics. This can be accomplished by meeting with the successor to gauge actual transition and reviewing metrics, for example, working hours on client files by the successor, transfer of origination or billing/matter credit. Any successes in specific succession transitions should be communicated, recognised and rewarded.

5. Transitioning knowledge

An important area of risk when addressing succession is the potential loss of knowledge and intellectual capital which we are defining broadly. It could be in the form of unique institutional knowledge a senior partner has of the firm, it could be a distinctive area of expertise that no one else in the firm has fully developed or it could be other important community-facing connections and ties. Any one of these could diminish something valuable the firm currently benefits from.

Once a firm has determined likely retirements over the next 10 years, it is important to consider what special skills and knowledge each partner aged 60+ contributes to the firm and to assess the strategic importance of senior partner expertise, roles, gaps and threats. There are a number of considerations and steps to take:

5.1 Practice specialties

Practice group leaders should take a close look at specific areas of expertise that might be lost when senior partners retire including an assessment of the marketplace for that specialty and whether clients and the firm would continue to benefit from this service offering. If the specialty is deemed critical to the practice going forward and others have not been groomed, the firm may need to hire laterally and be sure the senior partner is committed to the eventual transitioning of that practice and client base.

5.2 Firm history and culture

Unfortunately, a focus on short-term profits and immediate gratification, the influx and outflow of partners from departures and lateral hiring, and a diminished sense of institutional loyalty means that many firms struggle to maintain a sense of culture and history. Building and maintaining a sense of history and firm culture and values can be a differentiator in an otherwise competitive environment. Before founding partners or others who have been at the firm a long time retire, conduct video interviews with each of them about the firm's history, their stories and what the firm's mission has been.

5.3 Community involvement

Especially in regional firms or global firms with 'local' roots, many senior partners have played key leadership roles in civic and charitable organisations, serving on boards and contributing to the success and vibrancy of their communities. Traditionally, a substantial amount of business was generated for firms through these activities and relationships. It would have been hard to find a major rainmaker 30 years ago who wasn't actively involved and visible externally. If a firm is committed to a tradition of philanthropy and community involvement, it should map out a strategy for key organisations and develop a succession plan for next generation replacements while senior partners still have sway to put younger partners on those boards.

6. Transitioning to the next generation of leaders

Most law firms' attorney talent strategies focus on new and lateral associate hiring, associate training and advancement to partner and lateral partner hiring. Few have designed the kind of leadership pipeline and development programming that is more often seen in the corporate sector where leadership and succession are considered integral and ongoing components of the talent life cycle, not as occasional events that focus on individual leaders and retiring partners.

Too many firms today are still led by managing partners and department chairs who have been in those roles for 10, 20 or 30 years. With today's rapid pace of change, pressures and risks, leaders cannot maintain the energy and insights required over decades and may not be able to initiate or adapt to change as quickly and nimbly as needed now. It is common that many firms today find themselves with a dearth of qualified future leaders. The following are recommended as steps to design an institutional leadership development and transition programme.

6.1 Identify the most critical leadership roles needed for the future

Dramatic changes in the economy, globalisation and the need to focus on new ways of approaching the delivery of legal services and the traditional law firm model necessitate that most firms take a fresh look at leadership needs. Future leaders will require additional or alternative skills than those of past leaders. Reflecting on their strategic plan and priorities, firms should develop profiles of key leadership and management roles and skills. Many of these may be filled by professionals who do not practise law.

6.2 Delineate the traits you seek in your future/high-potential leaders

Different leadership roles may require different skills, although there will be a baseline set of qualities all leaders must have, for example: business and financial savvy, integrity and trustworthiness, vision and innovation, ability to inspire and motivate, high emotional intelligence (self-awareness, self-regulation, motivation, empathy and social skill), ego drive (the desire to persuade) and ego strength (resilience to bounce back and to help others to deal with rejection or failure).

6.3 Define the job/role and devise a core competency framework

Each leadership role should have a well-defined job description with attendant core competencies. The skills and responsibilities likely will vary so these should be identified and clearly articulated. Key leadership roles today include firm managing partner/CEO, office managing partner, practice group leader, industry group leader, client team leader and important committee leaders, for example, finance, strategic planning, compensation, talent management and innovation.

6.4 Recognise high-potential candidates early

Leadership traits should become an important segment of early performance reviews and skills assessments. Many lawyers have advanced into the partnership despite not having the leadership qualities. Firms should put a premium on leadership talent sooner, as early as the recruitment process and certainly by their third to fifth year in practice.

6.5 Beware the 'in my own image' or the top rainmaker trap

Many senior firm leaders fall into the trap of identifying future leaders on the basis of their own traits and success path. This inevitably leaves out many of the best future leaders – women and other diverse lawyers. (This tendency also is true and should be considered when looking for client relationship successors.) Firms also often promote key rainmakers into positions of leadership regardless of leadership skill. This may be done at the rainmaker's insistence either out of desire for control or recognition. While it may be difficult to resist these demands, top revenue generating partners do not always have the time or the acumen to lead effectively.

6.6 Start training/grooming your high-potential leaders early, as much as two–eight years in advance

Firms that are doing this well are transparent about their leadership transitions, especially at the managing partner level. Often they will appoint the successor as the Vice, Co- or Deputy two or three years in advance to allow for ample time for mentoring and a seamless transition. When looking for future leaders beyond the top spot, large firms will have to identify three or four times as many high-potential leaders at a time given the large number of important leadership roles in the firms. This is even more reason why high-potential candidates should be identified and groomed even as mid-level associates.

6.7 Offer training and resources

A number of firms send their future leaders to external workshops run by law and business schools. Other firms have designed their own internal programmes supplemented with internal sponsors and mentors and external executive coaches.

6.8 Provide good training ground

Future managing partners and other key firm leaders can learn a lot about leading and managing by serving as deputy office heads, practice group leaders, industry group leaders, client service team leaders and by serving on and then leading key committees. Put young partners onto committees early, even as non-equity partners, perhaps even as senior associates who are on track. Just as rainmakers are not born overnight when awarded the title of partnership, neither are leaders. Institute effective formal performance evaluation and feedback for your leaders including 360 reviews to allow for improvement and alignment.

6.9 Give new leaders the authority and space they need

Provide ample time for future leaders to facilitate relatively smooth transitions into leadership roles. For the managing partner role in particular, this can be a difficult transition for both the leader handing over the reigns as well as the successor (and others in the firm.)

6.10 Keep former leaders engaged and access them as the valuable assets they are

Leaders that are transitioning out have invaluable perspective, knowledge, leadership experience and institutional memory. Former leaders who are nearing retirement can still be used as leadership mentors and sponsors. Others may provide value serving as general counsel, providing substantive training or client development training and in *pro bono* or corporate social responsibility initiatives. As more firms put younger partners into key leadership roles, there will also be a need to support those partners as they re-enter their practice, re-engage with former or new clients, and continue to mentor new leaders.

7. Senior lawyer transitions and next career support

Perhaps the most challenging aspect of succession management is managing and supporting individual senior partner transitions. A recent study by Major, Lindsay & Africa projects that nearly 40% of law firm partners in the US expect to retire over the next decade. Whether or not firms have a structured policy and framework in place, firm leaders still report that their most difficult task is discussing the future with partners that reach a certain age.

Figure 7: Transitioning senior partners checklist

- ✔ Establish criteria to identify partners eligible to continue employment past a certain age.
- ✔ Put senior partners on fixed salary/benefits by a certain age that are scaled back gradually.
- ✔ Gradually reduce billable hours – days per week.
- ✔ Provide whole life key man policies to help finance buy-outs.
- ✔ Have each partner develop an annual, written plan that includes specific steps for client, practice and community transitions.
- ✔ Encourage and identify new roles in the firm – one firm has a programme called 'Phase 4' where senior partners play important internal roles.
- ✔ Provide individual financial planning to alleviate fear about income; host monthly lunches with firm's benefits consultant.
- ✔ Establish a policy for 'Reduced-Time Equity Partner' and for phase down options perhaps using the same flex-time mode/policy as used now for younger partners who want/need flexibility.
- ✔ Engage in big picture/legacy conversations with transitioning partners.
- ✔ Develop a robust alumni programme for retired partners.

Trying to force or demand that senior partners leave or transition usually is not productive and likely will cause resentment and tighter control. There are many reasons why senior partners are reluctant to either discuss or contemplate retirement. For example, many partners genuinely love what they do and have no desire to do anything differently, they may have a fear of loss, identity and self-esteem, financial concerns, feel resentment that younger partners didn't have to do the hard work of bringing in clients and now just want to inherit their clients without working at it, feel disrespected, undervalued and 'tossed aside', have a desire to maintain control/power, have no bridge to life after retirement and fear ageing.

Leaders of firms often lament how difficult it is to raise the topic of their future plans with senior partners. Many partners are very sensitive to the idea of retiring and worry about becoming irrelevant. One managing partner told me, "One of my big rainmakers who is nearing retirement hates the word retirement and asked us to change the name of the committee from Retirement Committee to Transition Committee. He said, retirement makes me feel like I am old, decrepit and decaying!" A former managing partner nearing retirement himself reflected the bitterness that can develop as he posed the question, "One could ask: as these senior partners are driven into retirement, what is it that they are expected to do? Is the theory that chasing a white ball around a green is all that they should be able to do once they reach a certain age? Perhaps no one cares. (That actually does seem to be the case.) And what of the skills and knowledge they have accumulated and the work that they enjoyed?"

Direct, ongoing and respectful conversation will be required for both the partner and the firm to devise plans that are of mutual benefit. Lack of meaningful dialogue often leads to distrust, misunderstandings and resentment.

Making transitions gradual will help ease individuals into their new schedules and roles. A former general counsel confided that one of the things that made his transition to retirement so effective was that he was able to scale down over a two-year period, during which time he worked with his successor and gradually transferred his time and skills to an important external role for the state bar foundation. This enabled him to feel he was still valued and relevant and was able to more successfully transition his skills to active involvement in a not-for-pay job. He said many of his colleagues who retired from law firms suffered when their departures were more sudden – one day they felt relevant, the next day irrelevant.

Instituting consistent and transparent firmwide policies such as beginning discussions with partners at a certain age, requiring annual business plans of all partners that at a certain age begin to incorporate relationship successors and expertise/knowledge transitions, is important. However, the timing and conditions of each partner's retirement transition must allow for flexibility and customisation. No two partners will be exactly the same.

For many partners, their worth has been measured in their compensation and origination credit. 'Entrepreneurial' firms (which often are described as eat-what-you-kill cultures where compensation emphasis has been on what you bring in for the lifetime of the client) pose more difficulties in negotiating 'fair' compensation during transitions. Some senior rainmakers continue to horde or hold onto client relationships as a way to leverage/control their own compensation. Firms need to design flexible options for compensating partners as they phase down and perhaps even after they retire, for example, time-period for compensation for work-in-progress (WIP) and accounts receivable (A/R), doubling up credit for both senior partner and identified successor during transition, compensation for new clients referred to firm, etc. Since many senior partners still generate significant revenue for their firms, it is important to reach a 'fair' (which can be at odds with what a partner perceives his/her value to be) and reasonable compensation plan.

Senior partners fear becoming 'irrelevant' and not valued. Firms should articulate, recognise and treasure the skills and contributions individual senior partners have and continue to make to the firm, the profession and often their communities. This can be done through oral histories, spotlight profiles on your intranet and asking partners to play key roles in mentoring, professional development and external activities on behalf of the firm.

In addition to determining compensation arrangements, the firm will have to decide whether and within what parameters it encourages partners to continue a presence and even to practise after formal retirement. Conditions and options will include title, for example, senior counsel, of counsel, retired partner, special counsel, office and any administrative support, and whether the firm will retain and pay for the lawyer's bar licence and liability insurance.

As with any lawyers who leave their firms, building a robust alumni programme is an excellent way for firms and former lawyers to stay in touch and maintain a sense of loyalty and belonging to their firms. An alumni programme for retired partners and former lawyers who went to other firms or in-house is a terrific way to help your lawyers stay connected and get social value and resource ideas from others at similar life stages. Retired lawyers should continue to receive firm announcements and be solicited for feedback and ideas. Some firms continue to invite retired partners to their partners' retreats and other social events.

Important roles for senior partners

Internal/firm-related options:

- corporate social responsibility;
- *pro bono*;
- professional development, training and continuing legal education (CLE);
- pusiness development/sales;

- diversity;
- special task forces/initiatives for firm and practice improvements;
- firm history;
- ombudsman;
- client interviews and feedback programme;
- firm advisory board (one that also includes clients and other 'influentials').

Outside options:

- faculty at law school, college or high school (others have served as deans);
- consulting and coaching;
- *pro bono* (often through bar foundations);
- leaders and directors on boards of profit or non-profit organisations;
- volunteering in civic and community organisations and causes;
- hobbies, for example travel, gardening, photography, writing.

Faegre Baker Daniels hosts a Retired Partners Group. The retired partners mentor younger lawyers but also mentor other partners nearing retirement. They also are involved in *pro bono* efforts and community/civic activities like the United Way. They get together as a group twice a year and meet with the firm's managing partner once a year. The firm profiles retired partners in its internal newsletter and hosts a dedicated online social network so retired partners can communicate with each other and share stories, advice and resources.

Few senior partners have grown up with the more recently prevalent practice of providing coaching for leaders and future rainmakers. Given how emotionally challenging and anxiety-provoking retirement and even the years leading up to it can be, firms should offer resources to partners for personal coaching and support. Such coaches can help design the partners' plan for how to build a personal legacy, develop and oversee client transition plans, coach on successor relationships and mentoring, etc. Financial consultants can help develop sound financial plans.

8. Conclusion

Recent surveys show that managing partners in firms of all sizes consider succession planning and transition of client relationships from senior partners among their top three priorities and concerns. Despite better health habits and medical advances, advancing age does bring more risk of diminished capacity, illness or sudden death. Succession planning is essential for firms to better protect their client relationships and revenue and manage the risks associated with partners leaving or having emergency health issues.

Clients want and expect their firms to be well run and managed and appreciate transparency about this. Having and articulating a sound succession plan sends a clear message to clients that the firm is looking to its future, putting the building blocks in place to adapt to changes, meeting the needs of clients, transitioning relationships and continuing its legacy.

Succession planning should be incorporated into talent management as part of a lifetime career path and addressed effectively in compensation models and options. A flexible but structured transition programme should alleviate firms' fear that their most productive partners will leave and take their 'book' to another firm. At the same time, firms must develop sound policies and practices that encourage younger partners to grow and lead in order to prevent future, high-potential leaders and rainmakers from leaving their firms.

With so much focus on per partner profits, productivity, rising costs, more competition and partners who strive only to maximise their own profits each year, firms are losing their collective visions and values. Building the expectation of and roadmap for smooth transitions of senior partners, firms can use a well-designed succession management programme to ensure a legacy that their firms survive and prosper into the next generation.

Leading and creating a rainforest: how leaders build a business development culture

Deborah B Farone
Farone Advisors LLC

1. Introduction

For most lawyers I've met, there comes a time in their career when developing new business can seem like a daunting and isolating endeavour. Lawyers have told me that when marketing their own practices, they often feel like they are out on a limb, with no support and no branches to grab in sight. Whether it's a reality or not, their feelings are genuine. They sense that they have been sent out into the wild with little guidance to determine when to reach out to a prospect, how to ask for a piece of business and how much is too much when following up with a lead. If the lawyer is a partner at a law firm, there are even more complexities and layers of decisions that come into play, all compounding the confusion and lack of direction for a lawyer who wants to develop a practice.

Law firm partners often struggle with issues such as potential conflicts in bringing in a new client, when and how they should collaborate with their fellow partners on a new business pitch, and how they should market their practice in a way that is effective, yet in keeping with the firm's culture. They may be stuck by not knowing which of their partners, if any, should join them in a new business presentation and which types of clients are appropriate for them to pursue. It's no wonder that a partner may hesitate or opt out when it comes to cultivating their own practice. They may believe they lack the fortitude to face what they see as a rocky and challenging climb.

There is a great deal of individual decision-making that occurs along the path to developing a practice. And while the initiative ultimately lies with the individual, there is a tremendous amount within the purview of firm leadership that can be used to promote the chances of their lawyers' marketing success.

The choice to foster a firm with a strong marketing culture is not one that can be approached lightly. The commitment to creating this environment needs to be purposeful, communicated clearly throughout the firm, and agreed upon by the most senior layer of management. Fostering a culture takes leadership, commitment and investment, but once that culture is in place, it is a valuable asset. In a firm with a strong marketing ethos, where partners have the right mindset and the access to the proper tools, lawyers will feel empowered to develop business. Proper leadership allows for practice plans to work, resources to be strengthened and role models and rainmakers to thrive.

With the right leadership, partners work together on business development efforts and look for opportunities to help one another grow each other's business. Together, they maximise the firm's resources in a strategic way. Good leadership helps in creating a culture of collaboration and confidence in developing business.

There are several aspects to leadership that make a difference in a firm's successful marketing. The steps to take are clear.

2. Serving as and creating role models

Lawyers are trained to look for precedent and examples of problem-solving approaches that have worked in the past. The same is true when it comes to modelling acceptable behaviour at a law firm.

We know that as a group, lawyers are risk-averse. Much like other professionals, they avoid failure. While making a pitch for business often doesn't lead to a binary result – either winning the business or not – lawyers tend to view the pursuit of new business as a short-term risk, much like asking someone out on a date, facing a fear that they might be rejected. They may see it as an immediate objective, rather than a process of working towards a long-term goal. We know from research, including the work done by Dr Larry Richard, that lawyers are the least resilient groups/professions within the population. In "The Essence of Leadership for Lawyers", Richard writes, "Most lawyers are also very low in psychological 'resilience', which means that they will be more thin-skinned and sensitive to criticism or rejection."[1]

Part of this aversion to risk leads partners to look for precedence in the form of role models. It's common to hear of lawyers looking to their colleagues to see what steps the person in the office next door is doing in terms of business development. In particular, they want to know what highly regarded and successful partners are doing, and therefore, they look towards the firm's leaders and place a significant value on their actions.

While the firm's goals and mission may be discussed at partner meetings, it's important to know that for behaviours to change within a firm, actions, especially those of role models, speak louder than words. Having a firm chairman say, "You should develop business by spending more time with your prospects," is different than having that same chairman demonstrate how they spend their own time developing business. And even better than knowing that firm leadership is active in developing business, imagine how powerful it is when leaders involve, and thereby sponsor, their fellow partners in

1 See www.lawyerbrainblog.com/2016/12/the-essence-of-leadership-for-lawyers/.

participating in those pitches. Utilising the concept of role modelling, and sponsorship by role models, can provide a huge leg up for a firm.

I have seen great leaders who actively demonstrate and speak to their partners about how they grow existing clients and actively pursue new pieces of business. I have also worked with those who go the extra mile to work collaboratively with their fellow partners to involve them in new business activities and make introductions to benefit them. Those who do the latter are more likely to lead firms where various forms of marketing and business development are embraced.

It's interesting to ask rainmakers about their earliest work experience and it's not surprising to hear many say that at the start of their career, they did something related to sales. They may be more comfortable taking the risk of hearing 'no' to a request for work, or perhaps they have a greater level of resilience. If they are out in the world pitching business on a regular basis, or view business development work more as a long game, they may not expect the quick turnaround of a 'yes' but instead approach business development as the need to plant lots of seeds for future cultivation. Regardless of their approach or mindset, that experience of business development needs to be shared.

In addition to their own business development activities, firm leaders should praise examples of others who are marketing effectively throughout the firm. Not only is this a way to provide important positive reinforcement for those exhibiting the right types of behaviours, but by highlighting others who are trying to develop business, perhaps with a completely different approach or style, the partnership is provided with additional role models. I often advise my law firm clients to set aside time to have a diverse choice of rainmakers with various styles speak at partner meetings. It is a great way to demonstrate how various lawyers bring in clients, build their practice or approach developing business. Providing several examples for role models, particularly those that demonstrate a range of styles in doing so, can help serve as a multiplier effect and let partners know there is no one-size-fits-all way to developing business.

3. Creating and supporting the marketing department

Look at any strong business and you are likely to see a strong marketing department. Law firms are no exception. A key part of creating a firm-wide culture for a business development function is having the proper resources in place to ensure that partners are supported in their marketing efforts. A well-run marketing department led by experienced professionals helps provide support to lawyers throughout the various stages of the development process. The department's staffers can focus on offering insights on existing clients and ideas for potential business. They can create strategy and garner competitive intelligence to assist with the firm's positioning, and tactics to garner possible matters based on news, client surveys and the use of technologies to track pipelines of business. Today, there are hundreds of dedicated professionals in legal marketing, and many who are multi-talented advisers, understanding the nuances of both internal and external marketing and communications and impactful business development approaches. These tenured professionals can be incredibly strong advocates for the firm. Even a decade ago it was tough to find the people with the right skill set for a law firm's marketing department. Today the Legal Marketing Association, the recognised trade association for legal marketers, counts more than 4,000 members in 30 countries.

However, even the greatest marketers can't spin gold from straw if they don't have the proper support. Firm leadership plays a significant role in fostering the work of a marketing department. One of the biggest mistake marketers see in firm organisational structure happens when the chief marketer, in many cases referred to as the chief marketing officer (CMO), does not have a direct or open line to firm leadership. In order to retain a talented marketing chief and produce effective work from the department, leadership must take an active role in communicating the firm's strategy to the CMO and others in the department. Together, firm leadership and the CMO should help set an agenda of marketing priorities for the year. The firm's leadership should provide constructive and honest feedback to the department whenever possible.

Victoria Reese, Global Practice Managing Partner, Legal at Heidrick & Struggles, says, "I am impressed by how many senior law firm management and marketing professionals are collaborating around the need for firms to innovate, engage and evolve." According to Victoria, "Marketing and leadership, for example, are transparent to clients regarding their commitment to diversity and inclusion and what the firm is doing to advance women and professionals of colour."

Rieta Ghosh, Managing Editor of Chambers and Partners, points out that these relationships and their impact on a firm's marketing, are evident in all areas of the firm.

Chambers research analysts often see the positive influence on client relationships forged when senior law firm leaders empower their marketing group. Clients talk about their need for well-rounded teams of attorneys, who balance technical expertise with practical, commercial advice. Collaboration between the marketing group and fee earners is the foundation to success here. A strategic marketing focus ensures these elements of industry understanding and high-quality client service are intrinsic at all levels.

Rieta continues, "The most effective marketing teams help attorneys develop a compelling narrative; one that identifies the firm's USPs (Unique Selling Propositions) and provides differentiation. Working together, they identify the key drivers for in-house counsel and how law firms can meet – and exceed – expectations."

Many firms have created marketing committees or appointed marketing partners, and this can work if the right partners are in place; however, if not set up properly, this line of reporting can also be the seed of great dysfunction for a firm. Marketing partners who have a vested interest in using the department for growing their own reputation inside or outside of the firm can be detrimental to the firm's marketing. It is important when selecting someone to be a marketing partner, that the individual has the firm's best interests at heart. In either case, with a marketing partner structure or not, firm leadership should have consistent and candid two-way communication with the CMO.

Firm leadership should ensure that the work of the marketing department is properly aligned with the firm's ideas for growth. For example, if the firm's strategy is to grow its corporate securities practice and hire several lateral partners within the next few months, it is key for the marketing department to know as early on as possible. The CMO and their team will begin to think about how to roll out a marketing plan for the new hires, and how to introduce them to the firm's existing clients in order to create cross-selling opportunities.

In addition, when firm leadership shows support for the firm's marketing department's efforts, other partners follow the lead. Not only will the department be more effective in marketing once they are brought in to strategy discussions, but if the marketers are more involved in the firm, they will be more productive, turnover will be reduced and the firm will see a greater return on their investment in its marketing.

Figure 1: Qualities of a functional marketing department

Job responsibilities are defined and are communicated within the department and throughout the firm.

The department is engaged with the partnership. They are brought in to practice and firm strategy meetings.

The department's members are provided continuous training in both the legal subject matter as well as marketing techniques.

The department's suggestions regarding new technologies to help the marketing function are taken seriously.

The department avoids silos by the use of technology and maintaining constant communication with one another.

The CMO reports in to firm leadership.

Source: © 2019 Deborah B Farone

4. The value of consistent messaging

Messaging that business development is an essential job for every partner, not just some, is key to growing a marketing culture. Articulating the specifics as to what the firm is doing in terms of its focus, such as which practices may receive specific emphasis over the next year, is equally important.

An explanation to the partnership behind those decisions is key. Author Simon Sinek points out in his speeches and book *Start With Why: How Great Leaders Inspire Everyone to Take Action* (Portfolio, 27 December 2011) that leaders need to explain not just simply what decisions are being made, and in which direction or how people should mobilise, but they must explain 'the why'. Once people understand 'the why', and the reasons that have contributed to the decisions being made, they are more likely to follow, adopt and even champion the direction.

Communicating encouragement, both informally and formally, about the importance of marketing the firm is another example of where, again, actions speak louder than words. Take a firm chairperson named Paula. Paula makes sure that at each of her firm's monthly partners' lunch, there is at least one item on the agenda about new business. She also asks a different partner at each weekly firm lunch to address how they brought in a piece of business. In conjunction with her management committee, she has asked the marketing department to focus on three core practice areas that the firm plans to grow this year. Paula makes sure that at each firm-wide retreat, there are opportunities for the firm's partners in various practices to get to know one another across practice areas, both through socialising and through various business get-togethers. Paula ensures that groups of clients are regularly brought in to the firm to talk, particularly from the three practice areas on which the firm is focusing this year. She also involves all of the lawyers and staff at these client forums. The presentation is well-received and gives clients the chance to talk about their companies' needs and what factors contribute to a successful relationship with their legal departments. Paula works regularly with the firm's CMO and a few of the people in the business development department, and while she doesn't have much spare time, she makes sure to have a regularly scheduled breakfast meeting with the CMO.

Now imagine a leader named Sue. Sue is a great lawyer and is responsible for a number of the firm's largest clients. She attends most of the monthly partner lunches, but if she can't, she selects another partner to oversee the lunch and set the agenda. While Sue feels partner retreats are important, she delegates the subject matter and arrangements to one of her more junior partners. Sue doesn't know the people in the marketing department and would prefer that the CMO report in solely to an executive director or a marketing partner. She doesn't feel that regular check-ins are important.

5. Communicating goals and values

Clear communication of goals and values is essential. Macfarlanes LLP in London is one firm where this is a strong tenet of management. Charles Martin, Senior Partner at Macfarlanes, says:

Getting our firm truly aligned with our distinctive vision and place in the market is all about fostering the right culture and attitudes, supported by small quantities of clear communication. We have an almost unfair competitive advantage in going about this, being a partnership of only 90 or so partners, all but one of whom works in our single office here in London. Communication is as unstructured and informal as possible and keeping the messages consistent (possibly to the point of being repetitive) is much easier if they come from as few sources as possible.

Charles continues:

The critical thing to engender in all our people is an instinctive feel for clients, the type and quality of work that we want to do for them and the style/tone of voice that we bring. Our aim is to be uninstitutional, unstuffy and to be very good at listening to individual clients and meeting their particular needs. We believe that the organisational agility that we have gives us an advantage over larger, more complex, competitors in trying to achieve that.

Delivering the key messages of being a single team of highly talented lawyers and fighting the scepticism and cynicism to which lawyers who fit that description are prone can only be done through leading by example. That requires a huge amount of energy, passion and commitment.

While some firm's methods of reinforcement may be informal, some may be more formalistic in nature. Charles also says:

For over a decade now I have sent partners a monthly letter (hard copy, I am afraid) talking about the practice and our clients as well as more administrative matters. I rarely mention individual partners in that as a deliberate part of ensuring that the successes of individual partners are the successes of the firm collectively. Some of that feel is also carried through the monthly lunches and occasional evening partners' dinners that we hold. We also have an annual Partners' Conference with a summary of the achievements of the year and goals for the year ahead. This is underpinned by an annual review of the performance of each partner which I conduct personally with the head of each department. That is where specific feedback is given on performance. Metrics play very little part in any of this as we pride ourselves on having no individual chargeable hour or billing targets for either associates or partners. Targets are generated on a firm-wide basis, then broken down department by department. More importantly any individual targets are self-imposed through a healthy degree of internal competition and a culture which ensures that partners feel accountable in a very real way to other partners. Command and control could never work here.

Stressing what matters most by reinforcement and recognition by individual or by practice area is essential. Mark Kelly, Chairman of Vinson & Elkins, says:

In an era where the legal market is increasingly competitive, it's my belief that you cannot stress excellent client service and business development enough. At V&E, we pride ourselves on making sure that we get to know our clients' businesses and work tirelessly for them to deliver exceptional results. We believe it's equally important to communicate those successes across our firm. For example, we spend significant time recognising our lawyers who demonstrate excellent client service at firm-wide meetings with partners and counsel, practice group meetings and through various internal/external communications.

6. Succession planning with clients and practice areas

In the past, the phrase 'succession planning' usually referred to the issue of ensuring that there was a plan in place to have continuous and strong leadership at the helm of the firm. Grooming talent and planning for future firm leadership is a vital aspect of strategic planning. While this type of planning on the most senior levels is becoming more commonplace, there are other forms of succession planning and training that are often overlooked.

Practice or department group leadership is vitally important to a firm's operations. Leaders of these groups should maintain a closeness to the practice and be involved in day-to-day management. However, often the criteria for these positions is based on a partner's success with particular client relationships or their own lobbying for the role.

Skill set should be the major factor when considering who should be given the role of practice leader, and like any other role at the firm, there should be an articulated and agreed-upon job description. For example, is the role to help manage incoming assignments or ensure business is being developed? Will the practice leader manage a budget for the group and ensure the partners are attending the right conferences? Who will help oversee conflicts between clients? These tasks and expectations should be carefully defined by leadership before putting someone into any type of practice management role.

Reinforcing a marketing culture should also be the responsibility of practice leaders. These should be individuals who know how to lead, how to encourage and how to foster talent. If some of these traits are there, but others are missing, coaching should be offered. A coach can help identify the partner's strengths and weaknesses, gather peer feedback and guide the partner as to the traits they need to improve. Practice heads should spend time with the firm marketing department in order to understand the firm's resources, learn about past successes and failures in marketing efforts and be provided with any available training. In sum, the practice leadership role should be defined and the candidate should be groomed for the role.

Succession planning also needs to take place on a client by client basis. There are several factors that make succession planning on the client level so crucial. With the pick-up-and-leave ability of partners and practice groups an expected part of law firm life, having a single strand of relationship maintaining the client relationship is a precarious stance. In addition, with surveys showing that a larger portion of in-house counsel's budget will go towards building in-house department capability than deploying more work to law firms, the strength of the relationship between the firm and a client needs to be bolstered by several strands of relationship. (Altman Weil Inc's 2018 Chief Legal Officer Survey). If one strand snaps, due to a partner leaving or a client reassessing their work, having these various relationships works as an insurance policy towards maintaining clients. Firm leadership can play a large part in encouraging these relationships to be both wide with several connections and deep with relationships that are meaningful and strong.

Succession planning for key relationships should begin several years before responsible partners are due to retire. A matrix including those clients that have billings over a certain dollar amount, with a list of those where the primary relationship partner is less than five years away from retirement, is a good place to start.

Mentoring and training younger partners to engage in business development and in connecting with clients is a vital part of succession planning. Training associates to solidify relationships is vital. Firms can accomplish this in several different ways. While some firms have a series of various programmes in place, including lectures and more interactive sessions, other firms have a natural structure that supports this training.

Charles Martin says:

The trainee system in the UK fosters mentoring and support from an early stage. The vast majority of our partners share rooms with associates and very few of our lawyers sit alone. So there is much informal mentoring going on. We are also constantly trying to improve our internal systems for supporting this. We have now introduced a formal training academy approach for lawyers of five or more years post qualification in which we give them as clear a picture as possible of the step-up that we expect of them and what it takes to make partner.

Charles also states:

Our experience with formal leadership training for partners has been patchy … Our partners are independent of spirit and that is an essential component of what it takes to succeed in an environment like ours. That tends to mean that received wisdom of a business school type is not well received. I like to think that there is a huge amount of informal training that goes on through operating on a single site where good/bad practice is clearly visible up and down the firm.

Could we do better in this area? For sure we could, but it is important to us to remain as informal as possible in our approach to these type of things … It is a way of increasing our differentiation. Clearly that comes at a price in that we could be better organised and more consistent in the way that we do things. That would take more structure and administration.

7. Client-based business and monetary incentives

Compensation needs to be a gauge to reward those actions you want to see, but beyond that the firm must support those behaviours by helping to provide partners with the training to develop those skills.

Mark Kelly of Vinson & Elkins, says:

One of the considerations in our compensation system is based upon the successful business development efforts made by our partners. Encouraging our younger lawyers to develop their skill set in this area is also emphasised. We routinely do so via training sessions, mentoring events and practice group meetings. We're even utilising our digital content hub, V&E +, to highlight the great client service efforts made by our lawyers.

Mark explains it by saying, "We try to drive home the point that there is more than one component to maintaining our success as a law firm. Business development and excellent client service is a significant part of the equation."

Francesco Tedeschini, Senior Partner of Chiomenti, points out:

The importance of Business Development ('BD') is key for any 'client based' business, including law firms. For Chiomenti, BD has always been linked to – and fostered by – the quality of the professional services. Therefore, for all our partners, the ability to win new mandates has always been inevitably tied to the good quality of the assistance rendered. ... In most (if not all) cases, the good quality of that client service is the result of team work with many professionals deploying different and specialised skills and expertise. ... From this simple observation, we gathered that our professionals not only deserve to be adequately compensated for their contribution, but also to feel (and be recognised as) part of the firm's success ... Starting from that, we decided to extend team-working also to BD, aiming essentially at two connected goals: (i) the first being a message to all potential clients that Chiomenti provides not only quality professionals but also, and more importantly, very well-integrated teams, and (ii) the second being a message to all our partners that BD is not reserved to (nor the prerogative of) 'rainmakers' but is a task and duty to which all the partners have to dedicate time and effort in a coordinated manner. To better reflect the above principles in our culture, we have recently strengthened in our remuneration system, the essential 'lock-step' principles, which encourage all the partners all the more to row in the same direction.

Monetary incentives set by leadership have one of the most significant influences in how partners act when it comes to developing business. Misalignment between compensation structure and the goals of firm management can not only be a wasteful way to spend money it can also be a negating factor. If partners are compensated solely by the revenue they generate and not by factors such as sharing origination, training, and providing leads or actual business to other practices in the firm, the behaviours that lead to building a collaborative environment will not be reinforced. In fact, if the compensation system is misaligned with the mission communicated verbally by firm leadership, it may promote a great mistrust between the partners. While compensation is not the only aspect of rewarding partners for bringing in business, it is an essential tool to be used properly.

8. Practice planning leadership 101

Chief marketing officers often say that lawyers who market without a goal or solid mission are "marketing without a licence". Those that market most effectively have a practice plan in place. After all, what other type of business could run effectively without a plan? Practice plans should be created in conjunction with professional marketers and firm leadership should be brought on to approve and help socialise the plan.

Even when this is done correctly, one thing leadership often forgets to do is to communicate these plans throughout the firm. By sharing these plans with other partners there are a number of benefits. First of all, when partners first learn of the practice plan, they may think about new opportunities for the practice. Secondly, it helps demonstrate to the rest of the firm that these plans are an expected part of operating the practices and serve as an example as to what to do right. Lastly, practice plans give other partners the chance to understand and further promote the practice, either by cross-selling to existing clients or by recognising new opportunities.

A fully functional marketing department is integral to the operation of any business and the creation and execution of practice plans. By hiring a professional who is experienced in running a multi-prong programme and providing them with the necessary financial and political support, they can provide the firm with ideas, support and execution. This means that firm leadership should include the marketing department in conversations regarding strategy and involve the CMO as a member of firm leadership.

A practice plan should be based on both internal information from the firm as well as external data. Internally you want to know who the practice's clients are, what revenue they are generating, what is their realisation, the trends in billings and which partners are most involved (see chart below). You would then turn to the external picture and ask: What does the market indicate? Will there be new changes in regulations that may impact the practice or what other external factors might impact the practice? Only after a thorough assessment is made of both internal and external factors should a plan be put in to place. The goals of the plan should be actionable and accountable.

Why are individual practice plans a vital ingredient in law firm marketing? According to Lisa Smith, Deputy Executive Director and Director of Client Relations at Patterson Belknap Webb & Tyler LLP:

> *Individual practice plans are an important tool for uniting a team around common goals and agreeing on the actions necessary to achieve those goals. Once a team*

agrees on where its members should focus their efforts, enthusiasm builds for shared objectives. Fresh, often innovative ideas for working together can emerge. The team also develops its identity as to who they are and, perhaps even more importantly, who they are not, which can spare members from wasting time on efforts not likely to succeed.

Lisa points out that there is a big difference between a practice plan that works and is effective, and one that never gets off the ground. "A practice plan can only work if it's implemented," says Lisa. "Going through a planning exercise at the beginning of each year is meaningless unless that plan is a living document that includes action items with accountability on the part of those who agree to undertake specific efforts." She adds, "The most effective practice plans I've seen are generated through a structured, inclusive planning process, followed up on with regular team meetings, and consistently updated and adjusted to reflect what is and isn't working." Lisa says, "In order to carry out this kind of plan, it is necessary for the team leader and/or others assigned to managing the execution of the plan to work closely with the firm's business development and marketing group to maximise the opportunities that planning creates."

In order for firm leadership to foster a culture where lawyers are encouraged to develop business, several things must happen. The firm must find ways to seek out examples of the various forms of business development taking place within the firm and give credit and recognition by communicating those stories. Lawyers look for precedent and role models. In addition, leaders need to do their part to support the efforts of a strong marketing department, while consistently emphasising the importance of client service, business development and the firm's values throughout the firm. Lastly, leadership must ensure that planning takes place, and that goals are set for individuals, practices and the firm as a whole.

Figure 2: The law firm leader's role in marketing

Know how to use the power of role models.

Support the role of your marketing professionals.

Communicate what matters most and promote the message through compensation.

Know your mission and values and be consistent in your communications.

Keep an eye on succession planning for management positions and for client connections.

Ensure you have a strategic plan and it flows down through your practices. Don't leave practice planning to chance.

Source: © 2019 Deborah B Farone

Building consensus for a merger[1]

Peter Zeughauser
Kent Zimmermann
Zeughauser Group

1. Introduction

Evolving Big Law market realities tracing back to the 2008/9 stock market collapse and ensuing recession have forced many law firm leaders to rethink and revolutionise their growth strategies. In our role as strategic growth advisers to firms across the legal industry spectrum, we occupy front row seats to Big Law's accelerating interest in consolidation. More and more firm leaders are concluding that a merger will be in their future.

We hear chairs, managing partners, executive committee members, and other leaders at firms that rank among the Am Law 100 and 200, and Global 100, many of them near the top of their markets, express mounting concerns that their firms cannot keep up with new market leaders who are encroaching on their turf and poaching their talent, even from historic Wall Street firms. Even some of the strongest regional, national and international market leading firms that produce solid revenue and profit gains annually recognise client- and talent-driven benefits provided by scale and differentiation, with the former complementing the latter.

Indeed, it is common wisdom that relying exclusively on traditional lateral partner and group hiring has proven too slow and error-prone for any firm – other than those at the very top – to achieve the scale needed to move up the Big Law ladder and stay within reach of the newly emerging group of mega and ultra-successful top-branded firms, which is pulling away from a largely undifferentiated second and third tier of firms.

This dynamic has transformed the notion of large-scale mergers from hypothetical conversation to high-priority strategic growth initiatives at firm after firm. Forward-thinking law firm leaders want to determine what their merger options are, and they want to begin bringing their partners along to better understand the evolving competitive landscape and the thinking of leadership.

1 The authors are principals in Zeughauser Group, a legal consultancy. They serve as trusted advisers to the leadership of market leading firms in Great Britain, Europe, the US and China. In 2018, they advised on six combinations, including the five largest combinations of the year.

The journey may be long, but provided that a merger accelerates the achievement of a sound business strategy for the firms involved, these forward-thinking law firm leaders believe two firms can achieve transformative results with a merger more quickly and with less risk than any other growth strategy, producing a more resilient firm better positioned as a market leader for the foreseeable future.

But, 'getting to yes' in a merger is hard. Firm leaders who decide to go down this path find one of their first and greatest challenges in their own backyard; to wit: building a consensus among their partners for a transformative combination. A surprising number of well-conceived deals fail for lack of a consensus about the wisdom of a merger.

Even for law firm leaders at the height of their leadership, achieving the requisite super-majority partnership vote in favour of a merger required by their organic documents, much less the 80% to 90% plus vote they perceive is necessary for the combination to succeed, is an enormous challenge.

In this chapter we lay out a multi-step process that begins with a firm's leader making the decision to build a consensus around a merger strategy among his or her partners. We illustrate the crucial role leaders must play in educating their partners on the dynamic market forces driving industry change. We explain how smart leaders involve partners in developing a shared vision of a successful firm that can be created by a transformative merger. We outline the factors leaders consider in evaluating merger prospects and flag the obstacles that can potentially kill a deal. We also set forth how to proceed once potential merger candidates are identified.

We should note at the outset that the chairs and managing partners at some firms who have laboured long and hard to build a following among their partners may be able to short-cut some of the steps we've set forth in this chapter. These leaders often benefit from a successful incumbency. But, in the minds of partners at the vast majority of firms, transformative change carries with it the risk of losing something about their firm that they find important; something that makes the firm 'sticky' for them. We are hopeful that this chapter will be especially useful for leaders of these partnerships.

We should also note that we have learned over time that as similar as Big Law firms are, they are that much different. There is no 'one-size-fits-all' for Big Law. Our intention here is to provide not only a cohesive process, but also a menu of options to use and tweak to create something tailored for a particular firm.

2. Start by forming and building consensus among a working group of firm leaders about the benefits of a merger

The first step for law firm chairs and managing partners who have concluded their firms should consider merging as a way to achieve their strategic growth aspirations is to build consensus among a 'working group' of formal and informal leaders of the firm. This 'working group' typically includes some or all the executive committee members and other opinion leaders in their firm. Some may be important practice group, industry sector leaders, and office managing partners. To the extent they're not already included, the group might also include influential rainmakers, next generation leaders, opinion leaders, and senior partners who played a key role in building firm lore. This 'smallish' coterie of partners must come to possess a strong sense of the firm's culture and knowledge of its demographics, current and historical financial performance and its strengths and weaknesses.

Building consensus in the working group around market dynamics driving the need for transformative change at a firm is critical. Some of the key premises around which consensus should be built are:

- The market[2] is consolidating. At the time of writing, in early 2019, Big Law remains a highly fragmented market. Among the 100 top-grossing firms worldwide, only two can claim as much as a 3% market share. However, just in the last few years, one of them has inched from 3% to close to 4%. They have increased their market share by a third, a remarkable and noteworthy accomplishment. Another 18 firms each have 2% to 3% of the market. Another 80 are competing with 1% or less market share. Having 1% or less of a market is not a desirable market position.[3]
- The competitive benefits of acquiring market share[4] are many. They include:
  - Greater 'known-for' and higher favourability status in the minds of clients and talent.
  - A larger profit pool to use to attract and retain sought-after lawyers and for investments in technology, client service, marketing and business development.
  - The benefit of compounding annual revenue and rate increases starting from a higher base, which produces a 'fly-wheel' effect for year over year performance.
  - Reduction of the 'single-point-of-failure' risk presented by poachers seeking to pick-off star performers.
  - Reduction of the risk and cost of lateral growth that results from lack

2 When we refer to 'market' here, we are referring to the market for work for which the Am Law 100 compete, an approximately $99 billion market.

3 Forgive the understatement.

4 Implicit in 'growing market share' is defining your market. Size relative to the market(s) in which you compete is what's important. When thinking about defining your markets, we think in terms of geography, practice areas, and industry sectors. Within each of those markets, each firm competes for clients and talent. It is worth noting, that clients and talent are often interwoven, and less likely to unravel in a merger transaction than a lateral transaction. A firm can differentiate itself by competing only in selected practice areas, locations and industry sectors which, by shrinking the size of the market in which it competes, enables it to grow market share faster with fewer resources.

of visibility into a lateral's performance at their old firm; in a merger, each firm has full visibility into each other's finances (and there is no loss of accounts receivables as there is in a lateral acquisition).

- Capacity (more depth and teams) to grow larger client relationships, which data indicates drives greater pricing power and training opportunities for young lawyers.
- More opportunities for collaboration and innovation in deal structures, dispute resolution, and practice management.
- Longer deal and matter experience sheets.
- The growing reality that compounding will make it impossible for second-tier firms to catch the top tier if the top tier continues to leverage the benefits scale provides them.

Building firm-wide consensus around a transformative merger is a formidable task. Building consensus among the members of the working group is the place to start. Once they are on board, the chair and managing partner can be satisfied that they have crossed an important first threshold and are ready to begin exploring possibilities.

3. Exploring possibilities

A current briefing on the competitive environment from consultants like us and a peer group presentation by either Citi Private Bank's Law Firm Group or the Legal Specialty Group at Wells Fargo, or both, on how their firm stacks up against their peers and aspirational peers are good places to start the process of exploring possibilities. The knowledge imparted at these briefings and in the reports also prove useful later in the consensus-building process when it comes time to assess potential merger candidates in the context of the relevant competitive landscape and available alternatives.

The second step for the working group is to identify the markets (again, the practice areas, industry sectors, and locations) the firm will prioritise for growth. The working group looks at how their firm's existing platform might best be built out to achieve their aspirations by combining with another firm. This group asks itself questions along these lines:

- In the industries we serve, which firms have the greatest brand equity, and where are our commonalities?
- Which firms occupy market leading positions in markets that would enable us to gain preeminence and bench strength in our most desirable high-rate markets?
- Which firms have complimentary depth, quality of service, and distinctiveness in our less rate-pressured markets?
- Are there firms in overlapping or complementary markets in which we don't have a presence that excel in our top areas of expertise?

- Which firms, or partners within firms, appeal to our biggest clients' most pressing wants and needs?
- How could our firm add genuine value to these firms' platforms?

This exploration often relies on outside consultants, with deep knowledge of non-public information about the competitive landscape and the cultures and strategies of individual firms, working with the firm's marketing and finance teams, to put together a package of data and presentation for the working group that addresses these questions.

4. Canvassing the working group and others for ideas

One of the most frequent stumbling blocks to getting a deal done arises when partners think candidate firms appear before them by happenstance. Following a thoughtful process for identifying what attributes attractive candidates would possess – answering questions on what the 'right firm' would look like – not only enables the partners to see the value proposition that each firm presents, but it also allows them to evaluate the value proposition against the kinds of attributes that their partners are looking for in another firm and relative to available alternatives that exist in the market.

We can use a set of desired attributes later in the process to identify potential candidates that may not be top-of-mind or even known by members of the working group. In the end, we want the working group to focus on choosing from the available alternatives in order to focus on what we call a 'doable deal'. It is easier to expand the universe of 'doable deals' looking for attributes as opposed to only the firms that are top-of-mind.

Interviewing partners also allows us to tease-out partner thinking, providing partners with a voice in the exploratory process, which is critical to consensus building. We find that interviewing a cross-section of partners and then having a facilitated discussion about the criteria that surface during the interviews is an effective way to determine, evaluate and decide on the criteria.

For all these reasons, we find identifying the criteria the firm intends to rely on in evaluating merger candidates to be an early-on critical step in building consensus for a deal. Having said that, one-on-one interviews – to identify points of consensus and where they need to be built – are often most important when leadership is new to the job. On the other hand, a facilitated discussion may suffice when an established leadership group has trust and their finger on the pulse of the partnership.

It's imperative that partners be open about expressing their views at this stage of the process. 'Not for attribution' interviews are a way to accomplish this end. We recommend wide-ranging interviews with a cross-section of partners, including practice group and office leaders, those with the greatest influence, up-and-comers perceived as future leaders and often some respected former leaders.

We recommend using an interview guide with open-ended questions for which there are no wrong answers. Our intention is to get their gut reactions to the idea of a merger and the qualities and practice attributes they would like to see in prospective merger candidates. We include a focus on attributes, because we want to avoid an exclusive focus on potential candidates. The latter often winds up with interviewees naming firms that will be out of reach.

From there, we segue to how the partners see the firm in five-to-seven years. As appropriate, we might cue them on current market trends, and bring them up to speed on the firm's recent financial performance compared with peers. Our most specific questions hone in on the partner's client mix, and the industry sectors and geographic regions where they feel they might need to expand.

We conclude every interview by asking partners to name the number one firm they would choose to merge with. The overwhelming majority name more than one.

Once we've completed the interviews, we prepare and present to the working a group a set of takeaways in which we identify the areas in which there is consensus and the areas in which views are disparate. As part of the presentation, we facilitate an interactive discussion with the goal of gaining consensus on the disparate views. The discussion often highlights and addresses:

- Deal breaker candidates
  On occasion, partners have a visceral objection to a firm based on personal experience. While it's important to separate fact from fiction in these scenarios, if a partner feels strongly that a firm should be stricken from consideration, the working group typically accedes.
- Slaying unicorns
  Some partners pin their hopes on unrealistic candidates, most commonly a Wall Street corporate dreamboat firm or a bite-size boutique in a high rate market that does high-end corporate work that probably does not exist or want to be acquired if it does. We try to reframe their thinking on a doable deal. Generally speaking, we encourage partners to consider firms with revenues-per-lawyer and profits-per-partner within 15-to-20 percentage points of theirs.
- Debunking myths
  Some partners take the view that all mergers are doomed to failure. Despite the view of some of the legal media, we stand ready to cite mergers that stand on their own as smart deals even in the minds of deal sceptics. We also explain the alternatives to not doing a deal.
- Winnowing out unbelievers
  We generally regard post-merger partner defections as a setback, so we like to surface potential undesirable defection risks early in the process.

Leadership should always be prepared to listen carefully to pushback to reduce the risk of a regrettable pre- or post-deal departure.

In addition to presenting the takeaways from our interviews, we find a facilitated brainstorming component of this working group session to be very helpful for identifying candidates.

Practically speaking, most of a firm's peer group set of competitors will meet many of a moving firm's financial criteria for a doable deal. When firms are in overlapping markets, the fact that they are competitors can satisfy many credentialling requirements. But, when complementary practices are involved, providing a way for each firm to enter new markets, credentialling becomes more important. Chambers rankings and other independent ranking authorities, such as Acritas research, and elbow grease scrubbing other firms' websites are important.

The working group's discussion should also be used to begin to establish some important boundary criteria. Asking the working group questions about these factors can help in building a list of compatible, prioritised candidates:

- Capitalisation and debt
  To what extent does the firm expect a candidate firm to mirror its capital and debt structure, and how far would it be willing to go in meeting the other firm's structure?
- Governance
  Few partnerships relish the idea of giving up control. The leadership must nonetheless consider what it would look for in terms of a governance model, and its flexibility in adapting to and accommodating change.
- Partnership structure
  How important is it that candidate firms have similar partnership structures? How do firm lawyers progress from associate to equity partner? What does the process look like, what are the various 'levels' and what are the criteria for movement?
- Compensation
  How are compensation decisions made? Is there flexibility on open systems v closed systems? What data is looked at in compensation? Can credits be split and, if so, by who and how? What ratio of highest-to-lowest paid shareholders is leadership comfortable with?
- Technology
  Use of and investment in technology is of growing importance in deals. What are the firm's baseline expectations concerning technology? Which candidate firms could offer the moving firm enhanced technology-driven tools and capabilities?
- Culture

Among law firms, culture is an amorphous term. Peter Drucker called culture a 'temperamental fit' – a core understanding and appreciation of candidate firms' business goals and values.

- We find that a shared work ethic and a partnership satisfied with how its partners divide the pie among themselves at year-end are important drivers of culture. But, importantly, culture also embodies core beliefs and values. When two firms combine, partners at each firm expect to see similar contributions at the two firms compensated similarly.

5. Familiarise the partnership with the upside potential of a merger

Once consensus is achieved among the working group about considering a merger and the aspirations and boundaries for a doable deal, leadership can safely begin to familiarise partnership with the growth options it is considering, including a possible combination.

Chairs and managing partners often make good use of partner retreats and practice industry sector group gatherings as natural opportunities to raise this topic

There's no one-size-fits-all method for conveying the requisite information, but it is important to go back to the beginning and enumerate the benefits of a material combination. It is also especially important for law firm leadership to emphasise the upside potential of a combination. In doing this, the principal goal is to head-off surprise down the road. This communication focuses on apprising the partnership of leadership's estimation of the importance of the endeavour to find a partner and building confidence in the process, which helps build confidence in the outcome.

Although some of the most successful deals have come as a surprise to many partnerships when they are first presented with an opportunity or choice, it is far more often the case that an informed partnership is more receptive to a deal than one that is surprised by a merger proposal.

Of course, communicating to the partnership always raises the risk of a leak. Hence, a note here on communications with the media and others outside the firm: firms are wise to be prepared at the outset of contemplating a merger for a leak to the press. Leadership should remind lawyers and professional staff that any and all conversations concerning prospective mergers are strictly confidential and should always be referred to the chair or managing partner, to avoid miscommunications and the risk of having outside interests kill a deal. Until two firms are confident of their ability to consummate a deal, the less it is discussed in the media, the better.

6. Prioritise a list of candidate firms and move forward

Once a firm has completed the overlapping tasks of understanding its partners' chief aspirations and drafting an exploratory plan, a sub-group of the working group, usually led by the chair and managing partner, analyses all its findings and knuckles down to creating a prioritised list of candidates best suited for achieving their goals.

Based on competitive market intelligence that reflects all the data points we've previously discussed, the firm identifies its chief target. The managing partner or firm chair might ask an outside adviser to serve as an intermediary and make introductions, and the chase is on.

If the first-choice candidate firm is open to a possible combination, then, at a second or third meeting, the firm will present a value proposition that lays out all the ways the two firms could be stronger together. Of crucial importance for leaders in this latter phase of the process is to nail a fact-based argument that supports the upside of the deal. As we've said, there's no such thing as a perfect merger candidate, and every deal has its downside.

On the upside, identifying shared clients and opportunities where one firm or both are leaving money on the table that they could capture together based on the combined firm's enhanced capabilities illustrates to partners that they can make more and have more interesting clients and assignments in the combined firm.

From this point forward, every Big Law chair and managing partner knows the drill: The parties sign an NDA, exchange lists of top clients, and run conflicts checks. If an initial conflicts check looks promising, the firms will begin their due diligence, which will include sharing anonymous data on partner compensation.

Gradually, the firms begin to include more partners in the discussions, introducing the chairs of their respective practice groups and offices, for instance. They might bring next-generation leaders into the mix, always with a goal of building consensus for the merger.

If all goes well (especially in mergers between big firms of comparable size), the courtship culminates with the target firm agreeing to look at a term sheet, which is a key milestone.

Of course, there will be discussions on how to share management duties, and a spirited debate on the new firm's name (best resolved based on market research). Both sides will naturally want to create public visibility that highlights their strengths. But at the end of the day, what's most important is that both firms' partners vote overwhelmingly to approve the deal and that it achieves transformational results. That's the ultimate proof that the consensus-building process has succeeded.

7. Conclusion

As we noted in the first edition of this book, since the great depression Big Law has been grappling with how to adapt to the so-called 'new normal' of pricing pressure, convergence of client relationships, global mega-law firm vereins, and territorial encroachment by other professional services firms. In our view, putting mergers on the table as an option, to be weighed against other available alternatives to achieve a firm's strategy, represents the most forward-thinking response to this continually evolving market. We have advised on some of the most historic law firm combinations between firms in the US, Great Britain and the People's Republic of China, and we have observed first-hand how the process outlined in this chapter supports law firm leaders in building the consensus necessary to execute successful deals.

Recent combinations have increased firms' resilience and profiles while also growing their profit pools. Enhanced profit pools have, by extension, afforded the combined firms more money to spend on attracting and retaining sought-after talent, marketing and business development, AI, cyber security and other technologies.

We expect the pace of law firm mergers to accelerate, and we foresee many deals involving big-firm combinations, what we describe as 'mergers among equals'. Especially among firms with revenues in the $800 million to $1.2 billion range, their futures might hinge on how quickly they can reach the $2 billion mark.

7.1 Drivers for success in building consensus for mergers: a checklist

1. Acknowledge the market forces and client demands driving change and be open to the possibility of a deal.
2. Educate executive-level leaders on current market realities and challenges and opportunities on the horizon.
3. Familiarise all partners with the upside potential of mergers.
4. Charge a core group of leaders with forging an exploratory plan.
5. Identify the industries, practice areas, and regions where the firm needs to grow to achieve its aspirations.
6. Canvass partners' aspirations for the firm going forward.
7. Develop criteria that another firm would need to meet, informed by the consensus of key partners.
8. Identify candidate firms and seek 'doable deals'.
9. Nail the upside argument that supports a proposed merger.

Authentic gravitas in law firm leadership

Rebecca Newton
London School of Economics and Political Science; CoachAdviser

1. Introduction: "I need more gravitas"

As an organisational psychologist and coach, I have had the opportunity to hear the personal goals of hundreds of leaders and professionals in law firms. Clients regularly share, "Rebecca, do you know what I really need? I need more gravitas." This is from both people new to their professional journey, right through to – surprisingly – the most senior leaders in law firms. People want to be trusted and respected. They want to have their ideas taken seriously and for their words to carry weight – not as a consequence of their title but because they are valued by those around them. People with gravitas are described by others as being able to "lead the room", regardless of their position in it.

We know gravitas when we see it: silence among a group of peers when one colleague speaks; someone's contribution shapes the conversation or profoundly redirects it; one who is widely held in high regard and leads with personal not positional power. At the same time, gravitas can be elusive and intangible. We ask, "What is it about them?" Is gravitas something that can be developed? If so, how? For some, this question matters for them personally as they seek to increase their gravitas. For others, it is about their responsibility as a leader to foster the professional development of the people in their teams.

While there are powerful techniques and strategies for communicating with impact, the most challenging part of gravitas is authenticity: "I don't want to pretend to be someone I'm not. I want gravitas, but I still want to be me." This chapter is based on the research and practical recommendations outlined in my book, *Authentic Gravitas: Who Stands Out and Why*, combined with insights from my doctoral research on law firm change and working with partners of professional service firms for close to two decades as a coach and adviser.[1] In this discussion, we look at the true meaning of authenticity, and practical ways to develop a number of key components of authentic gravitas including influence, connection and wisdom.

1 Dr Rebecca Newton, *Authentic Gravitas: Who Stands Out and Why* (TarcherPerigee, Penguin Random House and Seven Dials, The Orion Publishing Group, 2019).

2. The misinterpretation of authenticity

There is much discussion in firms today about the growing need for integrity and authenticity in leadership. Whilst often used interchangeably, there is a difference between integrity and authenticity. Behavioural integrity is widely regarded as being consistent between one's words and our actions. Authenticity, however, is often misinterpreted, as though being 'true to yourself' equates to being fixed in beliefs, style and behaviours when interacting with others. Authenticity is not about being fixed; in fact, to be truly authentic, we must change. It is about understanding one's 'real self' (cognitions, emotions and beliefs) and acting in congruence with that.[2] To be authentic means:

- being aware of one's values, how we think, feel and what we believe; and
- acting in a way that reflects these (and authentic leadership therefore requires leading in a way that reflects these).

Authenticity can be a powerful driver of behavioural integrity. If we are clear about what we value and believe, and are committed to practically demonstrating those things in our leadership, our words and actions are more likely to align.

2.1 Clarifying your values and beliefs about leadership

Authenticity and integrity are easier said than done. Whilst most firms today give extensive consideration to defining their organisational values, each leader has a responsibility to clarify their own personal values and beliefs. Here are some example questions for leaders to ask themselves in order to articulate their personal values and beliefs:

- What kind of leader do I want to be?
- What matters to me personally when it comes to my leadership role in the firm?
- What kind of footprint would I like to have on others' professional journey?
- If someone were to describe me as a leader, what would I want them to say?

This is not a one-off exercise. While values may be fairly stable over time, personal beliefs about what is most important professionally, and the impact one wants to have as a leader in the firm, will be likely to change over time. Let's take the example of Michael, a senior partner at an established global firm, who believed in tough feedback. He knew that junior staff needed to be told what to

---

2 J Ménard and L Brunet, "Authenticity and Well-Being in the Workplace: A Mediation Model" (2011) 26(4) *Journal of Managerial Psychology* 331–46; UB Metin, TW Taris, MCW Peeters, I Van Beek and R van den Bosch, "Authenticity at Work: A Job-Demands Resources Perspective" (2016) 31(2) *Journal of Managerial Psychology* 483–99.

do differently, otherwise they could not learn and improve. Michael knew that he was regarded as tough and difficult to please, but the quality of the work at his firm mattered to him. He had no intention of accepting anything less than excellence. Why should he? He was a senior equity partner and he knew what his clients needed and expected of him. Anyone on his team should be under the same pressure.

Michael believed in straight-talking. When someone messed up, he told them. He couldn't hide his dissatisfaction with people, nor did he think it helped them if he did. In appraisals, he would open with, "Well, I'm sure you know what you're good at. Let's talk through what you need to change." Michael had been a senior partner for close to a decade, and knew what he was doing when it came to leading client teams and giving staff feedback. "Yes," he'd tell himself, "I'm tough. But this is who I am. And it's going to help them be better."

When the firm decided to open up 360 feedback to include senior partners, something that hadn't been done before, there were scores in Michael's report that surprised him. Technically he was highly regarded. Yet the data around his leadership and management were somewhat of a shock to him. He certainly didn't expect to come out as the 'favourite' senior partner but didn't anticipate the results he now saw in front of him. Feeling challenged and uneasy, he arranged lunch with an ex-colleague and old friend, needing an external perspective he could trust. When Michael shared his report, Nathan wasn't surprised by what he saw. He was surprised that Michael asked what he thought of his leadership style.

Somewhat caught off guard, Nathan started talking about some recent research he'd seen around engagement levels. A 'deficit' approach – focusing on people's weaknesses and what they need to improve, leads to poor outcomes. Taking a 'strengths' approach as a leader – what energises someone and focusing on where their strengths lie – leads to remarkable outcomes. One study found that when leaders adopt a deficit approach only 9% of staff were engaged; when a strengths approach was taken by leaders, 73% of staff were engaged.[3] Nathan had heard that a strengths approach led to greater collaboration. It was pretty compelling.

Michael argued that just telling people what they're good at seemed like a waste of time. Nathan went on to explain that it didn't mean Michael shouldn't correct people, but suggested he might be too focused on people's weaknesses. Nathan knew that Michael cared about and valued his team, but did they know? All they heard was what they did wrong. Perhaps Michael could be more open with what he valued about them and their work, and be more 'constructive' in how he fed back what they needed to work on?

---

3 T Rath and B Conchie, *Strengths Based Leadership: Great Leaders, Teams, and Why People Follow* (New York, Gallup Press, 2008).

This feedback and subsequent conversation were the first time Michael had felt personally challenged for a long time. He was used to debating – arguing – with his fellow partners. But this was different. This was about him personally and what kind of leader he was. Given what he valued, how should he be behaving? He wanted to be someone who helped the people in his team be the best they could, and therefore help the firm be the best it could. He was committed to being someone who developed exceptional lawyers and future leaders. Michael's values weren't changing. He did, however, begin to question what his real goals as a leader were. Was he truly committed to bringing the best out in people or did he actually just want to get the best work out of them? He wanted to believe it was the first, but for the first time in a long time, challenged himself and reflected on his convictions about leadership. Michael asked himself, "What kind of leader do I want to be?"

The foundation of authenticity is not being fixed in style, or true to habits that we've formed – most likely unintentionally – over time. It's about being clear about one's values and beliefs, and committing to behaving in a way that reflects these. Defining what kind of leader you want to be can be the missing step to authentically leading well.

2.2 Aligning intention and impact

Being clear about what one believes, values, thinks and feels is something that leaders need to consider on a fairly regular basis and certainly something to reflect upon in changing environments. Out of this comes our 'intention for impact' – a leader being clear about the impact they wish to have (based on their values and beliefs) on the people they encounter, both internally at the firm and externally (eg, on clients).

Once a leader is clear on their intention for impact, they are able to embark on the more challenging part of leadership authenticity: checking alignment between intention and actual impact. The challenge lies in the difference (often unknown) between the impact a leader plans to have on others from the way they act and interact, and the impact they actually have. This is why, regardless of a leader's values and belief, one requirement for authenticity is a commitment to obtaining genuine feedback. The more senior in the firm one becomes professionally, often the less feedback he/she receives. Many firms do not have a culture of feedback (other than down the hierarchy, and even then, sometimes feedback is only on the content of work not useful feedback on broader skills and behaviours). Leaders can feel this is a difficult practice to introduce.

What matters in obtaining genuine feedback is a foundation of trust. This requires a belief that the reason the leader is asking for input on how to improve is based on a commitment to everyone at the firm developing (including him/herself), and a real interest in understanding the other person's point of view in order to make informed decisions about how to progress. "I'd like to understand what I could do differently for us to work together more effectively," is just one example of a useful starting point. Leaders need to be equipped with data about their impact. Within the scope of organisational values, a leader defines his/her own intention, but only feedback provides insight into actual impact. With this insight leaders are able to minimise the gap between their intention and impact. It is alignment between these two that marks authenticity. Moving to minimise this gap highlights that to be authentic, we need to be open to change.

2.3 Practical steps to be an authentic leader

- Define what kind of leader you want to be. Write down your values and what is most important when it comes to the impact you want to have on others.
- Seek feedback from at least three people who work with you in different contexts (eg, one peer, a couple of people in the firm who work for you on various client accounts). Framing the conversation as wanting some feedback for your own professional development, ask, "How would you describe me as a leader?" They may only give you positive feedback, so it's important to listen not only to what they do say, but what they don't say. What values do you want to show up in your leadership and impact that are not being mentioned? Consider how you could demonstrate these values more in your leadership capacity. Also seek direct suggestions for your leadership development by asking, "What could I do differently for us to work together more effectively? What could I do differently (more of/less of) to lead more effectively?"

3. Influence and connection

Authenticity builds trust, which is a core component of gravitas. People with gravitas who 'lead the room' are not only respected, but trusted. One definition of trust suggests it is the willingness of others to be vulnerable with you.[4] Trust isn't just a nice-to-have; it enhances one's ability to influence and therefore is a foundational component of leadership. Leadership can be thought of as influencing and facilitating others towards achieving collective goals.[5] To lead we must be able to influence effectively. Of all the influencing techniques available to us, arguably the most commonly used in law firms is rationality: using logic and evidence to change the thinking, feelings or actions of others. One study showed that trustworthiness significantly enhances the positive

4 D Malhotra and F Lumineau, "Trust and Collaboration in the Aftermath of Conflict: The Effects of Contract Structure" (2011) 54(5) *Academy of Management Journal* 981–98.

5 Adapted from the definition of leadership offered by G Yukl in *Leadership in Organizations*, 6th edn (Upper Saddle River, NJ, Prentice Hall, 2005).

effects of rationality.[6] It's not enough to make sure we are gathering the evidence and sharing logical arguments. The trust that comes from authenticity enables us to influence more effectively.

3.1 Target assessment, preparation and influence techniques

Influencing success also requires that we change. We tend to draw on influencing techniques that come naturally to us from our personality or that we've seen modelled at our firm or prior firms. But professionals who are skilled at influencing draw on a wide variety of techniques. Perhaps one of the most challenging forms of influence in a law firm is not influencing clients but colleagues. One study looked at how executives can successfully influence their peers.[7] The researchers found that three factors made a difference to their influencing success (see Figure 1):

They found that target assessment matters a great deal. Giving significant consideration to the people we are trying to influence fuels both executive preparation and appropriate influence tactic choice. In the context of a law firm, target assessment and executive preparation are carried out extensively for clients and prospects. Where these can be overlooked is in the context of internal relationships.

3.2 Influencing peers

When Margaret wanted to increase her gravitas, she specifically discussed the context of internal meetings. She was frustrated that amongst peers she didn't feel she was effectively influencing. Margaret questioned whether this was a direct result of her being part of a smaller group within the firm. She didn't feel that justified her seeming inability to sway the partners to her way of thinking when discussing the firm's strategy and future. When we talked through the principles of influence, Margaret realised that it wasn't just the size of her group that was at play. She acknowledged that while she spent a great deal of time preparing for client meetings, she would rush into partner, project team and committee meetings without giving much consideration to the room beforehand.

Margaret certainly would have prepared documents or reports that she had committed to contributing, would have read the agenda and any notes sent beforehand, but she wouldn't give much thought to her colleagues. She might think about someone who she knew to be particularly tricky, or when meeting the Executive Committee, but that was about it. Margaret engaged in the principles of target assessment, giving greater consideration to the people she

---

6 AW Joshi, "Salesperson Influence on Product Development: Insights from a Study of Small Manufacturing Organizations" (2010) 74(1) *Journal of Marketing* 94–107.

7 HG Enns and DB McFarlin, "When Executives Influence Peers: The Role of Target Assessment, Preparation, and Tactics" (2005) 44(3) *Human Resource Management* 257–78.

Figure 1: How executives successfully influence their peers

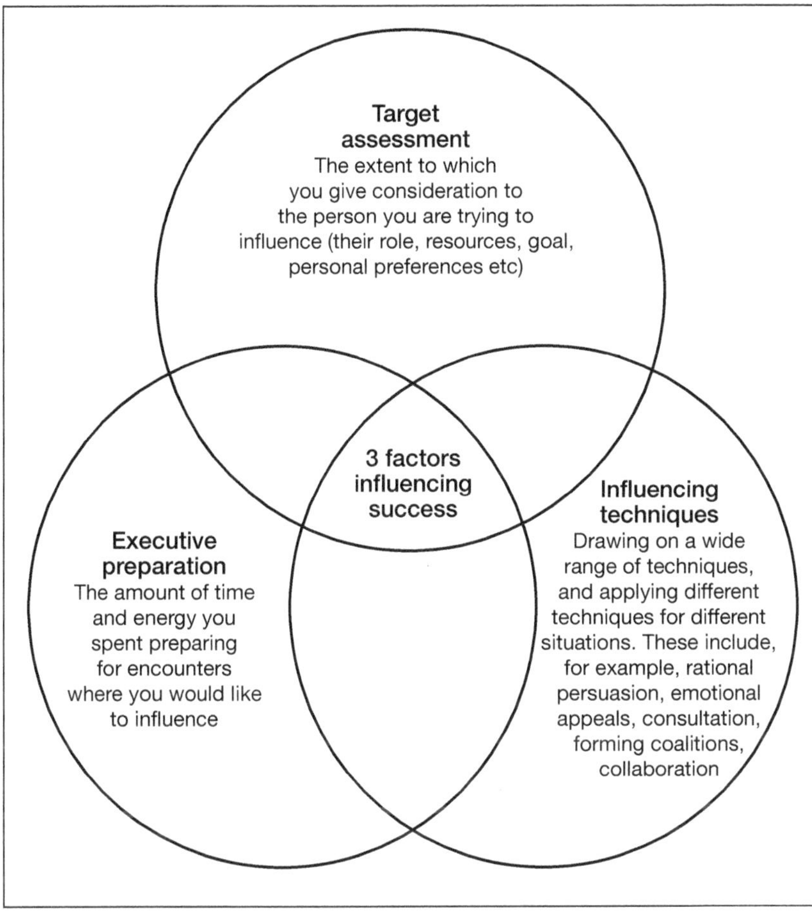

Adapted from HG Enns and DB McFarlin "When Executives Influence Peers: The Role of Target Assessment, Preparation and Tactics," Human Resource Management *44, No 3 (2005): 257–278*

was about to encounter, and committed to some more time preparing for those meetings. She reflected on the influencing techniques she used and decided on what she might do differently. As she implemented these changes she saw her ability to influence internally increase.

Leaders with authentic gravitas successfully influence others to achieve shared goals by being mindful of the people they're working with and their goals, being intentional about how they want to 'show up' as a leader, and drawing on a wide range of influencing techniques depending on the context. Studies which look at how to influence strategically show the need to adapt for different goals. One suggests that there are different ways to influence depending on whether you are deciding on the vision or guiding concrete decisions.[8]

In the visioning process, for example where you are strategically planning the future of a group or the firm consider using the following:

- inspirational appeals (drawing on values and invoking emotions); and
- coalition tactics (getting key people to support your idea before taking it to a wider group), which are effective.

Where you need to make concrete decisions about current issues, consider using:

- rational persuasion (drawing on logical arguments and factual evidence);
- inspirational appeals; and
- consultation (inviting participation and contributions).

Once again, we see that to lead effectively we need to adapt our style.

When seeking to influence, engage in target assessment. In particular, of the people you are seeking to influence, ask yourself what is most important to them right now and what is most challenging for them? When we engage in target assessment it can be disconcerting to realise we don't know the answers to the questions we ask. However, what we now know, is what we need to discover.

3.3 The trap of expertise

We invited 55 partners from different law firms around the world to answer the following question: "In the context of the legal sector, think of specific people you know who you consider to have a high degree of gravitas. What are their characteristics and skills?" We then double coded the 179 results into categories. The two highest categories that emerged, which were considered essential by more than 50% of participants, were *knowledgeable* and *relational*. Interestingly, these ranked higher than the *experience* category. To be taken seriously, have your ideas carry weight, to be trusted and respected, technical excellence is necessary but insufficient. Legal expertise within one's specialism is expected. Taking knowledge and expertise as the starting point, the key differentiator of lawyers who build and keep long-term client relationships, and who are regarded internally and externally as someone with gravitas, can be interpersonal skills.

One of the greatest barriers to building strong, trusting relationships is the trap of expertise.[9] We are confident within the realms of our expertise, and appreciate being valued by clients and colleagues for this knowledgeable contribution. We naturally feel 'safe' in conversations within the realms of what we know. This can

8 JL Jensen, "Getting One's Way in Policy Debates: Influence Tactics Used in Group Decision-Making Settings" (2007) 67(2) *Public Administration Review* 216–27.

9 R Newton, *Authentic Gravitas: Who Stand Out and Why* (Seven Dials, 2019) 43–44.

lead to a reluctance by lawyers to broaden the conversation with clients or even colleagues to wider business discussions. This reduces one's ability to understand the broader context of another's position and restricts one's ability to meaningfully translate expertise for the person he/she is interacting with.

Demonstrating a genuine interest by asking broader business questions is a powerful way to increase understanding and ultimately, trust. At the end of this section you will find a resource list of example questions designed specifically for professionals in law firms to open up conversations to go both broader and deeper. Even the most senior leaders at professional service firms have found these questions to lead to powerful changes in their ability to connect and add value. Carving out windows to ask such questions creates an opportunity to show empathy and understanding. This helps a lawyer pre-empt the danger of a client thinking, "You don't know my industry well enough," or "You don't understand my specific context."

Whilst some lawyers are excellent at using such questions externally, many do not apply these techniques internally to drive stronger relationships with colleagues across the firm. Applying the same connection principles internally as they use with clients and in the context of business development, can lead to significantly more collaboration across the firm. Furthermore, this can increase personal and firm-wide performance as connection increases and social isolation decreases. Researchers at the University of Chicago found that perceived social isolation may contribute to poorer cognitive and executive functioning (such as verbal reasoning, problem-solving, utilising feedback and the ability to deal with novelty).[10] Consider the importance of this in the context of significant change within the firm. Partners in firms need to create a culture of engagement and connection not only with clients, but within and across the firm.

3.4 Practical steps to influence and connect

- When you would like to influence – either externally or internally – give consideration to the interests, personalities, goals, resources and challenges of the person/people you are meeting. Conduct a brief target assessment, identify what you don't know and still need to explore before the meeting.
- As part of your preparation, consider which influencing techniques are most appropriate for this situation, taking into account the person/people you are meeting and your particular goals (eg, is this about vision or do you want to influence around a specific, concrete decision that needs to be made?)

---

10 JT Cacioppo and LC Hawkley, "Perceived Social Isolation and Cognition" (2009) 13(10) *Trends in Cognitive Science* 447–54; RCK Chan, D Shum, T Toulopoulou and EYH Chen, "Assessment of Executive Functions: Review of Instruments and Identification of Critical Issues" (2008) 23(2) *Archives of Clinical Neuropsychology* 201–16.

- Use powerful questions to open up conversations and avoid the trap of expertise: go broader into others' wider business interests and concerns, and deeper into what they are thinking and how they feel about particular topics and plans.

Open and directed questions[11]

The below are examples of questions which, when used with a genuine interest, can broaden and deepen the conversation. This builds greater understanding and trust, and can be used internally with colleagues across your firm, or externally with clients and prospective clients.

Opening up the conversation

- What are your biggest opportunities right now?
- What does success look like for you in the season ahead?
- What matters most to you at the moment?
- What's your main motivation?
- What's most important in your wider business right now?

Identifying challenges

- What are the disconnects in this situation between what's happening now and what you want?
- What is frustrating you most right now?
- What obstacles are you facing?
- What is your biggest concern?
- What are you finding most difficult to resolve?
- What is standing in the way of the outcome you want?
- What is the main thing stopping you making progress?

Follow-on

- What is the impact on you/others?
- What is at stake?
- How does this fit into the bigger picture?
- What excites/concerns you most about this?

Moving forward

- If you could change one thing today, what would it be?
- What is your instinct telling you is the right way forward?
- What opportunities may you/we be missing?

---

11 Adapted from the questions offered by R Newton in *Authentic Gravitas: Who Stand Out and Why* (Seven Dials, 2019) 45–46.

4. Developing wisdom

By three methods we may learn wisdom: First, by reflection, which is noblest; second, by imitation, which is easiest; and third, by experience, which is the bitterest. Confucius

In the research for *Authentic Gravitas: Who Stands Out and Why*, we conducted semi-structured one-to-one and group interviews with over 200 leaders and professional development experts across a range of industries and countries. The results highlighted wisdom as being one of the key factors in whether someone is regarded by others as having gravitas. This finding was regardless of the age or experience level of the interviewee. Being wise is about more than what we know and how effectively we reason. When we consider a lawyer to be wise, it is not only his/her knowledge or ability to rationally persuade that accounts for this conceptualisation. Studies of wisdom consistently note the importance of connection and understanding of life – particularly intra- and interpersonal matters. A German study with over 300 people found that wisdom is positively associated not only with valuing personal growth and life insight, but also prioritising the wellbeing of others.[12] Can we learn to be wise? Aristotle argued that both good character and practical wisdom could be trained.[13]

4.1 The practice of reflection

Once we have established the practices of connection outlined above, wisdom can be further built through habits of reflection. Whether in 4-, 6- or 10-minute groupings, law firm practices of accounting for their professionals' time perhaps exceed those in any other industry. This can create a culture whereby it is challenging to build in regular reflection. The role of reflection in learning has been studied by researchers from HEC Paris, Harvard University and the University of North Carolina.[14] Those people in the study who spent 15 minutes at the end of the day reflecting on lessons learned performed 23% better after 10 days than those who didn't. Importantly, the impact was not a one-off but appeared to endure over time. For increasing practical wisdom, professionals need to build in a habit of reflection at the end of the day. This is only one example of the self-leadership practices which ultimately shape one's ability to lead others in the firm.

4.2 Self-leadership

If we are looking to lead in the firm well, we first need to lead ourselves well.

---

12 U Kunzmann and PB Baltes, "Wisdom-Related Knowledge: Affective, Motivational, and Interpersonal Correlates" (2003) 29(9) *Personality and Social Psychology Bulletin* 1104–19.

13 PB Baltes and J Smith, "The Fascination of Wisdom: Its Nature, Ontogeny, and Function" (2008) 3(1) *Perspectives on Psychological Science* 56–64.

14 G Di Stefano, F Gino, GP Pisano and BR Staats, "Making Experience Count: The Role of Reflection in Individual Learning" (2014; revised June 2016) *Harvard Business School Working Paper* no. 14–093.

Two studies with over 600 participants in total, found that effectively leading others is associated with first effectively leading oneself.[15] These findings were consistent regardless of age, sex and even leadership experience.

When Dominique, a partner of an established European firm, asked for coaching on gravitas, to be able to 'lead the room' well, we quickly identified that one of the greatest barriers was the way he led himself. We looked at cognitive and behavioural strategies for increasing his own personal effectiveness and performance. In addition to connection and reflection as discussed above, Dominique chose to commit to the following three strategies:

- *Clarity.* Dominique needed to be clear about his intention for impact in each encounter. Before meetings he would now ask himself, "How do I want people to think, feel and act, as a result of this encounter with me?" This was true for both internal and external meetings. Dominique would be certain of his own personal goals and point of view before any encounter, whilst remaining open to new ideas and to being persuaded of the merits of alternative viewpoints. Dominique would simultaneously commit to clarity and curiosity.
- *Resource.* Dominique realised he needed to find windows to stay on top of both broader business news and industry updates. He would regularly read the paper on the way into work but admitted his thirst for knowledge had deteriorated over the years. The immense amounts of necessary data which flew at him on a daily basis regarding individual cases made broader reading or learning seem like a luxury he could not afford. Knowing he was not on top of developments, however, made him feel on uneasy ground, and reduced the scope of the conversations he felt comfortable to have with both clients and colleagues. Perhaps worst of all, Dominique had regarded himself as a thought leader, hoped he was regarded by others within the firm in this way, and could see that without making a change his potential for continued thought leadership contributions would diminish. He built regular windows into his daily working life and commute to ensure he was keeping up with both business developments in his own and his clients' fields.
- *Calm.* Dominique acknowledged that people with gravitas were able to bring a sense of ease even in the most pressurised moments with clients or at the firm. We talked through moments when he feels the most stressed, introduced some practices for managing nerves, and in particular, analysed his internal dialogue. Dominique had high self-expectations and struggled with negative self-talk. Constructive self-talk

15 MR Furtner, U Baldegger and JF Rauthmann, "Leading Yourself and Leading Others: Linking Self-Leadership to Transformational, Transactional, and Laissez-Faire Leadership" (2013) 22(4) *European Journal of Work and Organizational Psychology* 436–49.

has been found to be associated with reduced job strain and increased ability to lead others.[16] Negative self-talk, however, across many studies, has been found to have minimal impact on performance. One study of 189 senior executives with leadership responsibility for at least 500 people each and 15 or more years of management experience found that destructive self-talk was only related to one outcome (decreased leader creativity). It was unrelated to their ability to lead others. So, while negative self-talk for Dominique was frustrating, he was encouraged to learn it likely had little impact on his leadership. This knowledge led to an increase in his ability to handle pressurised situations and meant he was able to increase the sense of ease he brought to the room in challenging situations.

4.3 Practical steps to develop wisdom

- Spend 10–15 minutes when finishing work or on the commute home reflecting on the day. Did you act and interact in ways that align with the kind of leader you want to be? What did you do well as a leader; what might you have done differently? Are there any decisions you want to make about changes to your style and the way you lead going forward?
- How can you lead yourself more effectively? What practices or habits could you build in to your professional day, that would make a difference to: (a) the extent to which you have gravitas – you can 'lead the room' regardless of your position in it, you are trusted and respected, your words carry weight and your ideas are taken seriously; (b) the positive impact you are able to have on others; and (c) your ability to lead in the firm? Identify practical steps you can take, what resources or support you need to implement these changes, and what might stop you from successfully and consistently building them into your professional life.

5. The myths of gravitas

There are a number of myths around gravitas in law firms. First, the myth that gravitas is something we have or don't have, "I'm just not like that." Gravitas is something that can be developed with an acknowledgment that authenticity requires change, and a commitment to developing skills to align one's intention and impact. Secondly, the myth of confidence exists within firms. When people describe lawyers whom they regard as having a high degree of gravitas, they often use the term 'confident'. However, when those people describe themselves, they disclose that they do not feel consistently 'confident' but

16 SG Rogelberg *et al*, "The Executive Mind: Leader Self-Talk, Effectiveness and Strain" (2013) 28(2) *Journal of Managerial Psychology* 183–201.

instead they regularly have to choose to be courageous. Courage and integrity are recognised as two of the strongest predictors of executive performance.[17] Interestingly, other studies suggest that integrity fuels courage.[18] Here, we see the potential for a self-fulfilling prophecy when it comes to becoming the kind of leader we want to be. As we choose to lead with conviction that our actions align with our espoused values, our courage builds. This equips us to change and behave in ways that further enable us to close the gap between our intention and impact to lead consistently with authentic gravitas.

17 JJ Sosik, WA Gentry and JU Chun, "The Value of Virtue in the Upper Echelons: A Multisource Examination of Executive Character Strengths and Performance" (2012) 23(3) *Leadership Quarterly* 367–82.

18 ME Palanski, KL Cullen, WA Gentry and CM Nichols, "Virtuous Leadership: Exploring the Effects of Leaders' Courage and Behavioral Integrity on Leader Performance and Image" (2015) 132(2) *Journal of Business Ethics* 297–310.

Leadership and decision-making in emerging legal markets: how structures and dynamics shape success

Mariano Batalla
Batalla
Jaime Fernández Madero
Fernández Madero Consulting

1. Leadership beyond founders

When it comes to organising their legal practice, most lawyers tend to think in simple terms. They want to serve clients, not deal with administrative matters. In founder-led firms, these issues are usually reserved for those who started the firm. These firms are informally organised and intuitively managed, and few lawyers mind how founders run them as long as they can keep a high degree of freedom. This allows for a healthy sense of partnership while lawyers maintain their much-wanted autonomy.

This seemingly attractive model begins to show its deficiencies as firms grow. Effective founder-led firms combine camaraderie with the comfort of a natural, vertical authority that makes most decisions in an informal, intuitive style.

As firms transition, who makes which decisions becomes less obvious. The autonomous nature of lawyers and their informal management processes increases the need for negotiation among founding and non-founding partners. This leadership vacuum creates tension and lack of clarity in decision-making, leaving a fragmented group of professionals looking for reasons to stay together. This transition demonstrates the importance of examining decision-making processes in law firms. For most, it is through these processes that leadership is defined.

This is very particular of law firms but not of other industries, making decision-making processes a good measure for examining leadership. Lawyers have a particular aversion to authority, struggle with following predetermined management processes and do not usually appoint leaders based on the skills required for each role.

This chapter seeks to understand how law firms can overcome inherent leadership challenges through productive and sustainable decision-making processes. Drawing on the experience of three leading Latin American firms, we examine the tensions facing law firm leaders and the role decision-making processes have in law firm leadership in order to understand the journey each firm took to overcome these challenges.

We argue that law firm leaders can make better decisions and set their leadership for success when firms:

- become institutions with a particular purpose shared by the partners (vision);
- develop a cohesive leadership that is based on constant dialogue among partners (dialogue), and;
- establish organisational systems that allow an effective operation within the firm and with clients (structure).

2. The tensions faced by law firm leaders

It is generally accepted that compared to other professions, lawyers struggle with the concept of leadership. In fact, traditional management theory has always seemed distant and inapplicable to law firms. Predictable processes, specific roles and clear authority figures do not always fit with the ambiguous world of lawyers where autonomy is second nature. When it comes to leadership and decision-making processes, law firms are subject to different tensions that co-exist with one another.

2.1 Autonomy v control

This tension lies at the heart of the nature of a law firm and reflects the struggle between the individual and collective interests at the firm. Most lawyers seek to be autonomous so they can practise how they wish. But collaboration and some degree of control are also necessary for the effective functioning of the firm. This natural autonomy also has professional and economic consequences, since lawyers tend to control their clients and their economic results. This 'client ownership' increases the fragmentation impact of autonomy and makes it more challenging for lawyers to accept being 'controlled' by other partners. This struggle between individual and collective interests is key in understanding the leadership approach and decision-making processes in each firm.

2.2 Ambiguity v certainty

The opaque nature of professional work makes it difficult to assess the quality and role each partner plays within the firm. Who is a good partner? What contributions should be more rewarded? Is it influence or competence? Who should be a desirable leader for the firm? These questions are difficult to respond to and the answer to them may change depending on the specific circumstances of each law firm. To mitigate this ambiguity, lawyers normally resort to two different approaches: (1) analyse reality from a simpler perspective, normally from a financial standpoint; and (2) exercise direct power and authority to influence decisions in a particular direction. This oversimplification of solutions through basic compensation and governance systems does not produce the expected results of bringing certainty and clarity in a sustainable way to the ambiguous and highly political environment of law firms.

3. Influence and competence in leadership roles

When selecting leaders, most law firms tend to favour those with greater individual influence than the ones most capable for management and leader roles. Many times, this means the most respected leaders are those with the highest financial performance and professional recognition, irrespective of their personal and leadership skills. This is likely to be rooted in the founder-led stage, where professionals gravitate around the most influential members of the firm. Most firms we encounter struggle to find adequate leaders that will be respected as such. Law firms need leaders that are professionally respected inside and outside the firm ('Individual Influence') in order to be legitimated as such. However, many tend to disregard the importance of having the attitudes, skills and knowledge to be successful ('Leadership Competence'). The challenging goal is to find professionals that can achieve the balance that is right for each law firm.

Table 1 below describes basic features of leadership styles based on 'Individual Influence' or 'Leadership Competence' and their interaction with the tensions described above. Although 'Individual Influence' is a required condition that provides legitimacy, when considered alone it does not guarantee effectiveness in exercising the role. Therefore, 'Leadership Competence' is also required. Since the perfect combination is difficult to find, law firms face constant difficulties and trade-offs to find the right balance.

Table 1: Basic features of leadership styles

Individual Influence	Leadership Competence
• Focus on autonomy • Focus on individual results (narrow and financial) • Leadership based on respect (vertical, limited dialogue)	• Focus on collaboration • Focus on collective results (broad financial and non-financial) • Leadership based on personal skills (horizontal, open dialogue)

4. The role of decision-making processes in firm leadership

Table 1 shows the interplay between these tensions. Firms that favour Individual Influence over Leadership Competence are not necessarily led by those best suited for such endeavours, but by professionals with the most individual accomplishments. As a result, decision-making processes are rudimentary and little more than the wishes of the most influential lawyers. As a former managing partner of a prominent Latin American law firm once told us, "If someone can single-handedly choose the colour of the office carpet, you know who the leader is."

These firms have strong formal or informal vertical chains of command with high levels of professional autonomy, and little dialogue before decisions are made. In the long term, relying on Individual Influence for leadership could be problematic. Decision-makers in these firms do not want to lose their power and are thus likely to make key decisions with that in mind. Engaging in these erratic processes could hinder productive and sustainable decisions, affecting the firm's stability in the long term.

On the other hand, firms that tend towards Leadership Competence (which also means redefining the concept of Individual Influence) are led by those most capable of driving a business, while balancing the individual autonomy of professionals with decision-making processes where collaboration, dialogue and negotiation are key.

This approach requires driven partners who have a vision of what the firm should be, are committed to a more horizontal and open relationship among all lawyers and have the courage to face discussion of key firm issues with respect. In these firms, leaders overcome lawyers' traditional difficulty for communicating non-technical information to bring about a common firm purpose that every professional recognises as important enough to give up some of their autonomy. Unlike the first case, the professional success of these leaders is only important relative to their individual strengths to run a law firm.

Navigating these tensions would be hard for any leader regardless of profession. But lawyers are in a tougher situation given their most common personality traits. The particular nature of lawyers demands strong and outgoing personalities in order to be effective with clients, judges, counterparts and even their own peers. In our experience, this makes introverts and less outgoing personality types an ineffective profile for leadership in law firms in legal markets with a high individual component like Latin America.

Not surprisingly, there is no single path leaders can take to manage these tensions. And yet all efforts undertaken in this seemingly never-ending process require humility, decisiveness and a common cause to catalyse the right decisions. The firms studied showcase three different ways of dealing with this challenge, albeit with the same ingredients and a single goal: to jumpstart productive and sustainable decision-making processes that can help their firms thrive.

5. The firms

In order to study the leadership in Latin American firms through their decision-making process we have chosen three firms from three different jurisdictions. After some reflection, we decided to keep the names of the firms confidential, mostly to avoid potential preexisting opinions of readers about these firms (all three are very well-known and successful in their respective markets). The three firms started as small firms in the 1990s with clear expertise in transactional work, which evolved into full-service and diversified structures, but which maintained their strength in complex work. Two of them have similar sizes of between 130 and 140 lawyers and between 25 and 30 partners. The third one is bigger with close to 300 lawyers and 70 partners. All have proven to be successful and leaders in their respective markets, with several recognitions and awards for their accomplishments.

Their founders, or some of them, are still active in the firms but with different roles than originally. All of them have struggled and found ways to go beyond the initial founders' influence, and they have not stopped trying to improve the systems, processes and culture to achieve higher levels of performance in an increasingly competitive region. As one of them said, "We are still learning how to do this right; it is a challenge you never solve completely."

We have interviewed the managing partners or senior partners in each firm. Our aim was to understand the leadership structure in each firm throughout their history and how they have learned to develop a decision-making system to discuss relevant issues and reach consensus. Although they have many things in common they also show differences in the way their leadership concept developed, and that influenced the way the firm evolved.

6. How firms build a stable and productive leadership environment

The firms we have analysed in this chapter have a very clear perception of their leadership challenges and developed different formal and informal strategies to deal with strong egos and overcome their worse consequences.

We have identified in our interviews three main categories that concentrate most of the relevant strategies and behaviours the firms use to produce a stable and productive decision-making process in which the firm ultimately is the main beneficiary and produce positive results in terms of service, client satisfaction, market reputation, firm cohesion and, consequently, a more profitable business. Those are: (a) strategic vision of the firm; (b) communication and culture; and (c) professionalisation: systems and information.

Each of these firms, anonymised as Firm A, B and C, experienced different paths in developing their leadership model and finding a stable format for their decision-making process. Counterintuitively, firms with a more open and less centralised type of leadership from the beginning found a smoother path that led from the vision of the firm, into a dialogue dynamic that enhanced communication and mutual understanding and respect, which was then resolved in finding the adequate systems and rules needed to run the firm through different stages. Firm B and Firm C were within this pattern, although Firm B took longer to reach a clear vision due to an initial more unstable period with some leading partners, but their commitment to a culture of dialogue and respect helped them in finding that clear vision within a market still dominated by strong individuals. That commitment led them to later find a solid set of rules and systems to operate the firm. Firm A, on the other hand, with stronger founders leading the firm in the first stages had to work harder in finding an adequate communication dynamic among partners, so its initial strategy was to work on systems and rules based on their vision.

Firms that gave priority to dialogue in the first stages found an easier path towards what is called 'institutionalisation'. The term 'institutional', refers in broad terms to a variety of features and traits that firms incorporate including acceptance of rules by partners, systems that prioritise the firm's interest over the individual partners, and the intention of developing a collective project for the professionals in the firm and a unified brand towards the market and the clients. This is always a moving target in law firms, but those who work harder and understand the need for that objective achieve a more stable and productive environment.

As Figure 1 below indicates, as firms transition, they begin to recognise the need for balance between the respect and reputation of a lawyer and the respective leadership role and as a result, 'drift to the right'. Firms B and C enjoyed institutionalisation more rapidly due to their commitment to partnership dialogue in the organisational process. Success was achieved by the three firms, but Firm A had a tougher road ahead.

6.1 Strategic vision of the firm

In different ways and contexts, these firms had from the beginning a clear idea of what they wanted to do and how. Interestingly, the stronger the leadership of founders in the initial stages, the hardest it was to get this clear idea of a firm as an independent entity with a particular vision and purpose. Very strong leaders in the initial stages tend to identify the firm with themselves, so it is hard for them and the rest of the firm to understand something that can be described as 'the vision of the firm'. This particular element appeared with different levels of intensity in the initial stages of the three firms, but leaders were clever enough to find its importance as a way to divert the attention from strong individuals' wishes and desires to the firm's interest. Firm C, for instance, understood from its early stages that founders should not concentrate the power and management of the firm.

"Management should not be in the hands of the best lawyers," one of the law firm leaders told us. Founders understood that they didn't have natural

Figure 1: The relevance of leadership skills and individual influence in law firm leadership roles

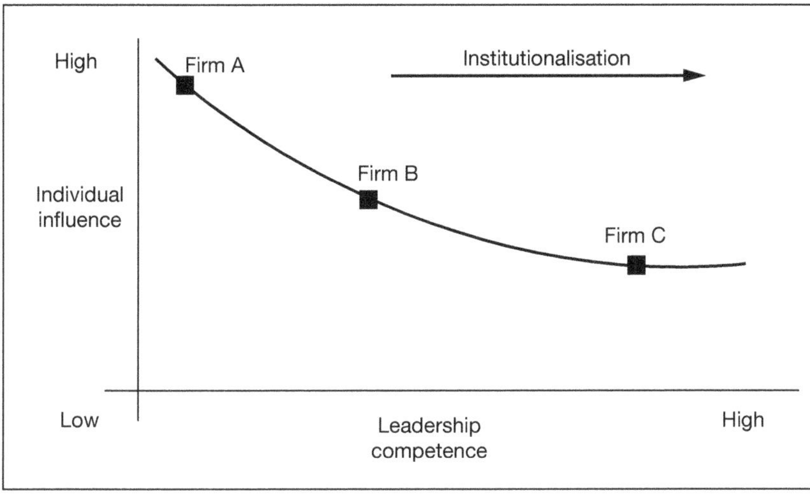

inclinations or skills for that task so they delegated it in favour of younger partners. This retraction from founders to participate in the management of the firm almost from the beginning and the humble attitude they took towards their role in the firm, is considered by its members as one of the secrets of their success. "This created a depersonalised young firm, opened to new ideas." In this context, power was better explained by the term 'delegated authority', under which partners with formal management authority were exercising its role based on certain rules and prescriptions. "No partner feels that he or she is above the firm's brand." This indicates a clear order of priorities, goals and values when partners discuss their interests and make decisions. "To be a partner in our firm requires a great capacity to resign."

In the other firms the process was slower, partly because of a stronger founder presence but also (in one case) due to a local market 20 years ago with a clear culture that gave preeminence to the individual over the firm (although that has been changing in the last few years).

The senior partner in Firm B said, "First, we had to look at the business and the vision, and then we understood that we should become more strategic and, to accomplish that, we should be more institutional." One activity that has helped in getting the partners together around the goals of the firm has been the strategic offsite meetings conducted every three years, to discuss the direction and business of the firm. These meetings, prepared in advance, gave the opportunity to the partners to concentrate around the needs of the firm as a whole and have an open discussion among them (including laterals) outside the daily environment of the office.

Firm A also had a vision from the start of becoming a leader in sophisticated transactions, but that was strongly related to outstanding individuals with high levels of financial productivity, without a strong sense of a unified firm in the initial stages and sometimes with a prima donna style. This vision, dependent on strong individuals, undermined the importance of rules or dialogue, so the firm evolved with a vision of a sophisticated group of lawyers working under the influence of a smaller number of very successful individuals. In this case, vision looked like the sum of individual visions which might coincide or not at different phases of the life of the firm.

6.2 Communication and culture

During the founding period, firms tend to concentrate the decision-making process in the founders. That makes sense since founders are the professionals with more experience and relevance in the market, and also with the higher stakes in the firm's ownership. But founders have different approaches to communication. Some use a more vertical style, where decisions are taken by them and then informed to the rest of the partners and lawyers. Other founders prefer a horizontal style and prioritise dialogue and exchange of ideas. This format tends to be slower and even cumbersome at times, but it is more stable since partners give more support to decisions where they have been consulted in advance and not simply informed after the decision is taken. Although lawyers are autonomous and expect little interaction with the firm as a whole, they also like to feel they are part of the firm and participate in significant decisions.

In the case of Firms B and C, where the leadership style of founders was open and moderately strong, dialogue was an essential part of how the partners learned to build the firm and the cohesion between them. Some had a clearer idea than others of where the firm should go, but all of them understood that without dialogue and respect it was difficult to move forward in any meaningful way. Another aspect that both firms described as essential was the concept of a horizontal partnership, where decisions need an appropriate consensus and partners trust each other. "All important decisions were always agreed with a broad consensus. That assured a stable environment," said one of the leaders.

In the case of Firm A, where the founders' influence in the beginning was more significant and they tended to concentrate the decisions, the transition to a more open dialogue was more difficult for those founders. However, they all found a way to learn and move forward with a different strategy. In this case, partners agreed with the structures to make decisions (governance arrangements) although dialogue was not as fluid. When difficult decisions were not agreed by some powerful partners (which in the past meant a complete deadlock), the new systems provide for majority vote even when powerful partners would not agree. Initially this created difficult situations, but the partners evolved and adapted. "We started to learn to live with different opinions. We learned to disagree," said the managing partner of Firm A.

An interesting observation is that despite the differences in leadership style (stronger and more vertical, more open and horizontal) all ultimately understood that a culture and dynamics of dialogue and respect were essential to develop into a more mature and productive firm. "We need to have open discussions among partners, even if we disagree. Respect is key to achieve that result," said one of the managing partners. The high stress and individualistic environment of law firms could prevent the levels of dialogue and respect that a partnership needs to remain strong and cohesive.

That idea produced other results. For example, all the firms, although at a different pace, have learned that they should not hire or make partners that are prima donnas and have an egocentric view of the firm and the legal profession. They strongly prefer 'team players'. Even if founders have a strong personality, as in the case of Firm A, who tend to concentrate attention on themselves, second and third generation partners are more collaborative and open to dialogue (which also indicates the willingness of those founders to let the firm evolve to a new model).

The other related idea is the concept of 'non-personalised management', which means that the firm is not dependent on one particular individual or individuals but rather on certain structures, rules and dynamics that enable a more productive way of running the firm. The goal of becoming more 'institutional' and building a culture around it, which was mentioned several times by the three firms, reflects this belief that an exaggerated dependence on specific individuals for a long period weakens the firm and its future success. This is more expanded in the next section.

6.3 Professionalisation: systems and information

A third category of ideas came around the objective of becoming more 'professional' in the strategy and management of the firm, which included the need for using management tools, systems and information to support a more efficient professional practice. This perspective includes a number of topics that relate to the other two categories:

(1) Open information: information about the firm should be open to all partners. This not only helps partners make better decisions but also creates a partner-inclusive culture. Since this is always a difficult topic for lawyers these firms have made it a priority to make sure all partners have access to all information and understand it, at least in the most important aspects. "An inclusive partnership requires open access to information for all partners," mentioned the senior partner from Firm B.

(2) Rules and processes: management needs to be organised around rules, systems and processes that give certainty and also limit individuals that

want to do things their own way. "We have powerful partners but they are subject to the rules and structures of the firm. Prima donnas are controlled," said a managing partner.

(3) Professional managers: management becomes more professional by:

a. Selecting management partners who have better skills for that job, not the best and most reputable lawyers. Firm C took a clear path in that direction and named two managing partners with leadership skills (Leadership Competence) but also with high levels of internal respect (Individual Influence). However, this last feature was not defined by the highest billing record but by a general recognition of a professional competence in the market. "Management should not fall into the hands of the best lawyer," said one of the managing partners. Firm C elects two managing partners for four years, and they can be reelected. They invest approximately 50% of their working time for this task. "The management structure should be diverse, not formed by just the more financially productive," said the senior partner of Firm B. The same approach was taken by Firm A.

b. Hiring professional managers in different areas that would give knowledge in fields where lawyers have little or no knowledge.

7. Lessons for leadership and decision-making processes

The way a partnership makes decisions is probably one of the best ways to understand how real leadership and power work in a firm. Given the structural limitation of lawyers with communication, matters seem to be decided often by elements of power and influence more than by the specific merits of a particular decision in an open dialogue among partners. Communication is one of the recurrent complaints of partners in law firms, but they don't always contribute to solving the problem when they have the opportunity. Exchanging information could be seen as a risky activity and searching for consensus a waste of time unless strictly necessary.

Under this perspective it is no surprise that lawyers tend to resolve matters through direct power and by establishing objective systems that could reduce the ambiguity, instead of facing them and trying to deal with them using open dialogue and a consensual approach. The result is that, except during the first stage of law firms when founders are powerful, this way of dealing with decisions means that matters that are already decided are often not complied with or implemented since they receive a silent rejection from partners who feel they are not part of the process.

As the table below indicates, the three firms followed different paths and ordered their priorities in different ways, depending on the market conditions and leadership style of their founders.

Table 2: Key strategies for sustainable and productive decision-making processes

Order of appearance			
	Firm A	**Firm B**	**Firm C**
Vision The firm as an institution with a particular purpose	1	2	1
Dialogue Cohesiveness through dialogue dynamics	3	1	2
Structure Organisational systems for firm success	2	3	3

Firms B and C used a clear decision-making pattern from the beginning based on open dialogue and respect for different opinions. At times, that may have provoked some inefficiencies, but these firms chose that approach to strengthen the partnership and provide a more stable environment for partners. In the case of Firm C, that approach was enhanced by founders who relinquished having a significant role in the management of the firm almost from the beginning. Firm B had a different leadership process in its first stages, but it still developed a strong dialogue culture. Firm A had a much stronger founder influence for a longer period and that created a concentrated decision-making process where open dialogue was more difficult. However, the founders in Firm A understood the need to create an organised structure with different partners taking part in management roles. Therefore, after an initial stage with founders active in management, partners from the second generation (and later, from the third generation) were appointed as managing partners. That in itself created a more open environment for discussions, even if at times the founders were not comfortable with this situation.

Our cases show that a culture of dialogue and respect enhances a more effective decision-making process, where partners feel more comfortable. The vision and strategy, as well as the systems and rules, tend to align more smoothly within a culture of dialogue. Firms B and C prioritised vision and dialogue in the early stages, which later produced a natural definition of the appropriate systems and rules to start a more professional and strategic stage of evolution. Firm A defined early their governance and compensation structures (also driven by the needs of fast growth), but with a dialogue culture still needing to be developed. Although Firm A also grew significantly and achieved high levels of success, cohesion was weaker and it created some difficulties in the process. Although the three firms indicated some level of effort and even difficulties in nurturing dialogue and consensus, Firm A showed the bigger struggle in this matter. "We are still learning how to do it," was the managing partner's comment.

The 'strategic vision of the firm' was a relevant driver in all firms despite the different stages of evolution in each of them. "No partner feels above the brand of the firm," indicated one of them. "To be a partner of this firm you need to have a big resigning ability," mentioned another. "We need to accept the concept of 'institution'," concluded a senior partner.

This strategic vision was connected to the ability to understand the changes in the industry and the capacity of the firm to innovate. "I am concerned that we might not develop the ability to change and adapt," expressed a managing partner. "We need to anticipate changes when we take decisions, so we can avoid a crisis. We need to be open and willing to embrace change," mentioned another.

The vital importance of 'communication and dialogue' was stressed by all firms and became a key element in building a strong sense of partnership, developing a clear collective vision and agreeing on appropriate systems to allow the firm to function effectively. Also, it was the channel to create trust among partners. "A culture of sharing and consensus was important to build the trust of the partners," mentioned one of them.

It was interesting to see that this commitment to dialogue was not interpreted as avoiding having difficult conversations. "You have to learn to say no," said one of the managing partners. Even in firms with a clear strategic view and an open culture of dialogue and consensus building, some decisions are always difficult to take. The ambiguous and opaque nature of professional work creates a constant clash between the individual and collective interests in which it is difficult to come to a consensus in all instances.

Part of creating a constructive leadership that operates with a stable and efficient decision-making dynamic is learning how to deal with difficult matters and make hard decisions. A consensus system that is unable to make difficult decisions is inadequate for a firm that wants to operate efficiently in a competitive market. This included cases like excluding non-performing partners, or delaying payment of an expected bonus. In these cases, partners were unable to reach a consensus about what to do since the alleged trade-offs were significant in either of the decisions to be taken. There was, however, a general perception of which were the right decisions to take – they were just too difficult. In these cases, the partners expected the leaders to take the risk themselves and make a decision. This was hard because if the decisions were ultimately right, the partners would express their gratitude and acknowledgement, but in the opposite case they would probably criticise the leaders for taking the wrong decision. In our cases, the decisions taken under these circumstances ultimately strengthened the leadership.

The observation of this evidence indicates that effective leadership in law firms works in a paradoxical manner. On the one hand, autonomous lawyers feel reluctant to accept a traditional leader working in a hierarchical and vertical way. Such a leader, even if sufficiently powerful due to a strong 'Individual Influence', will progressively lose recognition and support from the other partners creating a crisis or a demotivating environment. A leader seeking consensus and dialogue would be more adapted to this type of professional situation. But on the other hand, lawyers also expect strong leaders that are able to make difficult decisions and lead the way within a fragmented organisation. This combination of strength and dialogue is what normally defined good leaders in law firms, and it is not the more typical type within lawyers.

8. Conclusions for future leadership and decision-making processes

Law firms in less mature markets like Latin America tend to struggle with the concept of leadership, as it is normally related to specific individuals with particular qualities. Successful founders tend to be identified with the model of leader that lawyers seek. This personalised and individual approach poses the challenge of defining what the firm is about beyond these individuals. The whole concept of leadership is questioned and the ability of the partners to make effective decisions might be weakened. However, successful firms seem to find ways to deal with this conundrum and resolve the leadership challenge in effective ways.

We decided to observe the decision-making processes of three successful firms to understand how leadership evolved in one of the most relevant aspects of law firm life. As highly politicised organisations that have to face ambiguity in their everyday functioning, decision-making is an arena where leadership is defined and construed.

The need for an 'institutional' framework mentioned several times by all three firms indicated the clear view that only when firms are transformed into a business organisation beyond the founders' influence can they reach sustainable success and build a strong partnership. A necessary tool for that purpose is a culture of dialogue and communication where uncertainties and different perspectives can be discussed and analysed. A strategic vision and the structures and processes to make it effective only become possible when permanent dialogue and respect among partners occur.

As our cases indicate, firms might encounter different situations and challenges to achieve that result. Founders' personalities and market conditions will influence that process, making it harder or easier to find progress. But the results tend to go in the same direction, especially when you observe them in longer periods. An initial culture and vision of becoming 'institutional' will smooth the way from the beginning, and systems and processes will align later without significant struggle. Very strong founders might help a faster growth in the initial years due to their individual capacities, but the downturn might be a slower process in becoming a more institutional firm.

The stories indicate that good firms find different ways to build sustainable partnerships and successful businesses. Their decision-making processes indicate how that objective is pursued in the firms' everyday life, and the type of problems they face. Leadership tends to become effective when the seemingly paradoxical combination of strength and dialogue is pursued. Under this approach, a courageous leader that is willing to take a difficult decision does not need to preclude dialogue. On the contrary, finding the right balance between strength and dialogue seem to be the right strategy and dynamic to achieve significant results.

Leaders in less mature legal markets can benefit significantly from developing cultures of open dialogue and communication within the partnership, while developing their vision, strategy and operating systems. Organisations so dependent on autonomous individuals require a dynamic where cohesion and sense of belonging can be developed. An open discussion about leadership in forums and academic environments could also help in bringing more depth into a difficult but also critical aspect of law firms.

Leadership, power and politics in law firms

Laura Empson
Cass Business School

1. Introduction: the reluctant leader

Leaders, by definition, must have followers. In most studies of leadership, this statement is self-evident. Such studies assume that hierarchical relationships within organisations are relatively stable, and take for granted that the most senior people in an organisation have the formal authority to lead it.

In law firms, however, the distinction between leaders and followers is more difficult, as traditional hierarchies are replaced by more ambiguous and negotiated relationships among professional peers. As the client relationship partner in one global law firm expressed this to me:

Empson: *Does anyone have power over you?*
Partner: *Not as far as I'm concerned, no.*
Empson: *Does anyone think they have power over you?*
Partner: *I don't think so.*

In recent years, I have undertaken two major UK government-funded research studies into governance and leadership in global professional service firms. Through these studies I have conducted more than 400 interviews in almost 20 countries with leaders and partners from many of the world's leading professional service firms. These interviews have been supplemented by archival and observational analysis. With regard to the legal sector, through my research and consulting I have worked closely with 15 of the world's leading law firms in the United Kingdom, Europe and the United States.

I have found that in law firms, which are filled with highly educated, independent thinkers, who do not like being told what to do, it is not easy to find lawyers who are happy to identify themselves as followers. Finding lawyers who are happy to put themselves forward as leaders is even harder.

We tend to assume that the most ambitious people in an organisation will aspire to leadership roles because they crave the opportunity to influence decisions and exercise power. In a law firm, however, taking on a leadership position can potentially entail losing power. In any organisation, as in most areas of life, power comes from controlling access to valuable resources. In a law firm, or indeed in any professional service firm, the most valuable resources are specialist professional expertise and lucrative client relationships. Lawyers who take on major leadership roles necessarily reduce their fee-earning work and may find their hard-won client relationships migrating to their colleagues, or to other firms. By taking time away from frontline client work, they will struggle to ensure that their professional expertise remains at the cutting edge.

Individuals who take on leadership roles in law firms risk exchanging their most valuable assets (ie, their client relationships and professional expertise) for a title which brings with it relatively little formal authority but a great deal of responsibility.

2. Extensive autonomy and contingent authority

Leadership in law firms presents a complex and fascinating set of challenges. These challenges are encapsulated in two interrelated concepts: 'extensive autonomy' and 'contingent authority'.

Experienced lawyers require, or at least expect, extensive autonomy. This autonomy is justified by the requirement for professionals to preserve the right to make choices about how best to apply their specialist technical expertise to the delivery of customised professional services. It is perpetuated by the fact that the core value-creating resources of a law firm – technical knowledge and client relationships – are often proprietary to specific individuals. In the very largest so-called 'corporate' firms, a partner's autonomy may be less than it was in the past, but it is still nevertheless considerable. As long as the delivery of a legal service requires considerable customisation, the senior lawyer delivering that service must be free to exercise discretion. So, while the partners in the largest firms may be required to submit to formal performance evaluations and feel increasingly removed from the leadership of the firms, they nevertheless retain a high degree of operational autonomy.

Extensive autonomy is associated with contingent authority. In a law firm, senior executives are typically elected by their peers to formal positions of leadership and can be deposed at any time if they fail to retain the support of their fellow partners. While formal votes of no confidence are unusual, more discrete 'palace coups' are commonplace. As a result, senior executives can only lead by consensus and need to be acutely aware of the implicit power structures and shifting networks of influence among their colleagues.

As the chairman in a partnership I studied explained:

My experience of authority is that it lasts about an hour if you stop refreshing it … We've seen people get killed very quickly if their teams stop following them.

In my book, *Managing the Modern Law Firm* (Empson, 2007), I described partnerships as the best means of reconciling, or at least attempting to reconcile, the tension inherent within any professional service firm between the needs of the individual and the needs of the collective. At the heart of this tension sit the leaders of the firm who must absorb, embody and resolve that tension. It is no wonder so many lawyers refuse to take on these roles. In my most recent book, *Leading Professionals: Power, Politics, and Prima Donnas* (Empson, 2017) I examine the leadership dynamics of law firms in comprehensive detail. What follows is a brief overview of selected themes from my book.

3. Leadership constellation: a plural model of law firm leadership

This combination of extensive autonomy and contingent authority means that leadership in law firms needs to be conceptualised differently from the way we typically understand leadership. To date, very little leadership research has been conducted in the context of law firms and most conventional approaches to leadership simply do not apply. Most studies of leadership focus on the individual leader (eg, their personality traits and behaviours) but this conventional approach is not particularly useful when it comes to understanding law firm leadership.

Fortunately, a developing area of leadership research provides useful insights into law firm leadership. In recent years there has been growing interest among leadership scholars in what has variously been termed 'collective', 'distributed' or 'shared' leadership. In this plural conceptualisation of leadership, leadership roles are shared among multiple actors, and authority relationships are ambiguous and potentially contested. Unlike most conventional leadership research, a plural model of leadership views leadership as a collective process, unfolding over time and arising from the actions and interactions of a group of individuals. Leadership, in this sense, is not something that is done by people but something that happens between people seeking to influence each other. As a result, it can be more temporary, more insecure and more subject to negotiation than traditional individualised notions of leadership.

As part of my research on leadership in law firms, I developed the concept of the 'leadership constellation' as a means of expressing this plural model of leadership (see Figure 1 on the following page). Rather than view leadership as a quality that an individual has, or something that an individual does, the concept of the leadership constellation emphasises that leadership happens in the interactions between key actors in a firm. In some firms this may be a very small group and in other firms it may appear more like a series of concentric circles. Whatever form it takes, the power structure which the leadership constellation represents is implicit and often highly opaque to those outside of it.

Leadership is represented by the arrows that connect the members of the leadership constellation (ie, the processes of influencing), as much as by the circles representing the leaders themselves. As a senior partner in a law firm I studied summed it up:

The interesting thing in this role is that you find that you can't achieve anything

Figure 1: Leadership constellation

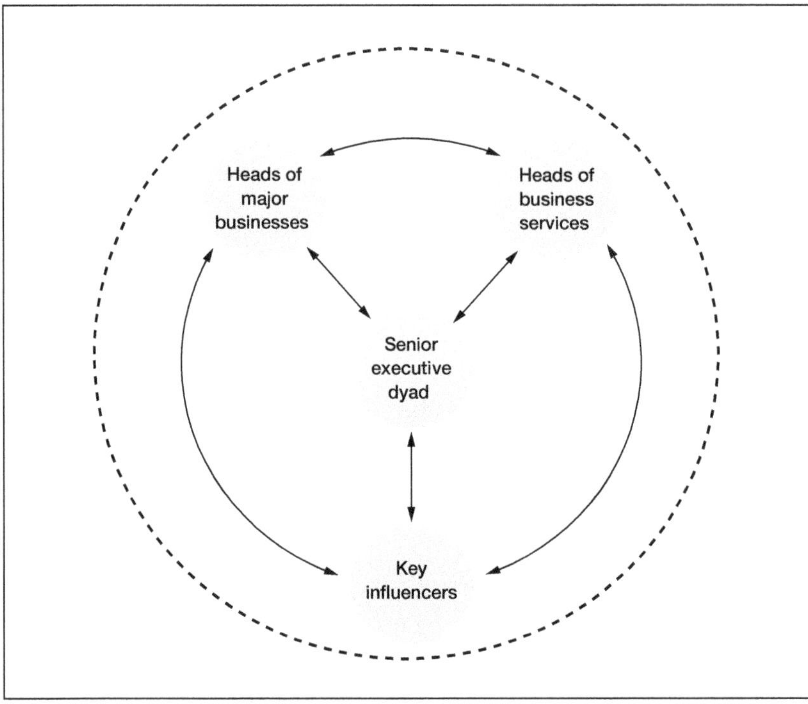

except through other people ... You can only make things happen by essentially working with this group [of powerful individuals] who in turn influence the wider group.

So who are these powerful individuals? In the context of a law firm the potential members of the leadership constellation are:

- Senior executive dyad – typically a managing partner and senior partner, or chairman and chief executive.
- Heads of businesses – leaders of major fee-earning areas such as specific practices, offices and market-sector groupings; many fee-earning areas may be excluded from the inner circle of power.
- Heads of business services – in some firms the chief operating officer, the chief financial officer or the head of human resources may have considerably more influence than most law firm partners; the partners may not realise this.
- Key influencers – these people have power derived from control of key client relationships, valuable expertise or a strong internal and external reputation; they might not appear on an organisation's chart if they have no formal role.

It is important to remember that members of the leadership constellation do not form a leadership team in any explicit sense because the constellation as a whole has no formally defined boundaries or overt identity within the firm – it can overlap with and coexist alongside formal bodies such as the executive committee or the board. The organising hierarchy within the constellation is opaque, and roles and relationships are negotiated between members as required. They recognise each other as powerful, but others may not fully recognise their power. Individuals within the firm may see themselves as leaders because they have important-sounding titles but may not be part of the leadership constellation because they are not recognised or accepted as leaders by their colleagues.

The leadership constellation therefore expresses the informal power structure of the law firm. An effective leader is one who is able to navigate this complex set of dynamics to achieve a particular purpose.

4. Identifying the leadership constellation

In my most recent research study I asked interviewees to identify where they were placed within their firm's formal governance structure and informal power structure relative to other members of the leadership constellation. I asked them to identify specific critical incidents and then recall who had been involved in the process of addressing and resolving them, at what stage they had been involved and what had been the nature of their involvement. I sought to verify their recollections by comparing them with others' recollections. I then cross-referenced interviewees' statements with formal documentation such as minutes of board meetings and transcripts of conference calls.

I was seeking to verify individuals' perceptions of their position within the power structure, to identify who recognised each other as a peer, who they deferred to and who they felt was marginalised. I used this data to map each of the firm's leadership constellations. Figure 2 is an example of the leadership constellation in a major global law firm I studied.

As the senior partner in this particular law firm saw it:

There's probably an inner core of leaders which is about 15, yes something like that, and then there's an outer core which is probably around 10 or 12 people, something like that.

In fact, my research revealed that there was a hidden inner circle of around eight people in this law firm. Interviewees identified these people by observing who was invited by the senior and managing partners to key meetings (and who was excluded) and whose opinion the senior and managing partners sought at the earliest stage about the most sensitive issues (and whom they consulted at a later stage). As one practice head in this law firm described it:

I would say there's sort of the inner group. There's one or two from [A] practice, me from [B] practice, one from [C] practice. This is quite sensitive; I wouldn't pass this on to anybody. I don't know whether this is accidental or on purpose but I think

Figure 2: Mapping the leadership constellation in a law firm

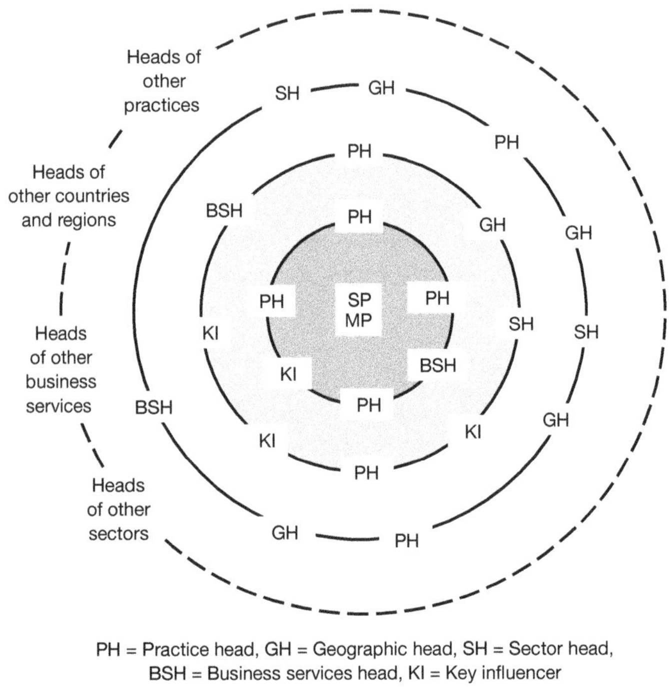

it's on purpose. There's [the senior partner], there's [the managing partner], then probably two from [D] practice. The other head of [B] practice is not included ... The group doesn't include the other head of [A] practice, and didn't include my predecessor in [B] practice.

So some practice heads considered themselves to be peers of their fellow practice heads and were unaware that they were in fact excluded from the inner circle. And there were some heads of business services (who were neither lawyers nor partners) who were closer to the inner circle than board members (who were both lawyers and partners).

5. Negotiating leadership relationships

Even for those supposedly at the centre of power in this particular law firm, the power dynamics are complex and opaque. For example, all major practices have multiple leaders who negotiate shared roles as required. How then are the members of the leadership constellation able to work together so effectively? The answer lies in the concept known by sociologists as 'social embeddedness', which helps to explain the way in which deep social ties can influence supposedly transactional and rational economic exchanges.

Many partners in a law firm may have known each other for many years. They may have studied for their law degree together or trained together when they first joined the firm. They will have been thoroughly socialised into the firm so that they share many of the same values and the way in which they understand the reality of their business world has been shaped by the organisation which has been their home for the past 25 or more years. During this time they will have built up close working relationships which enable them to negotiate their shared role space through intuitive mutual adjustment. Or as two joint practice heads explain:

The reason it works for me and [joint practice head] is that we've worked with each other for years and years and years. We like each other. We share the same values and we find the same things amusing by and large.

It's a very easy relationship. We're on a very similar wavelength. We seem to be able to anticipate what each other will think on things. I don't know whether that is healthy or unhealthy, but it feels quite easy.

For global law firms that have grown by a series of smaller acquisitions this social embeddedness exists for the partners of the legacy office (eg, the London office in the case of the magic circle firms) but not for the partners in other offices. This may cause difficulties for those from outside the legacy office who seek to exercise power within the firm they have joined. Where a firm has grown suddenly as a result of a mega-merger between firms of similar size, the issue of social embeddedness may present a different kind of problem. The challenge then is how to bring together two pre-existing leadership constellations to create a new power structure which functions effectively.

But before members of the leadership constellation have the opportunity to engage in intuitive mutual adjustment, how can these individuals come to be considered as leaders or potential leaders? More generally, how does a lawyer become a leader? The following section deals with these questions.

6. Gaining and retaining legitimacy to lead through market success

To be perceived as a potential leader in a law firm, a lawyer needs to gain the respect of colleagues through professional work. Few lawyers are happy with the idea of being led by someone who has not already done their job at least as well as, if not better than, them. As one practice head in my study explained it to me:

I've dealt with some of our most difficult clients. So I've been the partner on [major client] having won that. I'm also still currently the partner on [major client] and that's not the easiest one either. And, even now I've become head of the practice, I'm just going onto [major client]. ... So if I put my little ego hat on for a moment I was sort of, you know, seen to be a good partner. You know, one of the top partners, I suppose, and one that can get out there and win work.

While providing high-quality advice and delivering exemplary service are important ways of gaining respect, it is market success that matters most. According to another interviewee:

I think a lot of the leadership in a firm is linked to your practice and the position in the market because those people have the credibility, those people are in the market, they actually know the client and so on and in the end all that we do is ultimately directed towards clients.

Why should lawyers assume that, just because a colleague is particularly effective at rainmaking, they are in any way fit to lead their firm? My study suggests three important reasons why market success is taken to be an indicator of fitness to lead.

First, the ambiguous nature of professional work means that it can be difficult for lawyers to judge the absolute quality of a colleague's work. Market success thus comes to symbolise professional proficiency – a tangible measure of the intangible. By succeeding in selling work, aspiring leaders demonstrate to their colleagues that they are more than just highly skilled technicians; they have a broader understanding of their clients' needs and, by implication, possess the commercial acumen to lead their fellow partners to commercial success.

Secondly, the partners value an individual partner's commercial success because it will ultimately generate income for themselves. This is most marked in lockstep firms but also applies in law firms where remuneration is more directly linked to individual performance. A successful business generator creates a halo effect for his or her colleagues, whether indirectly in terms of the reputational benefits for the firm, or directly in terms of passing on additional work to colleagues. Those who prove they can feed their partners are also deemed to be qualified to lead their partners.

Thirdly, being successful in the market has strong symbolic qualities. It demonstrates to colleagues that you know what it means to work hard. You have already made the personal sacrifices that you will be asking of your colleagues. Demonstrating you can bear the pain is the ultimate demonstration of authenticity as a leader – you have pushed yourself to your limit as a professional and you have earned the right to ask your fellow partners to do the same. Or as one interviewee explained:

I think that professional service practitioners ... will accept almost unlimited decision-making and authority from someone that they think understands the things they are going through.

The leader has been through it all before. But it is not enough just to have done so in the past. Claiming or being granted the right to be seen as a leader is not a one-off event, you have to keep proving your leadership eligibility by continuing to be involved in winning business and working with clients.

One practice head in a law firm I studied contrasted his own experience with that of a less politically astute colleague:

I did more billable hours than any other practice group head ... I always find if you ask people to do something, you get a lot more respect if they think 'well he's doing it', so therefore they follow that. The banking guy who's very, very good, made a classic mistake of cutting right back on his practice and becoming full-time management. And that doesn't work in a firm like ours. You do lose credibility doing that. You have to be able to show you can still cut it.

As a lawyer in a management role, showing that you can still cut it and demonstrating your continuing commitment to the firm is vital if your colleagues are to entrust you with formal authority to lead them. But that is not all. If you have been accepted as a leader in a law firm, you must be capable of leadership – but only as far as your fellow partners will allow you.

7. Enabling autonomy while retaining control

When partners delegate formal authority to one or more of their number, it is with the understanding that they will use it to achieve the partnership's collective objectives for the firm and further its commercial success. They are by no means promising unquestioning obedience or unlimited respect. Indeed, their tacit expectation is that their individual autonomy will remain unchanged. As one law firm leader acknowledged:

You can't really tell people what to do. You can say what you're going to do and then hope people will agree with it ... and the people you can least tell what to do are those who are most important for the success of the business. Because they are the ones who control the client relationships.

Yet these firms are not haphazard anarchies, they are highly successful global professional service firms. The leaders do in fact exercise a degree of control but within certain constraints. Control focuses on ensuring that the activities of individual partners are aligned with the strategic goals and performance targets that have been agreed by the partnership as a whole, even while encouraging colleagues to believe they are exercising autonomy. As one chairman described it, leadership in this context is like:

walking a tightrope of helping my partners feel like owners, helping them feel involved, helping them be engaged, not dominating them, not getting out in front, not having a huge ego which makes them feel like the chairman's kind of off on his own trip. At the same time, being strong and providing them with a sense of confidence that we're going somewhere.

Constraints on individual autonomy (ie, managerial discipline) occur within the informal hierarchy, with partners accepting a degree of control in the interests of the partnership as a whole. This balance between enabling autonomy and maintaining control can be clumsy and hard to sustain. As one senior partner explained:

Partners say 'you're too tight' and they say 'get looser'. So you get looser and they say 'it's chaotic, get tighter'. If the money is going up, you can do what you like. If the money is going down, you can't do anything. But the money going up or down isn't within control of the senior partner.

Sometimes there are formal constraints, but the most powerful and effective controls are the desire to win and retain the respect of senior colleagues you respect by conforming to the norms of professional behaviour that they advocate and exemplify. In other words, professionals look to their chosen role models and attempt to act accordingly. As a senior law firm partner explained:

I think the younger partners want you to spend more time (than them) thinking about what the firm as a whole is doing and ... to provide thought leadership which they will either follow or not, because it's not telling them what to do; it's actually just coming up with the prompts and ideas to maximise the business and get the best out of people. I think that's what they expect some of the more senior partners to do. So it sort of happens.

It seems that leadership in a law firm can be something that 'sort of happens'. Partners will be likely to cooperate as long as the prompts and ideas are not positioned as bureaucratic incursions or excessive management. This is the essence of the contingent nature of authority in such organisations. Leaders have, in effect, a temporary mandate from their partners to interpret and implement partners' objectives for the firm.

It is important that leaders should not try to work alone in maintaining this balance. They are acting on behalf of the partnership and should not allow themselves to become portrayed as acting in opposition to it. It is easy for leaders in this situation to become isolated. Instead, they need to enlist the support of their colleagues within the leadership constellation and beyond to help maintain the balance between individual autonomy and managerial control. They also need to recognise when it is time to act in order to exercise stronger leadership. As one interviewee explained:

Lots of people here are crying out for leadership, you know, they just don't realise it. But they are. They do what they do but if somebody could inspire them and show them there was a better way of doing it, they'd follow that.

But such overt leadership activity may be perceived by partners as interfering with their autonomy and is likely to be met with resistance or disdain. Control of a partnership is maintained in more nuanced and less obtrusive ways and, accordingly, requires subtle political skills.

8. Interacting politically while appearing apolitical

In order to be accepted as leaders by their peers, professionals must appear to be apolitical. But in reality politics is simply a fact of life in law firms – it is the oil which lubricates the wheels of everyday organisational interactions.

Many interviewees in my study said, unprompted, that they abhorred politics and insisted that their firms were not political. But they have somewhat naive notions of political behaviour. Interviewees seem to understand organisational politics in rather simplistic terms as self-serving, duplicitous and unscrupulous. According to one interviewee:

To me politics smacks of alliance-building in the corridors, in offices behind the scenes. It smacks of people engineering agendas, which creep up on the firm and deliver a fait accompli *in a way that becomes disruptive. Or politics could manifest as someone undermining another person. I would like to think we don't have those behaviours.*

So lawyers who display these behaviours may be seen by their peers as unsuitable for a leadership role. As another interviewee in the same firm explained:

There are people who are clearly very ambitious in the firm who will say from quite an early age to you, particularly over a beer or over a meal or over a chat [slams hand on table], 'Do you think I'm in the frame to be managing partner or senior partner? What is it I need to do along the way?'... And they're regarded as quite pushy, will be more political in their views in terms of what they think people will want to hear and what they think people will want to vote for.

But how can someone become senior partner at a large law firm without learning how to negotiate between opposing partners, influence on a one-on-one basis and in large groups, take soundings among powerful individuals and build consensus across the partnership? These actions require social astuteness, interpersonal influence, networking ability and apparent sincerity – all key political skills.

This suspicion of political behaviour has a certain irony when you consider that the partners of the firms have explicitly and deliberately constructed political environments. They use political language, hold formal elections to senior roles and have candidates who issue manifestos and speak at candidates' debates. Senior leaders of law firms refer to their partners as 'constituents', and tell stories of rival candidates briefing against them and of leadership coups. Or as one interviewee described it:

The previous election for senior partner was a bit of a power struggle between two individuals who were dominant characters within the organisation and [Fred] held sway on the basis of support from a number of the more senior partners including the outgoing senior partner who had quite a lot of influence ... It was all closed doors – smoke filled rooms – lots of politicking etc etc etc – a variety of promises being made to various senior people to get them to support [Fred].

Interviewees describe political behaviours as rife, but curiously do not interpret them as such. As one interviewee explained it:

There was a time at a partner conference when I thought somebody was getting lynched. We were having a formal vote and discussion about electing someone to partner ... There were two or three people with a personal agenda, a particular dislike for an individual and they were trying to scuttle this person ... It was fighting in public. I mean the way this firm operates it should all be resolved before you ever go in the room.

In other words, the conflict resolution, trade-offs and compromises that inevitably must occur within a partnership were supposed to be made in private, allowing for a public show of harmony and consensus. This is of course a much more political approach than open disagreement during partner conferences, but it allows the partners to preserve the illusion that they are not operating in a political environment.

This apparent paradox (of denigrating political behaviour while creating structures which favour skilful politicians) can be reconciled by recognising that the more adroit leaders persuade their peers that they are not personally ambitious, even while they are climbing to the top of their organisations. These individuals appear to be ambitious for the partnership as a whole rather than for themselves (though, of course, the two are not mutually exclusive). Their peers are willing to cast themselves in the role of followers because they trust these individuals sufficiently to allow them a degree of formal authority over them. As one interviewee described it:

The partnership as a whole trusts our leader, that he's going to resolve it for the best – for the good of the partnership. As long as they believe that and trust that, then there's no reason to put any other kind of hold on him.

In fact, interviewees sometimes described successful leaders as above politics entirely:

Sometimes my sense would be [senior partner] doesn't necessarily always understand how influential he is. He's very modest about it, quite self-effacing, and he himself doesn't attach such great importance to some of those things that might be under the heading of creeping as in slightly sinister. He is not himself a player in that way at all … it's simply because his own motivations in this world are so, I think, very genuine and clean.

How can someone rise to be senior partner of a global law firm without being a 'player'? Perhaps some of the reluctance to take on leadership roles in law firms, referred to at the start of this chapter, may be professed rather than genuine? After all, most senior leaders need to put themselves forward for election in the first place and in some cases fight a very tough campaign to be elected. But to win the trust of their peers, leaders must be seen as 'genuine and clean' rather than 'creeping' and 'slightly sinister'. That is, they should be looking out for the good of the firm rather than for their own self-interests. As one interviewee saw it:

We have people in leadership positions who don't appear to be having to work politically to keep their position ... The one who does [leadership] more naturally, partners will recognise that, and [he] is more likely to sustain the role. And the others are more likely to crash and burn.

Yet individuals operating in a highly politicised environment who do not appear to have to work politically to keep their position are almost certainly deploying highly sophisticated political skills – whether utilising them consciously or not, and whether using them to fulfil their personal ambitions or their ambitions for the firm.

One interviewee, the global head of human resources in a law firm, who is not herself a partner, reconciles the apparent paradox of denigrating political behaviour while rewarding political skill within these firms as follows:

It is important to distinguish between the sort of political ego, which doesn't work, and political savviness, which is absolutely essential. And that savviness is born out of empathy and the ability to see and absorb and understand what is spoken and unspoken, and what goes on sort of implicitly. I think it is critical in this organisation ... Without it you are in real trouble because if you don't have it you can't have influence.

It is worth recognising that this political savviness, and the political skills that underlie it (ie, social astuteness, interpersonal influence, networking ability and apparent sincerity), are precisely the abilities lawyers need in order to handle their clients. In the client context they are not thought of as political skills, but just as being good with clients. This is another – albeit probably unconscious – reason why professionals infer leadership ability from market success. The client relationship management skills that make you good at winning business and retaining prestigious clients are the same skills that can make an effective law firm leader.

What makes an effective law firm leader?

It seems that leading a law firm can be reduced to three tactics:

- gaining and retaining legitimacy to lead through market success;
- enabling autonomy whilst retaining control; and
- interacting politically while appearing apolitical.

All of these are densely intertwined.

To achieve market success, lawyers must have mastered their technical professional work and be highly effective at winning and developing profitable client relationships. To enable autonomy while maintaining control they must perpetually perform a delicate balancing act between being 'too tight' and 'too loose'. And to act politically whilst appearing apolitical, they must be able to demonstrate social astuteness, interpersonal influence and networking ability, while all the time appearing sincere. To achieve this, to put in the hours required and not become discouraged by the scale and complexity of the role, requires very high levels of physical energy and emotional stamina. In a firm where your colleagues are highly driven and high-achieving, you need to remain just ahead of them to ensure they are achieving in the right direction. In a firm where your colleagues are not as highly driven and high-achieving as you believe they should be, you need to remind them continually of the goal you are supposed to be collectively striving towards. You must not lose faith in yourself or your colleagues when progress seems too slow.

So what sort of individual can effectively negotiate his way through the subtleties and complexities of a law firm's leadership? Looking across all of the firms studied, an effective leader should:

- be highly respected for his skills as a professional – especially business generation;
- not appear to be seeking power;
- inspire loyalty and commitment;
- have a strong personal vision and be able to communicate it;
- be able to build consensus and act decisively;
- transfer responsibility but intervene selectively;
- be comfortable with ambiguity and conflict;
- spend time massaging egos;
- not expect to have his or her own ego massaged; and above all
- be able to identify and navigate the leadership constellation.

9. A romantic ideal?

The plural leadership model typically found in law firms can be seen as the antithesis of the individual heroic leader, as mythologised by the business press. Lawyers do not like to see themselves as unthinkingly or even admiringly following someone who is out in front of them, winning the kudos and controlling their actions. Instead, they elect some of their peers into leadership positions, often for a fixed term, granting them the status of first among equals.

Yet, as they do this, they may be creating an alternative leadership mythology. Interviewees describe their leaders as self-effacing, modest individuals with 'clean' motivations who are above the political fray, reluctantly accepting office only because they are putting the interests of the partnership first. By perpetuating this belief in the purity of their leaders, lawyers are also reasserting their belief in themselves as autonomous individuals working within apolitical partnerships. The reality, of course, is far more grubby, complicated and compromised than that – leadership, power and politics inevitably are.

Acknowledgements

I would like to acknowledge support of the Economic and Social Research Funding Council of Great Britain for their support for my study "Understanding Leadership Dynamics in Professional Service Firms" (RES-062-23-2269). I would also like to acknowledge the work of Johan Alvehus of the University of Lund, with whom I am developing academic papers from this empirical material, and whose insights are reflected in some of the ideas presented in this chapter. Finally, I would like to thank the members of the Cass Centre for Professional Service Firms for their contributions throughout this study.

Selected references

Empson, L (2007), *Managing the Modern Law Firm: New Challenges, New Perspectives* (Oxford University Press).

Empson, L (2017), *Leading Professionals: Power, Politics, and Prima Donnas* (Oxford University Press).

For details of ongoing academic papers arising from this study and other relevant research, see: www.lauraempson.com

Generations in the workplace

Alexis Caught
Strategy Four
Kevin Doolan
Møller Institute

1. Introduction

The law firm model needs a flow of well-qualified and enthusiastic entrants to the profession to provide it with the leverage it needs; the ability to serve clients at different skill levels and prices; and from which it can select the best to take on the role of leaders and equity owners of the future firm. The model has been tried and tested in its modern form since the 1940s. However, we now see strains emerging in this model, especially over the behaviour and motivations of the Millennial Generation of lawyers. We are going to examine the impact of these changes on the current law firm model using the following structure:

- What do we mean, when we say, 'different generations'?
- The tension points.
- The traditional law firm model – what are the rules and how have they changed?
- The demands of the new generation of lawyers.
- The solutions – working successfully with Millennials.
- Our Top Six ways to work with Millennials in your firm.

Generations, we all belong to one. We're all aware of them, we grew up as part of families where care and compassion, power and status were passed down (and fought for) between age groups of our family. In our families, it creates tension as each generation seeks to grow and take the reins from an older generation who may be reticent to give up their power.

In the workplace, we see the same story playing out. For the first time in modern working history, we're really becoming aware of how these generational differences play out in the workplace. As businesses grew and became international, 'cultural competency training' and 'leadership across borders' took off as an understanding that different groups have different ways of working. The same applies for the generations.

It is this that we will be exploring in this chapter, looking at how changing generational needs and attitudes are causing issues in the world of work, and actionable, practical tips for solving inter-generational headaches. Millennials now make up over 40% of the workforce, and our research showed that they responded to a different management style from the more traditional law firm one. When the differences between the generations are understood, solutions to problems come easily, and great change and innovation can be harnessed to bring benefits to our workplaces. Moreover, we believe that those firms who are best able to harness the different skills available across the generations will develop a real and sustainable competitive advantage in the marketplace.

What millennials want, contrary to popular belief, is not pandering to their whims. They want to be active in their own futures, they want to make a difference, they want to contribute, and importantly – they want leadership. This is a big issue for law firms – there is a big difference between managing and leading, and we saw that success in retaining and motivating Millennials came to those who leveraged these differences.

2. What do we mean, when we say, 'different generations'?

Generational classification has its grounding in attitudinal research, which believes that the way in which we view the world, our core values and driving motivation, are heavily influenced by global events such as politics, economic trends, wars and changes in technology. These influences create step changes and differences in those that experienced them at formative points in their lives. It would be remiss not to point out the obvious flaw with this – we are all individuals, so the extent to which different events affect us will differ, so this is an exercise in broad-brush strokes to create an understanding of a broad demographic. There are generalisations here but our experience inside numerous law firms tackling these issues has convinced us that the differences between generations are real, and not to be ignored.

For the purposes of this chapter, the generations that we shall be focusing on are the Baby Boomers, Generation X, and Generation Y – the latter being the often demonised 'Millennials' criticised for ruining the world of work with their demands, and laughed at for their financial profligacy as they 'choose' to spend money on avocado-toast rather than mortgages and pensions. Of course, these are not the only generations alive today, but they are the focus of the world of work. Older than Baby Boomers, we have 'The Silent Generation' who lived through terrible world wars, and the young whipper-snappers about to burst into the world of work – Gen Z, young people who never experienced life pre-social media, let alone pre-internet. The Silent Generation, while now retired and out of the workforce, helped create many of the working ethics and practices that we still follow, their traditional values and 'do as you are told' beliefs are still the basis of most office hierarchies. Gen Z, at the polar opposite end, are currently too young to be shifting and changing the world of work ... but they're coming.

2.1 Who are they? What are the cut-off points, and what are the differences?

Exact dates of the cut-off points between different generations vary slightly from study to study (typically within only a few years). For clarity, the definitions, and their cohort demographic that we are using are as follows:

(a) *Baby Boomers*

Born between 1945 and 1960, making them between the ages of 59 and 74 in 2019. They grew up under the shadow of The Cold War, where the threat of nuclear destruction was ever present. This created a trust in government and power – an acknowledgement that a strong, militarised, state was crucial to survival, challenging this was a threat to personal safety. They saw the rebuilding of cities and the global economy after two devastating world wars, so believe in hard work as a real-world solution to difficult problems. As they reached adulthood, they experienced the economic boom of the 1980s, a time of unprecedented economic growth which saw them believe their hard work had earned them great rewards – a belief continually supported as they've seen their wealth increase with the global boom in property prices. As children in the education system, teachers still ruled with the rod, and strict familial structures were the norm; these combined to make them unused to feedback (it wasn't regularly given), and uncomfortable with conflict – authority was to be respected, not challenged.

(b) *Generation X*

Currently 39 to 58 (making them born between 1961 and 1980), these were the first 'latch key kids' who typically had both parents working, and so grew up more independently and autonomously than any generation before. They witnessed the 1980s economic boom, combined with free market political figures like Ronald Reagan and Margaret Thatcher, who promoted an Ayn Randian view that 'greed was good'. Thatcher's statement "there is no such thing as society" created a generation that were very self-focused, individual and self-reliant. Conversely, they matured at a time of ever increasing international travel and international trade, creating a cohort more aware of global implications than ever before. In the workplace, they can see the way ahead and want to 'just get on with it' – their schooling focused on independent learning, further enhancing their autonomy, while new testing regimes came in that rewarded hard work and study. As they started their professional careers, the introduction of email sped up the pace of work. Whilst this was the first generation that talked about the importance of work/life balance, they rarely saw it and tended to emulate the working practices of the Baby Boomer generation.

(c) *Generation Y – Millennials*

This cohort were born between 1981 and 1995, aging them at 24 to 38 in 2019. In their youth, they lived in pre-internet times before the digital and online revolution and have matured as technology embedded itself in our society. As such, they are a living link between a huge change in human history, the Industrial Era to the Information Era. But this does not offer them guaranteed security – globally, they feel that they have been increasingly let down, social contracts enjoyed by prior generations have been broken, indeed they are the first generation in history to be financially worse off than their parents, facing a future on a dying planet. In many ways they have both lower quality of life and lower life expectancy than their parents, being paid less, with home ownership permanently out of the grasp of many. They understand traditional institutions, but would say that they were repeatedly let down by them in their formative years. In school, like those before them, they were promised "work hard, you'll get to go to university, you'll get a great job, and buy yourself a nice house" ... and one by one those rewards vanished. Tuition fees in universities sky rocketed, the financial crisis in 2008 and resulting jobs crisis struck when they were graduating from university (with unprecedented levels of student debt), and since they've managed to get onto the career ladder house prices have globally become unaffordable and out of reach for the majority of workers. These factors combined to create a generation who will no longer wait for long-term payoff and reward; experience has taught them, it won't be delivered. They do not believe the promises of future benefits spouted by authority figures – they need to see much more immediate evidence.

3. Tension points

Contrary to the often deeply held belief of each, no generation has it all figured out and is doing it 'the best way' – each has its own strengths and weaknesses. The tension points come from where these fail to match up. Often, they are around issues such as:

- Attitudes and approach to work: Baby Boomers need to be in charge, Gen X want to be left alone to deliver, and Millennials want to collaborate.
- Differing styles in communication: Baby Boomers were brought up in a time of very little feedback and so find giving and receiving it highly uncomfortable. Gen X, ever the pragmatists, want to know how to get better results, faster. Millennials need the emotional nurture of regular constructive feedback. This is often a by-product of their schooling, which saw them tested and reported on more than any generation before them.
- Attitudes to team working: Baby Boomers are comfortable in intergenerational groups, when they're leading the team. Self-reliant, but also self-aware, Gen Xs will engage with teamwork when they see a benefit to it, but typically prefer to work separately with designated 'check-in points' for group work. Here Gen X will collectively assess the

situation, plan the next steps, and then individually action their own separate tasks. Millennials were raised on group projects and collective learning so crave the stimulation of multiple ideas, and look to older generations in teams to give examples and share knowledge, but don't assume age guarantees the best idea. In fact, they may have a tendency to assume the opposite.

- Values and attributes: Baby Boomers typically are sticklers for tradition – they grew up in a workplace ruled by order and hierarchy, and now they're at the top, they want it upheld. Gen X, made independent by their parents and empowered by email, were the first to push for more flexible working conditions as the autonomy they provide is a way they feel trusted and respected. Millennials went even further – while at university, they were empowered by the internet and the prevalence of fast laptops which meant that they no longer had to go to the library to study, they could learn anywhere, they could work anywhere. Naturally, they took this into the world of work with them and crave flexibility and freedom.

To help understand their motivations, each of the generations have a set of generally agreed upon key core values and drivers. These are only indicative and of course will vary in strength from individual to individual, but will broadly be applicable and help us to understand the differing perspectives.

4. The traditional law firm model – what are the rules and how have they changed?

The Baby Boomer joined a firm with a clear 'apprenticeship model'. Start as a low paid trainee, gain experience and the all-important qualification, then the route to partnership could be as short as a few years. No complex tiers, at most there might be a period in salaried partnership. The trainees had a high level of access to a partner (often sharing their office), would attend client meetings and be given high levels of hands on guidance.

By the time Gen X arrived, law firms were growing in scale and complexity and the route to partnership had become longer and more complex. To maintain high equity partner incomes, law firms had stretched the road to equity, imposing multiple layers of senior associates, directors or the like. Now it might take 15 years or more to reach equity, creating even more drop outs along the way. Equity was becoming a more exclusive club and the layering of lawyers meant that training would often be provided by non-partner lawyers.

Then, in 2008 the game changed again. At a time when Millennials were entering the workforce, demand for legal services had taken a big drop and law firms were shedding staff and reducing or cancelling training contracts. A young lawyer or trainee was competing for work with lawyers who had been made redundant at their firm. After so many years of continual growth, the rules had changed. A young lawyer entering the profession, duly trained in sceptical analysis of an opponent's arguments, would see law firms who had continually moved the goalposts, had ditched partners, lawyers and business services professionals pretty fast when times had got tight, and seemed to value existing equity partner earnings above all else. So, what is the chance that this Millennial generation of lawyers would buy into promises of equity jam tomorrow if they worked hard for 15 years or more?

This is not just about Millennials – any new generation of lawyers coming into this work environment would be strongly suspicious. The partner-led apprenticeship model has disappeared, they see that very few lawyers make it to the top (even if they work hard for many years) and they are going to be much more focused upon current rewards (what will I earn this year?) and the behaviour of their immediate supervisor (how am I treated in this organisation?).

5. The demands of a new generation of lawyers

The concept of work/life balance is certainly nothing new, Baby Boomers thought about it, Generation X swore they'd get it, Millennials are the ones demanding it. When an industry such as law depends so heavily on new recruits putting in effort now for future reward, it actually depends on the willingness of juniors to delay gratification and put their trust in the institution. Unfortunately, even at their relatively young ages, for many Millennials life has taught them that this does not pay off.

When Millennials went to school, they were told "work hard, and you'll get to go to university", then when they reached higher-education age, students' fees sky rocketed to unprecedented levels while maintenance grants were cut. "But it's okay" they were told "pay the tuition with an interest free government loan, and you can get a good job you like afterwards", so they took the loans and went off to university. Then they graduated, to find the Global Economy had crashed. Starting your career at a time when those with a decade's more experience than you are being made redundant, was not good for job prospects. Fortunately, those 'interest free government loans' didn't need to be repaid until earnings went past a threshold amount, except the rules were changed and formerly interest free loans were now the subject of interest, which immediately began to accrue. Those who got their foot on the job ladder faced extreme competition, often having to self-fund their lives while working unpaid internships in order to get a start in their careers. Eventually, they slogged away, to find that their salaries no longer matched inflation and wage growth had stagnated. They are the first generation to be financially worse off than their parents, at a time when the cost of living, and house prices, have never been higher.

For many Millennials, at pivotal points in their lives, inter-generational agreements and pacts have been broken by those ahead of them. As a result, they take a very dim view of 'promised' future rewards.

Against the backdrop of this, we have the arrival of tech giants. In these companies, run by up-start Millennials, offices changed beyond recognition, company perks took on new forms, pay packets grew, offers of equity came at much younger ages, and the best and brightest paid attention. Working in a tech company for their in-house legal team meant good pay, much more reasonable hours, free food, a relaxed office environment, flexible working, yes – they could even wear jeans to the office. Suddenly, in comparison, a law firm didn't look quite so prestigious. As one associate who left a global firm to join an in-house tech team told us, "I'd make maybe £20,000 a year more in a firm, but I'd get a whole lot more stress," while another when asked why they left 'big law' for in-house life said, "Have you ever had to cancel your holiday … while on that holiday?"

One day, we were finishing up a meeting with a large global bank and as we walked through the in-house legal department, an excited face rushed over. We'll call this person Helen, she was a remarkably talented Millennial senior associate that we had met when she worked in a large global law firm. It was no secret that Helen was on track to make partner, so seeing her as part of an in-house team – at a bank – was a surprise to say the least. "I'm so much happier here, I sleep, I see my kids" was her gushing response when asked why she had quit her law firm position. It wasn't a zany tech office that drew her away, she didn't leave a law firm over a desire to wear jeans and trainers to the office, or an inability to 'keep up'. Banks have their own high-performance cultures, but the hours, she said, were far, far lighter. As she explained, she had come to the decision that becoming partner was not what she wanted any more. "I looked at them, tired, stressed, always sick, paranoid – sure, they might earn loads, but for what?" Another former high-performing senior associate, when asked about his decision to quit law firm life said, "I want to go home to my kids in the evening, I don't want to be a stressed Daddy."

There are other factors at work though. Millennials are a highly ambitious generation. They might wish to change the world and claim to be less financially motivated than those before them, but they're also pragmatists, saddled with debt and facing rising prices, and know they need a salary to afford them the adventurous lifestyle they wish for – this is why so many conversations with Millennials turn to money, if their holistic needs and desires aren't met they easily become contractual. Even what the generations spend their money on has changed; rather than accruing possessions, research has found Millennials much prefer to spend their money on life experiences, eating out, events, travel etc. All of that needs to be paid for. They still crave reassurance about their position and progress, to develop themselves and improve. What they need are not law firm line managers in rigid hierarchies and tick boxes. Millennials crave leadership. Let's explore that in more detail.

6. The solutions – working successfully with Millennials

For us, the standout lesson is that law firm management is not enough. It was often sufficient in the past, but we do not see it as a recipe for success in the future. What do we mean by this? That in a relatively stable profession, with strong growth in demand for legal services, many firms could succeed without having a great vision or leadership mindset. There were some well-established formulae for success, that worked when firms faced a positive growth in demand. Work hard, look after your clients, recruit the best that you can, and so on. The first major bump in the road for many years (when demand saw a substantial drop) was just after the Global Financial Crisis. Until then we saw all firms rising on a tide of ever increasing demand and an ability to restrict the supply of new lawyers by only recruiting the number necessary to cope with each firm's growth curve. Firms had 'managing partners' – even the terminology gave it away – their role was about steady management of growth. His (sometimes her, but never frequently enough) job was to be the most senior manager in the firm. A key expression that we heard from these 'leaders' of firms was about 'accountability'. Complaining that really, partners weren't very accountable, and that they had few 'sticks and carrots' with which to 'manage people's behaviour'. Of course, that is because they were acting as managers and you cannot manage unless others agree to be accountable to you (whether for this month's bills or winning that new client). This assuredly is not leadership, because leaders do not gain their power because their followers are accountable to them. This is absolutely text book management behaviour.

For an explanation of the real difference between leadership and management we turn to Professor John Kotter at Harvard Business School and in particular the models in his seminal work, "What Leaders Really Do". Leaders behave very differently to managers. The focus of a manager is on the present, on delivering today's work, this month's numbers, on quality assurance and delivery. This was an extension of the task orientation that would come so naturally to most lawyers, who had grown to deliver ever more complex legal projects for their clients. Leadership could hardly be more different. Skills for a leader often started with a focus on the outside world and the firm's position in it, especially in future years (not for the next three months). Leaders used their understanding of the opportunities and threats that they saw to create and then articulate an inspiring vision – a destination that others could buy into. This was not command and control, much less micro-management of the numbers. Leaders seek to empower others to help delivery of a vision, where managers seek to direct and control subordinates who are accountable to them. Leaders recognise a responsibility to the people that they are leading. A manager will seek to use authority to drive behaviours of subordinates in line with budgets and plans.

Now here was the key finding from our research. With the legal market facing increasing competition and technological change, the next 10 years will be a period when law firms require leadership rather than management. Moreover, we found that Millennials respond overwhelmingly positively where their immediate superior behaved in a leadership style towards them, and adversely against being 'managed'. What do we mean by saying that a 'leadership style' worked well? It is that the behaviours that Millennials praised were in phrases such as:

- I felt my manager was really interested in my personal development, that I would gain new skills while working with her.
- He had time for me, gave me detailed feedback on my work and helped me to get better at my job.
- She knew a lot about me, I felt she cared for and wanted to hear my opinion.
- I really respect my team leader's integrity.

There was a valuable lesson here. Millennials were more likely to stay or leave an organisation based upon their assessment of their direct line manager, and that the most successful of these managers acted in a leadership role when dealing with their Millennial team members. We felt that there was something of a formula emerging here, of an approach that would bring great results not just for the Millennial and their manager, but for the organisation as a whole. Leaders listen, they empower, they invest in the development and success of those they are leading. The great leader is successful because they inspire others to follow their vision, a vision that has wins for all, not just for the leader. Let's now look at how we saw this playing out in practice in the most successful firms that we researched.

7. Our Top Six ways to work with Millennials in your firm

7.1 Listen

Millennials will typically have a strong point of view on any topic. It is not about saying that their view has to prevail, but they immensely value the feeling that they have been listed to. We work with firms which have developed sophisticated ways of actively listening to their Millennial lawyers – and understood that asking for feedback at a group meeting with partners was unlikely to lead to honesty. Millennials understand that criticising partner behaviour or decisions could be career limiting. We also saw them being given challenging issues and asked to work in teams to create new solutions, or external consultants employed to carry out structured listening exercises to truly uncover their views and attitudes in a confidential environment. Millennials hugely valued 'being listened to' and this seemed to be the platform for other, positive, cross-generational practices.

7.2 Communicate

Millennials grew up in a feedback intensive culture. They are used to being judged and commented upon daily. It feels odd and uncomfortable to them when they carry out work and hear nothing. Just like anyone else, neither do they crave constant criticism – but they are keen to learn and improve. For example, we saw a firm that trained partners to deliver instant feedback on work that was phrased "I really like that you did xxxxxxx on this piece of work" and "It could be even better if you did yyyyyyyy". Another had set up a closed group twitter feed where partners could keep in daily contact with associates working with them and had trained partners in the value of providing 'praise and guidance'. This is a real and very strong generational difference – silence lands hard with Millennials.

7.3 Mentor

Millennials crave the guidance and learning that can come from close contact with partners. If these, the leaders of the firm, demonstrated that they were too busy to spend time with the Millennial lawyer, then they could not expect much loyalty in return. In some firms they were using 'Reverse Mentoring' to bring the newest members of the firm into contact with the most experienced partners. For example, this could take the form of the Millennial teaching the partner about social media, establishing a good LinkedIn profile for them and showing how this could be used to build the partner's market reputation. In return the partner would take a formal mentoring role looking at the future plans of the Millennial and how they could help them to succeed (within the organisation or outside of it).

7.4 Empower

Millennials tend to have an almost arrogant assumption that if something has been done in a particular way for a long time, then there must now be a better way. This constant challenge can be wearing for their seniors, but well harnessed, you have a generation who excel in taking an innovative approach, using technology and fresh ways of thinking to drive change. This generation thrives on change – and we saw many examples of their being put in the front line with clients who wanted to see innovation and change in the way that services were being delivered. You have the most tech savvy, entrepreneurial and innovative generation sitting in your offices – are you using these skills?

7.5 Think career planning

It is clear that for the great majority of Millennials the traditional, lengthy, career structure was a turn-off. Too uncertain, too much future-focused and it assumed that the Millennial was keen on making partner. A much shorter career horizon was needed. In the accounting profession we came across 're-contracting' where the Millennial would have a formal meeting every 18 months at which there would be a discussion of the ways that the firm would invest in that person's skills and expertise (including formal training) if the Millennial was prepared to sign on for another 18 months (an idea we were told was copied from the Army). We also heard much about 'boomerang staff'. This involved an acceptance that their Millennials may want a change of scenery after a few years, so were prepared for them to leave, but would then stay actively in touch so that the best ones could come back into the law firm at some point in the future. This was no box ticking exercise but very proactive contact with the former member of staff, checking on their progress, finding out what they had learned in their new organisation, and looking at new opportunities if they returned.

7.6 Tell them why

Millennials have a need to understand the context for their work. That means spending more time explaining to them what you are asking them to do, how it fits in to the other aspects of this client's work and what you are trying to achieve overall. They want to make a difference, to feel that what they are doing is worthwhile. We saw that partners who invested time explaining the context for the work had a more engaged and successful relationship with their Millennials. At first, we heard partners complaining that this was a substantial demand on their time, which was already in high demand. But when partners saw the results from investing in this time, they quickly became convinced. They received back a much better, more usable, more valuable piece of work when they invested this time. It also paid off in terms of the Millennials' motivation and job satisfaction – and then ultimately into their retention in the firm. It harked back to an earlier age when there was a much closer relationship between partner and young lawyer – to the apprenticeship model.

8. What is the prize?

Some partners questioned whether investing in retaining Millennials was worth the extra effort. There was a recognition that they needed to nurture the next generation, but often a desire to identify Millennials that were 'just like them' and would follow the more traditional route through the firm. We came across examples where substantial effort had been put into psychometric test development in an attempt to recruit 'the right type' of Millennial. But our question was this, does the future of law need 'more of the same' personality types in charge? With much more frequency we came across a recognition that ignoring the problem was simply not going to work, and that this is an issue of growing importance. However, our interviews with clients revealed that there was a big prize for firms that integrated their Millennials into the firm. Clients told us both that they valued inter-generational teams, and we were repeatedly told that they gave the client better results. The combination of ideas and viewpoints from a mixed age legal team gave more value to the client. We reached the stage where we saw this as having the potential to give a firm a sustainable competitive advantage.

We saw another prize too – a very personal and important one. We had often heard the complaint from Baby Boomer and Gen X partners that Millennials simply would not regularly work the same hours as them, and that they insisted on having work/life balance and other outside interests. This was often followed by the statement, "Of course, it's possible that the Millennials are right – that there is more to life than work, and we should be giving a greater priority to ourselves and our families!" A little to our surprise, we started to see Gen X partners changing some of their behaviours, starting to pick up on the benefits that Millennials had shown them of the value of work/life balance. For example, we're seeing a number of Gen X partners who are deliberately keeping two phones – to segment and separate their work and private lives, to enforce a disconnect by not having work emails on their personal phones. It allows the Gen X partner to have family time, holiday or simply time off without work emails constantly pinging on his or her phone. Millennials could be an example of a more balanced, happier and less exhausting career model. One partner added, "As our clients are getting younger, we are starting to see a difference in client demands. If the Millennial client is not working all weekend, we have started to see them accept that neither will their lawyers – it is slow at the moment, but it's a promising trend."

Leading teams of lawyers in an increasingly global and virtual world

Mark Mortensen
INSEAD

1. Introduction

Success in today's economy requires collaboration. At its simplest, it is rare to find any meaningful work in today's professional service firms that a single person can complete. Teams have become the building blocks of almost all firms around the world – something which holds true across all industries and sectors. Beyond simply increasing the scope of our work, teams can foster the flexibility, innovation and adaptability demanded in our knowledge-driven economy. Teams increase intra- and inter-organisational knowledge flow, improving the skills of individual employees while diffusing culture, ideas, innovations and best practices.

Going a step further, global teams allow firms to provide integrated solutions to global clients who increasingly face global issues. Clients want counsel to address and solve their problems the same way they face them – globally. When a US-based multinational's trademark is being infringed upon in Germany, China and Australia, that client needs to know that discussions with counsel in New York are mobilising the necessary associates and partners in Frankfurt, Shanghai and Sydney. Clients want to know that their matters are being handled by individuals with deep knowledge of the distinct local contexts and the relationships needed to either settle or pursue litigation. At the same time, they must be confident that any local solutions will be well-integrated into a global outcome that matches their brand strategy. In some cases, global collaborations help firms to identify and capitalise on innovative solutions that may form the basis of new services and may even attract new clients. It is thus no surprise that many major firms have experienced substantial international growth in the past few years.

With the benefits of global teams, however, also come risk and expense. Global collaborations incur significant coordination costs, such as:

- project delays due to incompatible schedules;
- cross-cultural or linguistic misunderstandings that result in non-billable rework;
- technology failures that cause deadlines to be missed.

The stakes are higher as global projects tend to be some of the biggest and most important within a firm's portfolio. Because such projects are increasingly impossible to avoid, firms must learn how to reduce those costs and improve effectiveness. Those who are unable to master – or at least manage – these challenges will find themselves facing massively increased overheads without a corresponding increase in revenue.

This chapter explores the unique obstacles facing global collaborations within professional service firms and offers ideas on how best to overcome them. In the first half of the chapter, I outline the core effects of working at a distance – some expected and some unexpected. In the second half, I outline some tactics derived from observations of best practices in the field, augmented by research findings.

2. The effects of working at a distance

Global teams introduce distance. The most straightforward is physical distance, as team members are spread across different cities, countries or continents. Frequently, however, we introduce other types of distance at the same time.

Some teams also face cultural distance, bringing together team members holding different expectations and behavioural norms. Take, for example, a firm serving a Los Angeles-based multinational that has a trademark being infringed upon by a competitor in Brazil, the United Kingdom, Japan, Singapore and Australia. To effectively implement a global response requires collaboration among parties based in all of these locations and cultures. The directness that is highly valued by American and Australian counsel may well be viewed as rude or insulting to their Japanese counterparts – even while the Japanese and Brazilian partners disagree significantly on how deadlines are interpreted and managed.

That same team faces linguistic distance as a result of bringing together individuals with different mother tongues. The simplest incarnation of this is a language barrier in which only part of the message gets through. To combat this, firms introduce policies (eg, mandating English as the firm-wide language) and practices (eg, having each site recap key expectations and deliverables). The real barrier posed by language, however, is not about information flow, but power. Alex, an American associate, is able to rapidly craft complex, nuanced and subtle arguments in support of his points while Junichi, a senior partner in Tokyo, finds his arguments are slower, overly-simple and far more blunt than they would be if he were able to make them in his native Japanese. Alex, however, feels frustratingly confused when Mahesh and Jason, his counterparts in London and Sydney, compare aspects of the present case to the previous one while watching cricket at the weekend. On top of this, both Alex and Jason frequently fail to capture the real meaning of Junichi's points because they cannot read 'the words between the words' – a common problem when people from low context cultures and languages work with colleagues from high context languages.

Many cases also introduce temporal distance – collaborations that span time zones. When the lead partner in Los Angeles revises the litigation strategy during the morning, she must wait until the following morning before hearing the issues her changes raised for the senior partner in Singapore, who similarly must wait if he wants to get revised figures from the London office. When the team faces court-imposed deadlines or must counter opposing counsel's filing, delays like this can mean the difference between success and failure. Even in the absence of external deadlines, spanning time zones reduces opportunities for the real-time conversations that all teams need in order to produce the coordinated legal strategy that their clients expect. While important deadlines may provide more than enough cause for associates and partners to work late and through weekends and holidays, the same cannot always be said for other parties like contractors or parties on whom a case may depend. This adds significant logistical coordination: the team must keep abreast of differing schedules for national holidays or even – as in the case of much of the Middle East – what days constitute the weekend.

Lastly, every team that interacts with, for example, co-counsel in another firm, an investment bank on a transaction or auditors on a restructuring, faces organisational distance. While large projects or cases have long required collaboration across divisions within a firm, increasingly teams must work across the boundaries of firms themselves. Many smaller firms in the international legal arena – or those which have chosen to use a network, rather than mergers – routinely work with their partner firms in other jurisdictions. One driver of this is increasingly sophisticated clients who are unbundling legal services and sending different pieces of work to different 'right cost' providers. In such cases, firms must work together to provide services integrated with those of other firms. Similarly, consolidation through non-organic growth, such as mergers and acquisitions, frequently results in counsel collaborating across firm boundaries.

While the challenges of cultural, linguistic, temporal and organisational distance are bad enough independently, the effects are even greater when they line up (as they often do) in distributed teams. The effects of differences within teams multiply when so-called 'faultlines' – the group's divisions based on certain characteristics (eg, culture, language, time zones) – line up. Compare two versions of a litigation team involving partners from two firms, working in London and Sydney, and specialising in tax and real estate law. While any of those characteristics – firm, location or specialisation – might be a source of division and tension in the team, they can also be sources of similarity.

Figure 1: Differences between litigation teams

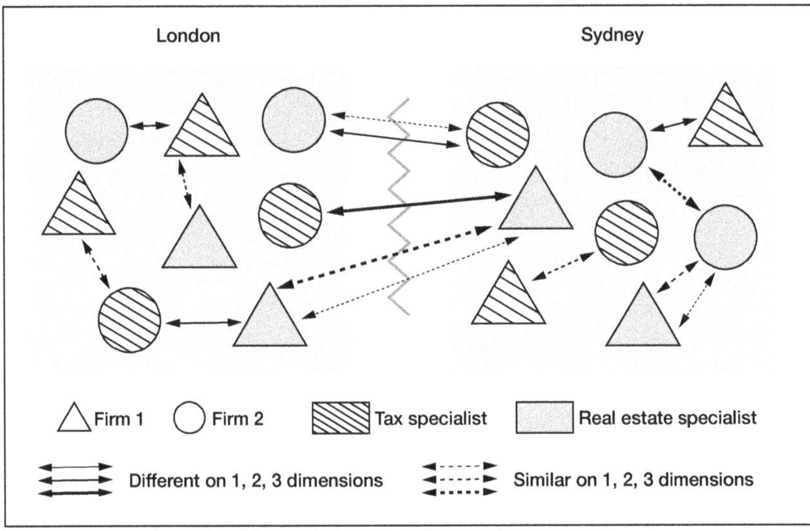

The situation becomes exponentially worse, however, if all the real estate specialists are working for one firm in London while all the tax specialists are in the other firm and working in Sydney. In that situation, the differences within the multi-firm team line up, with all the traits reinforcing one another. This strengthens the faultlines within the team which, like tectonic plates, are just waiting to fracture and draw attention to those differences within.

Figure 2: Aligned faultlines reinforce one another

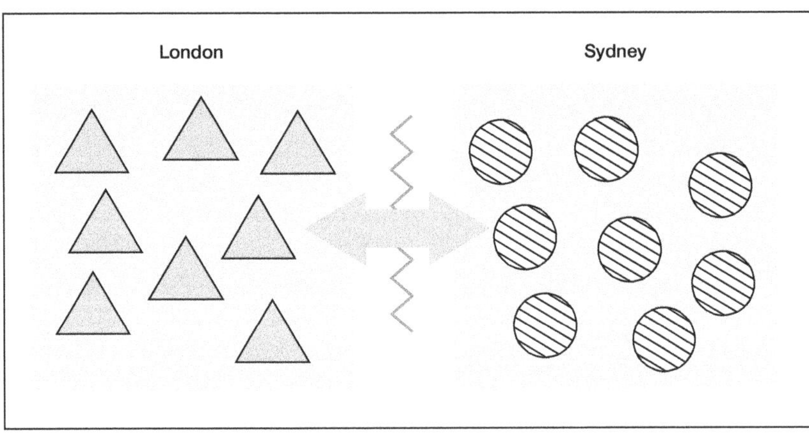

Obviously this is not always the case. Partners in New York working with colleagues in São Paulo have to deal with distance, language and culture, but not time zones; a team split between Washington DC and Sydney spans a larger distance and many time zones, but has the benefit of a common language. Nonetheless, different types of distance are frequently correlated.

Across all of these types of distance it is important to keep in mind the difference between the problem and how it is experienced. The best illustration of this comes from a discussion I observed in an American-Japanese collaboration that was reviewing how the team handled the large number of hours separating offices in San Francisco and Osaka. They had adopted the commonly espoused best practice of 'rotating the pain', that is alternating the timing of their meetings so that neither location had all of the late night calls. It was only during a face-to-face all-hands meeting that someone asked an eye-opening question: "Where did everybody take a midnight call?" The results were striking – everyone in Osaka took calls in the office while everyone based in San Francisco took their calls at home. While motivations ranged across cultural norms, language proficiency and the lack of a home office, the end result was the same. The Americans had dinner with their families, had a conference call in the comfort of their home office and stumbled down the hallway to their beds. The Japanese stayed in the office and hoped the meeting ended before the last train stopped running – lest they sleep in a nearby hotel or at their desk. As in this case, we frequently focus on bridging these different types of distance without addressing how they are experienced.

The types of distance outlined here should come as no surprise – they are well-known issues and the bread and butter of a whole host of consultants ready to help you optimise your global teams. They are not, however, the most direct shapers of global team effectiveness, nor where you should focus your efforts to get the most return on your investments. While you can spend substantial time and energy trying to tackle cultural differences, time zone issues and technology effects one at a time, a far more efficient strategy is to address them where they converge and impact team effectiveness. For this reason, your focus should be on two other types of distance with far more direct and far-reaching impact on team effectiveness: psychological distance and informational distance – both of which are triggered by each of the types of distance discussed above.

2.1 Psychological distance

The different types of distance identified pose problems in their own right, but also trigger psychological distance. To get a gut feel for this just ask yourself whether you feel closer to your local colleagues than those working in another office. The answer is probably "yes".

Psychological distance is at the root of the process we use to help deal with the increasing complexity of our daily lives. The world is incredibly complex and fast-paced, and it is beyond our cognitive ability to fully understand every person, process and social interaction we face. Instead, our brains simplify the world by grouping things together in cognitive buckets. Rather than thinking about all 23 people handling tax law as unique individuals, you find ways to group them: associates versus partners, litigators versus regulatory, London versus Hong Kong versus Sydney-based. This process, which psychologists call 'social categorisation', helps us to cope with overwhelming volumes of data.

A problem arises, however, when we place ourselves into one of our grouping categories. That placement fundamentally changes our view of people we view as in our same group (our 'ingroup') and those who are not (our 'outgroup'). We treat our ingroup more favourably and our outgroup more negatively. While unintentional, this distinction nonetheless shapes many dynamics critical to effective team functioning. We are less cooperative with and supportive of our outgroup, less likely to communicate and share information with them, less attached to them, and, ultimately, we evaluate them more poorly and are less satisfied with their work. All this just by creating a distinction between 'us' and 'them'!

Compounding things for global teams is the fact that our internal categorisation process is extremely easy to trigger – indeed, psychologists have been able to provoke it by grouping people using irrelevant criteria (eg, eye colour) or even grouping them entirely randomly. When given a basis for categorising others, our brains do so automatically (it saves us cognitive energy); and we then begin to treat each other differently. While this fundamental psychological process is at work in co-located and global teams alike, the types of distance noted earlier – physical, cultural, linguistic, temporal, organisational, and technological – all trigger the ingroup/outgroup responses. If you don't think you do this, ask yourself a simple question (and answer honestly): When working in a dispersed team, do you ever find yourself saying "WE do things this way, but THEY do it like that?" Just like a 'tell' in poker, this reflexive us/them distinction is evidence of your own psychological process of categorisation. It happens below the surface – and it introduces tension, damages trust, and reduces performance.

2.2 Informational distance

While psychological distance and social categorisation affect how we feel about distant colleagues, we face an additional obstacle based on what we know about them. The cornerstone of any effective communication and collaboration is common ground – information that all parties share (and know they share). This common body of information helps us to interpret situations and better understand one another, letting us calibrate our frames of reference and expectations. It makes us more efficient while simultaneously reducing misunderstandings.

When working face to face, we pick up and use a tremendous amount of this ambient data. Most of our information collection is unconscious, as is our subsequent use of it to better understand our colleagues. Think about the last time you walked into an important meeting; consciously or not, you noticed the dynamics of the people in the hallway. With one glance, you may have gauged the mood of the individuals in the room. During discussions, you picked up on subtle, non-verbal cues to predict the direction of the arguments. And you did all this against a backdrop of knowing everything from local news stories and recent office events, to personal information about the relevant parties, or even the weather. Every bit of this information is fed into the mental database you use to interpret, understand, and react to the events around you.

On its surface, the issue is simple – you do not (and in fact cannot) have the same amount of knowledge about your distant collaborators as you do about the people who are close to you. But this simple fact has far-reaching and complex effects that cause collaboration to break down. While millions of years of evolution have programmed us to pick up and use all of these data sources, we are not that good at doing so over intermittent visits or, even worse, over video links or phone calls. Think about your last phone or video conference:

- Did any of your distant colleagues' behaviours make less-than-perfect sense to you?
- Did you have any differing expectations for the content or timing of deliverables?
- Did you get a sense that there were other issues behind the scenes that may have been affecting your distant colleagues' decisions?

Laura, an associate based in San Francisco, shared this experience:

I had emailed João in our Lisbon office asking for an update on a pending motion. As he was usually very quick to respond, when I hadn't gotten a response in a couple of hours I resent my message. I immediately received a very angry reply telling me he was looking into it and that I was being unreasonable expecting such a fast response. What I didn't know was that João and his wife had just had a baby and he was terribly sleep deprived. Everyone in Lisbon knew it and were all pitching in and cutting him slack. Me, I had no clue.

Issues may not be due to a total lack of information, though – they may arise where some team members have only partial information, or where they mis-calibrate the information they do have. 'Rain' during the Delhi monsoon season and 'snow' during a hard New England winter are serious events – so when half of your team miss a meeting due to 'bad weather', if you've calibrated the meaning of 'bad weather' correctly, you know to cut them some slack. But what if you're in sunny California and don't appreciate that 'rain' right now means something very different in Delhi?

Both technological and behavioural issues can contribute to a lack of shared information. Despite recent advances in communication technology (and counter to the promises of technology vendors), telepresence is not yet 'just like being there'. Members of a litigation team split between San Francisco, Frankfurt, London and Shanghai simply cannot (yet) know as much about their colleagues and the context affecting their actions and attitudes as they do about the colleagues who work down the hall – at least in part because technology filters out the small, contextual cues and clues that our brains rely on.

At the same time, we also behave differently in global teams. Our communications are measurably more task-focused, which means that we share less of the contextual information required to efficiently collaborate. While this may seem appealing with respect to reducing billed hours, in reality it creates a net reduction in efficiency and productivity because we don't have a fully shared common context.

3. What can we do?

Addressing the issues posed by psychological and informational distance takes effort. Below are a few tried and true methods for overcoming these issues and improving distant collaboration.

3.1 Fight psychology … with psychology

Now that we recognise that our brains put people into categories, the risk you face is that the members of your team see each other not as 'one of us' but 'one of them'. The bad news is that there is nothing you can do to stop yourself – or anyone else – from this subconscious process of forming categories and playing favourites. The good news, however, is that while we cannot stop grouping people, things, events and behaviours into categories, we can influence what those categories are. Your objective should not be to try to eliminate categories – instead, we should be more mindful and choose them.

The categorisation is easily triggered, causing significant challenges. This very ease, however, also presents a great opportunity for creating the frameworks that allow effective collaboration. Just about any noticeable difference within your team will form the basis of categories. Your task, then, is to make sure that the categories your team 'chooses' are the ones that bring people together – and not the ones that drive teams apart.

As Penelope, the lead litigator in a global team, shared:

It was clear our team was not playing nicely. My associates' emails frequently placed blame on how 'they' in the other office weren't giving us what we needed, when we needed it, and the emails we got back made it clear that sentiment was the one thing both offices agreed on. I scheduled a video conference and reminded everyone on both sides that we all had the same objective and that if we weren't going to work together, we might as well just give up – because we certainly weren't going to win the case. Reminding everyone about our shared purpose and reliance on one another really snapped the team back together and turned things around – though I did have to remind them from time to time …

Penelope got the members of her team to shift their focus from their local offices to the team as a whole by using the most obvious and powerful thing everyone had in common – the purpose that brought them together in the first place. While her team still thought in terms of categories, she helped them shift the primary category toward the team as a whole (and away from their own local offices). This manoeuvre was built on some of the same foundations as team-building exercises like trust falls, ropes courses and wall climbs or the branded mugs, pens and T-shirts that litter our workspaces. But there is an important difference: such activities and trinkets are one-shot interventions at a single point in time. They are typically introduced at the launch of a project to distinguish and reinforce the identity of a team relative to the rest of the organisation. On a day-to-day basis, though, dispersed teams are faced with repeated and ongoing stimuli (eg, distance, time zones, culture, language, technology) that continually highlight the differences across sites. For these teams, a single injection of team spirit is entirely inadequate: they need an ongoing set of triggers that reinforce their similarities. The most powerful and strongest of these is your team's common purpose.

That common goal is the glue that binds teams together. Teams that work to remind their members both of their shared objective and their reliance on one another to achieve it, find that their differences are reduced in comparison to those that do not. This can be accomplished in very straightforward ways, including:

- revisiting progress towards the team's stated objective at the start of meetings;
- celebrating milestones and intermediate successes;
- highlighting situations in which members provided crucial assistance across locations; and
- having shared experiences, such as cross-site visits.

These are good practices in their own right, and engaging in them with an eye towards promoting a shared team identity illustrates and reinforces their value. This, of course, comes with an important caveat – if a team's members do not have interdependence across its locations, this strategy will not work. (And, if that is the case, you should be asking yourself why you are labelling this group as a team in the first place.)

3.2 Create shared knowledge to increase understanding

When working with distant colleagues, we lack much of the contextual information that we normally rely on to interpret and understand their attitudes, cognition, and behaviours. We must therefore find ways to affirmatively recognise and share that information. The sheer volume and scope of the information in question, however, makes this task extremely challenging.

No technology will ever be able to capture and transmit all the information that affects our cognition – and spending time trying to relay all of it is clearly unrealistic. There are, however, a few simple best practices that can start the ball rolling and better position your team for distance collaboration.

(a) Give (and take) a virtual tour to provide context

If you plan to work together frequently or for an extended period of time, the more you and your distant teammates know about each other's environment, the better you will be able to make sense of one another's behaviour. Ideally, your team would visit your distant colleagues and experience their environment and routine firsthand. When such a trip is not feasible, though, a few alternative steps can help dramatically. At the start of a project, give each person just a few minutes to share a bit of their context – and not just name, rank, and serial number (or not-so-self-effacingly recitation of pedigree). Rather, have team members share environmental elements that are most likely to affect the ability to collaborate effectively. Kai, a senior partner in the Copenhagen office, shared a helpful approach:

> *I started to work on a matter with a partner in New York and knew he and I would be having a number of late night – or early morning – video conferences. So I took five minutes to give him a rundown of my workspaces. It didn't take long but I focused on things that were most likely to interrupt future calls: my co-counsel on a major tax litigation, my occasionally over-eager assistant, and – when working from my home office – my dog. The interruptions were much easier to deal with when they came up because he was expecting them.*

Whether a quick pan of a webcam or a verbal walk through, this kind of context-sharing will help colleagues better understand each other's work environments.

(b) Gain direct and reflected knowledge to create perspective

Visiting your distant colleagues provides critical and often irreplaceable information. Once you have returned home, that information will help you better understand and interpret your (again distant) collaborators' behaviour. As Marcus, a partner from Boston, noted:

> *When I travelled to Delhi for a meeting during monsoon season, I discovered I had to recalibrate my understanding a bit. I suddenly understood that when my colleagues there cancelled a meeting because of rain, they weren't joking around. I had never seen rain and flooding like that, but they all took it in their stride. I just hope I get a chance to return the favour and give them a chance to see New England snow ...*

When members of your team have the opportunity to visit and learn about their distant colleagues, they gain important direct knowledge about their colleagues' local environment. That information can fill gaps in their understanding and, as in the case of Marcus, help them to more accurately calibrate what they already know. Visits can also provide 'reflected knowledge' of how your office is viewed by your distant colleagues. As Bente, a partner from the Berlin office, noted:

It's a totally different view: standing a bit aside and looking from outside of the system. Of course, I understand much better how Germany is seen by other offices of the firm worldwide. There is certainly a big difference between working in Germany, and dealing with Germany while working abroad.

In a recent field study[1] we found that when people are abroad, their interactions with their home office helped them learn how distant teammates understood the environment, people, dynamics and events that shaped their interactions. That knowledge significantly increased trust. While direct knowledge is the basis for the age-old wisdom of 'walk a mile in their shoes', reflected knowledge helps us to learn what contextual information our colleagues use to understand us. This, in turn, enables us to better understand and improve the contextual information we share when we get back home and return to business as usual.

The benefits of direct and reflected knowledge are one of the reasons that secondments are so powerful in supporting a consistent culture in global firms. By rotating associates, or even partners, on temporary assignments to other offices, firms gain a tremendous boost in their lawyers' ability to work efficiently and effectively on global, virtual teams.

(c) Keep knowledge current to stay relevant

Our work environments are constantly changing and, as a result, we need to continually update the knowledge that we hold and use to effectively collaborate with distant colleagues. The most efficient way to consistently keep ourselves and our colleagues up to date is with regular (but quick) context updates on major events or changes in each location.

Context updates are different to sharing information on details or information related to the matter you're working on; that information will (or at least should) come out in project status discussions. Instead, context updates address information that is outside the direct scope of the work at hand, yet likely to affect it. As Michael, a partner in Silicon Valley, explained:

I was working on an IP matter with colleagues in New York, and we got in the habit of taking a few minutes each week to fill each other in on what was going on locally. It wasn't directly relevant to the case but that knowledge ended up being critical because it helped me know which other partners or senior associates in that office had related experience and how busy they were in general. Others might

1 M Mortensen and TB Neeley, "Reflected Knowledge and Trust in Global Collaboration" (2012) 58(12) *Management Science* 2207–24.

question the value of this time investment – especially when we're supposed to be billing by the six-minute increment! – but we found that it paid off enormously because we got quick turnaround from an expert when a couple of critical questions arose.

This information takes many forms, including changes in personnel or office restructure that will affect the resources you might draw upon, new office or local practices or protocols that constrain the way in which your team works, or even non-work events (eg, local political change, strikes or other social movements, major news events) that are likely to affect people's thinking or perspective.

Some might argue that it is a waste of time to exchange such non-work information – particularly in the face of partners and associates who are suffering from overload. This would be wrong, due to the crucial fact that our brains and cognition do not obey work boundaries. Consciously or not, your teams' decisions are affected by their contexts. As a leader, you must be aware of these and ensure that the teams are as well-informed as possible if you want your teams to perform effectively.

3.3 Foster spontaneous interaction to boost shared identity and understanding

Some collaborations target the parallel issues of a lack of shared identity and understanding at the same time. One such two-birds-one-stone is spontaneous communication. For as long as people have worked together, we have recognised the importance of those unplanned, spontaneous interactions that occur during shared non-work activities, such as getting coffee/water or food, exercising, and commuting.

On the one hand, these interactions serve as a bonding agent, creating a shared experience that brings people together and helps them to form relationships. These interactions help to foster a sense of shared identity. Just consider whether those coffeepot chats help you better relate to your co-workers and you will likely realise that they do. Yet these conversations are also important conduits for the exchange of all kinds of information. We learn who and what others know, allowing us to better leverage their abilities or connections. We learn about successes and failures, gathering ideas we can apply to our own challenges. We learn what is happening and who is involved, and then we use that data to calibrate our understanding of the context around us.

The problem is an obvious one – when we are working at a distance, we just do not have the natural opportunities for these interactions to occur. While this is not surprising, our research has discovered an interesting twist. While spontaneous interactions occur less often and less readily in dispersed teams, when they do occur, they produce a marked improvement in shared identity and shared understanding – and those effects are much stronger than those in co-located teams. This means that, although it is hard to foster distant spontaneous connections, when you are successful, it yields huge benefits for your team.

So how do you get people to spontaneously interact across distance? Until virtual coffee becomes a reality, the short answer is that you have to work at it. Teams that wish to promote spontaneous interaction have to invest in doing so – in effect, they must formalise the informal. By definition you cannot schedule something spontaneous. You can, however, schedule opportunities for such spontaneous interactions to happen.

James, a partner in Chicago, occasionally creates 'scheduled, unscheduled time' – time at the beginning of a call that is explicitly off-agenda in order to provide his team with opportunities to informally and spontaneously interact. This tactic comes with a warning, as James explained:

You can't just go ahead and put "10 minutes of free time" on the agenda. It doesn't work unless your team understands why you're doing it and what benefit it offers them. I made that mistake at first, and everyone either spent the first 10 minutes texting or showed up 12 minutes late. Once I got them to realise how important those interactions were, things started to change. It was still awkward at first, but each time we did it, it became more comfortable and now everyone agrees it is a critical part of our process.

To use this tactic effectively requires two things: understanding and perseverance. Your firm (and team) have to understand (and buy in to) the value of spontaneous interaction, as well as the logic of scheduling time to promote it. At a firm level, there must be a recognition that informal interaction is not a waste of time, but rather plays a crucial role in information flow within your organisation. This is not new – as long as there have been law firms, breakthroughs have taken place in hallways, breakrooms and around water coolers. Changes in the structure of the modern law firm, however, are threatening this key pathway for critical knowledge transfer and intra-team connection. Perseverance is required because your team has to push through the first few times when the process feels awkward and forced. The meetings will feel this way for a very good reason – they are forced! But that forcing is necessary; after doing it a few times, the team will discover that each subsequent attempt feels more natural and normal.

Making all of this a tougher sell is the fact that the payoff of such interaction is not immediate. Instead, it is reaped over the long term as teams build the connections and shared context that will help them effectively overcome distance barriers. Team success requires the same kind of investment you already make in reinforcing your firm's culture so that associates and partners can better understand and work with one another. Distant teams can only get the crucial benefits of spontaneous communication by putting into place the processes and structures that are necessary to compensate for the sorts of interactions that no longer come for free.

3.4 Be predictable to increase trust

The most often cited breakdown in dispersed collaborations is a lack of trust. At its core, trust is about predictability – you know that your distant colleagues will behave in a certain way, and you can therefore plan accordingly. Critically, both shared identity and shared understanding are key drivers of trust. The more you see your distant colleagues as part of 'us', the more you trust them – because they are fundamentally like you. The more you share the same understanding of people, context, and events, the more you trust these colleagues – because you have a shared frame of reference for understanding behaviour.

Another source of trust is predictability itself, which makes it important to create as much predictability as possible within your global collaborations. A first step is regularising your meetings. When we work face to face, we often rely on impromptu check-ins as the need arises, but these cannot effectively materialise when colleagues are not down the hall from one another. Pete, a tax specialist in Baltimore, explained that his new managing partner introduced a fixed schedule for conference calls and site visits with their office in Denver. At first, Pete didn't understand why this was necessary, but it was not long before he realised the regularity of the meetings both helped him plan his work and interactions – and also helped him understand what to expect from his interactions with distant team members. Obviously when the need arose, the team scheduled additional calls and visits, but those were built on the existing foundation of the regular interactions.

Trite as it seems, one last way to build trust is to have an open and honest discussion about the challenges that you and your team face in working at a distance. Frank was struggling on a project with his colleagues in the Paris office until he decided to share his feelings:

> *Finally I called Anne, who I knew a bit, and said, "Look, I'm having a really hard time figuring out how to manage this distance thing." Turned out she was wrestling with the same things but didn't think it was appropriate to mention it. We agreed to schedule a video conference with the whole team to discuss it and that meeting was a watershed – we got a better idea about what each side needed and realised we were all in the same boat.*

As Frank and Anne discovered, being open and honest about the challenges serves two purposes. First, it sets expectations, putting team members on the same page and helping people understand each other's behaviours. This supports a greater shared understanding and reduces the likelihood of the surprises and expectation shortfalls that so often damage. Secondly, the act of sharing your concerns in and of itself builds the rapport and trust that underlies shared identity. It effectively creates a shared experience for the team – one of consciously working to overcome the obstacles of global collaboration.

4. Concluding thoughts

In the end, none of these tactics can guarantee a perfectly smooth experience for global, virtual teams. Given the enormous complexity of global collaboration, the only thing we know for certain is that distance-based issues will arise. However, by reinforcing your sense of a shared identity across locations, you increase the likelihood that your dispersed collaborators will give each other the benefit of the doubt when such issues do come up. Setting shared foundations and contexts enables team members to take a cooperative and constructive stance (rather than a competitive one) when trying to address these unavoidable challenges. At the same time, building your teams' shared understanding will also help them to better interpret the actions of their distant colleagues, as well as to ensure that their own actions predictably generate the most productive outcomes. In leading and working on far flung teams, it is critical to recognise and remember the inevitable role that human cognition plays in team success: fundamentally, the key to effectively managing distributed teams is not technological, but social.

Leading merger integration

Jenni Emery
Arup

If you want to build a ship, don't drum up the people to gather wood, divide the work and give orders. Instead, teach them to yearn for the vast and endless sea.
Antoine de Saint-Exupery[1]

1. Mergers – a fool's errand?

Report after report will tell you, almost irrespective of when you are reading this, that right now, no, right NOW, we have hit an all-time high for M&A activity across the globe.[2] And yet study after study will also tell you that the failure rate for mergers is anywhere between 70% and 90%.[3] M&A is one of the riskiest investments for organisations of their time, money and reputations – and yet the imperative for growth, or consolidation, or diversification is such that organisations across the globe and across sectors press ahead with this strategy time after time, convinced that they will be the ones to buck the trend. Clearly something is awry, and commentators are increasingly identifying an underestimation of, and a lack of investment in, the people and cultural aspects of an M&A integration process as one of the main reasons for failure. It is those people and cultural aspects that this chapter focuses on.

In early 2016, as Director of Strategy at CMS, I was asked to lead the team that would put together and then implement from a people perspective what became the three-way merger of CMS, Nabarro and Olswang to create a new top five global law firm. Now, organisational change is a difficult path to follow. Mergers are the highest craggy pinnacle of the organisational change mountain. And lawyers, and law firms, are probably amongst the more reluctant of mountaineers, and for good reason – they operate by consensus rather than command and control; their stock-in-trade is their ability to challenge, spot the catch, minimise risk and focus on detail;[4] their product is their people, and so they cannot afford to have them distracted; and their

1 attr. Antoine de Saint-Exupery, *Citadelle*, Gaallimard (Paris, 1959, reprint, first published in 1948).
2 ADP, *Achieving M&A Success*, at www.adp.co.uk/assets/vfs/Family-32/adp-files/Insights-Resources/Whitepapers/Docs/adp-unleashing-m-and-a-success-fy17.pdf.
3 Christensen *et al*, "The Big Idea: The New M&A Playbook" (March 2011) *Harvard Business Review*.
4 Research suggests that analytical thinking can reduce our capacity to empathise and care, in part because our brains use different neural pathways for each and we literally have to switch between the two.

ability to focus on clients and deliver seamless and uninterrupted service is of paramount importance.

All of this means that a merger integration project in a law firm has the potential to yield the richest possible learning about some of the challenges of leading organisational change. At the risk of ruining the suspense, let me say now that the CMS merger ended up epitomising much of what I have come to believe is the very best approach to leading merger integration in particular and organisational change more generally. For this reason, the story of the CMS merger is the core case study I return to most often in this chapter.[5] In summary:

- The new firm created by the merger was a product almost entirely of its own creation, put together under the strategic leadership and guidance of its senior management team, and integrated operationally by its own people.
- The leadership team understood that it was important that this process itself should become part of the story of the new firm, and that it would be by virtue of going through the process together that people would best be able to understand one another's existing stories, cultures and values and weave them into something new.
- The team delivered a co-located, single firm, operating as one team, on one set of systems, and delivering a fully integrated service to clients right from day one – an unprecedented and frankly astonishing achievement.
- In its first year, the new firm achieved a 19% increase in profits, exceptional client feedback and extensive industry recognition, flying in the face of the M&A trends.

The central focus and emphasis that the leadership placed on people and culture was one of the most – perhaps the most – critical factors in the new firm's success.

2. A change will do you good

The central thesis of this chapter, in a nutshell, is that complete clarity on purpose, an approach rooted in storytelling, and a very human approach to leadership can enable firms to navigate periods of profound change, including mergers, in such a way as to actively generate value and enable their business and individuals to flourish.

Read that again. There is a quiet revolution in this message. The widely accepted, and entirely understandable, response in times of uncertainty and

5 This chapter draws on and summarises much of the ground covered in my book *Leading for Organisational Change: Building Purpose, Motivation and Belonging* (Wiley, 2018). That book was written with the full support of the CMS leadership team, but is not 'the official story' of the CMS merger; that is for others, or history, to write. The learnings and observations are all my own.

change is to take control – to impose more structure, more systems, more rules, policies and reporting, to minimise risk and ambiguity and close down doubt. This thinking is symptomatic of an 'old' paradigm which can prevail in business, in our personal lives, and – notably at this moment in history – even in the global political arena, namely a paradigm that urges us to dig in, resist change and to cling to what we know.

At least in the context of merger integration, this chapter advocates for a different approach; one which is subtler and requires patience, and which focuses on changing behaviour by changing minds and hearts. It is rooted in an alternative paradigm which says that when change comes we should approach it with courage – with open hands, and an open mind – and seek to understand, include and transcend differences to create something new that is even better than what went before. This approach requires letting go when you want to hold on; opening up when you want to close down. It allows space for ambiguity and for mistakes. It is about planting seeds and letting them grow.

In this chapter, I will outline a perspective on change based on this alternative paradigm, and then explore how this alternative perspective, with its focus on purpose, stories and human leadership, can help firms to navigate many of the most significant challenges and opportunities which tend to present themselves throughout a period of merger integration.

There's currently a paradox, a dissonance, at the heart of our relationship with change. On the one hand, we hear that everything in our world is now VUCA – volatile, uncertain, complex and ambiguous – and that change is the new normal. We all need to be agile and able to turn our businesses on a hairpin – quick, quick, quick.

On the other hand, we are taught that change is something to be feared. The very language we use pathologises change, and we seek to minimise its impact and 'get through it' as quickly as possible. We use the Kubler-Ross 'Change Curve' model, first produced in the 1960s as a model for how people process and move through grief, to explain how people might be 'coping' with change, and fret about those salutary stories of the dire outcomes of M&A adventures, and about those almost weekly research reports showing that employee engagement is at an all-time low.

The most famous and enduring model for change management – the eight stage model presented by John Kotter in his iconic book, *Leading Change*[6] – betrays some of this thinking. Kotter elegantly identifies and defines eight important aspects of any change programme, but the very fact of his having presented them as a linear process, with an assumed degree of hierarchy and command and control governing them, suggests a mentality around change that sees it as something to be managed and 'got through'.

6 John Kotter, *Leading Change* (HBS Press, 1996).

This sort of mindset encourages a focus on process over people, and in so doing becomes a self-fulfilling prophecy. Back to those tales of doomed M&A: time and again, post-mortems reveal a chronic lack of attention, focus and investment in the people and cultural aspects as a key cause of failure. In a 2011 study[7] which surveyed more than 200 senior executives worldwide who had experienced M&A deals over the previous three years, more than two-thirds of the business leaders surveyed said they had over-emphasised traditional due diligence (on tangible assets such as finance and IT) at the expense of intangible assets (such as human capital, leadership compatibility and cultural integration), and only 13% said that they had prioritised engaging and integrating senior management and the workforce once the M&A had been completed. In this sort of context, people become victims against whom a merger is committed.

But what if, instead, we adopted an approach to change which had human beings right at the centre of it? What if we treated people not as victims, but as active participants in, and co-creators of, a change process which is valuable in itself – the coming together of values, the exploration of common purpose, the discovery and creation of stories? Now of course change inevitably involves loss – it involves leaving something behind, letting something go, moving on. And of course there is reluctance and grief associated with that. Change also involves moving towards something new and different – and while that can be exciting, it can also be daunting. But what is almost always overlooked is the value of the period of change itself. That period in time when things are uncertain and in a state of flux? That is not a period just to be endured and got through as quickly as possible. It's not all downside. Quite the contrary. It is a period – a place – which has inherent importance and, for leaders who choose to embrace it, it can yield huge opportunities for value creation and growth.

3. Change – this time it's personal

So, what might it look like to bring a truly people-centric approach into the heart of change theory for law firms? In bringing a purpose-centred, story-rich perspective to bear, what we are really doing is quite explicitly bringing some of the latest thinking in psychology and neurology into a business context. Curiosity, vulnerability, pleasure, pain ... it pays to remember that we are all human, and will continue to behave accordingly, even when we are suited and booted, and sitting inside glass offices and multi-million turnover businesses. If we are to build a new theoretical framework for change then it must, as far as possible, be consistent with, and draw on, the best of what we know about how people behave and how the brain works.

Traditional ways of thinking about organisational change see it as a process

7 Hay Group, *Touching the Intangible* (2011).

or a programme, with a beginning, a middle and an end. They promise jam tomorrow in exchange for a little pain now. But this is not how our volatile, uncertain, complex and ambiguous world works, and if we carry on trying to motivate people on the basis of false promises and false limitations, we are destined to fail. Change is our new steady state and we should be changing the whole paradigm such that we learn to accept, embrace, thrive on and even to drive change as something we are wired for, and something we actively seek.

Recent developments in our understanding of how the brain works can help us here. One thing that we are increasingly understanding, is that our brains are malleable. New connections can be made, new neural pathways laid down – this is called neuroplasticity. Our brains are built to do this – it is natural and healthy and the brain can do it relatively easily and over a short time frame, provided – and here's the rub – the brain's owner makes sufficient effort to focus attention on the change it wants to make. Attention is paramount. It's that simple – and that inordinately difficult.

The neuroscientist and author, David Rock, in *Your Brain at Work* says that three conditions are necessary to persuade someone – and, by extension, whole organisations of someones – to shift their attention and thus change their thinking:

- First, it needs to be safe for them to do so;
- Secondly, we need to help people to focus their attention in just the right way to create the right new connections;
- Thirdly, people need a reason to keep coming back and walking that new neural pathway again and again so that it becomes the thoroughfare of choice.

Rock uses what he calls the SCARF model to summarise five social domains that drive human behaviour and are instrumental in determining how threatened or safe an individual feels. The five domains are Status, Certainty, Autonomy, Relatedness and Fairness. If, in order to make change happen, our first aim is to increase safety and minimise threat, then we need to pay close attention to all five of these domains, because once a threat response – commonly known as the 'fight or flight' response – is triggered in the brain, a number of things happen which make any change process even more challenging.[8]

It is a commercial imperative to do all we can to keep people performing at their best during times of uncertainty. Paying attention, then, to Rock's five domains is important, and preserving a person's status or increasing their

---

8 Blood flows away from our pre-frontal cortex which is where we do our rational thinking, and manage our emotions, and make plans, and flows to our amygdala to help us get ready to run or smack someone. Our anxiety increases and we start to box at shadows and see threats that are not there. All of this makes us struggle with decision-making, creativity and problem-solving. We also collaborate less.

certainty, for example, can make a profound difference to their capacity to perform during periods of change.

Once you have reduced threat sufficiently that people have offered their attention, the next challenge is to help them focus that attention in the right way. Rock says that one of the more effective strategies for doing this is to ask people a question and so draw them in to the story of what is happening.

The final step in Rock's approach is to ensure that people keep their new circuitry alive. This means finding a multitude of ways to increase the 'attention density' around a new idea. Talking about the change, telling more stories, asking people to share ideas and collaborate – all of these things will help.

The case for this approach to change is further supported by the latest thinking in neuroscience about what it takes to keep us engaged and motivated at work more generally. In *Alive at Work,*[9] Daniel Cable's central thesis[10] is that organisations can, and should, keep their employees engaged – *alive* – at work by activating their 'seeking systems'; the parts of our brain that encourage us to explore and learn. When we activate this system, it releases dopamine – a neurotransmitter linked to motivation and pleasure, and this release in turn makes us want to explore and learn more. There are three triggers that activate the seeking system – self-expression, experimentation, and purpose. It is clear that an approach to change which includes people in the crafting of the journey itself, and allows them to create their own stories and discover their own purpose, will keep people much more engaged and motivated than a process which sees them as passive recipients – or victims – of change.[11]

Lawyers leading change need to transform their own view of the power and potential of change and, in so doing, give back agency and ownership to the

---

9 Daniel M Cable, *Alive at Work: The Neuroscience of Helping Your People Love What They Do* (Harvard Business Review Press, 2018).

10 *ibid.*

11 This chimes with Deci & Ryan's work around the three key components of motivation being autonomy, competence and connectedness (EL Deci & RM Ryan, "The Importance Of Universal Psychological Needs For Understanding Motivation In The Workplace" in M Gagne (ed), *Oxford Handbook Of Work Engagement, Motivation and Self-Determination Theory* (Oxford University Press, 2014)) and the work of Dan Pink who identifies autonomy, mastery and purpose as the three key intrinsic motivators of our behaviour (Daniel Pink, *Drive: The Surprising Truth About What Motivates Us* (Canongate, 2009)) and with the work of Amabile and Kramer (Teresa Amabile and Steven Kramer, *The Progress Principle: Using Small Wins To Ignite Joy, Engagement And Creativity At Work* (Harvard Business Review Press, 2011)), which concludes that the single biggest motivator is a sense of progress – the capacity to make small wins and make sense of those in terms of progress towards an ultimate end or a bigger purpose will impact on both productivity and creativity. Actively engaging people in co-creating and directing their change journey, rather just having them sit and wait for it to happen to them, not only mitigates their threat response but actively engages and motivates them. (This in turn chimes with the findings of the MacLeod Report, which, though not specifically focused on change, explores the link between employee engagement and organisational performance. The report identifies four critical factors for high employee engagement – visible, empowering leadership that provides a strong strategic narrative; engaging managers who give people scope to develop and treat them as individuals; employee voice throughout the organisation and integrity between espoused values and actual behaviour. D MacLeod and N Clarke, *Engaging for Success: Enhancing Performance Through Employee Engagement* (Department for Business, Innovation and Skills, UK, 2009).)

people in their firms to deliver more value and more engagement than they realised was possible, even while the change is ongoing.

But how? What does it take to lead in this way? Three things. A clear sense of purpose. Some compelling stories. And really human, vulnerable and engaged leaders. Let's consider each of these in turn.

4. On purpose

'Purpose' is without doubt a hot topic and a big buzzword for business. It is, however, poorly defined and often involves the conflation of a number of related but distinct ideas, in a way destined to irritate lawyers.

There is the corporate responsibility school of purpose, which frames purposes entirely as societal purpose – looking beyond short-term profit generation to positively impact individuals, society and the environment.[12] This interpretation of purpose is a close cousin of a second, older concept which can be found in the Quaker-founded businesses of the past 200 years, and which is now enjoying a huge revival – namely, purpose as part and parcel of enlightened capitalism, incorporated within a broader and longer-term definition of value generation. This argument says that businesses with a clear sense of purpose generate more long-term value – that is, are more sustainable – than those without.[13]

This longer-term perspective leads to a third 'start with why' theory of purpose, as posited by Simon Sinek, via his 'Golden Circle',[14] which places 'why' an organisation exists at the centre, surrounded by the 'how' of how it conducts its business, and then places the actual 'what' of what the organisation does as the outermost of the three concentric circles. Sinek's theory is that those organisations that follow this model are the organisations most likely to be resilient and successful.[15] This is similar to the evolutionary development perspective on purpose which says that as organisations develop over time, they become more focused on culture and more willing to consider the perspectives of multiple stakeholders, to focus on 'inner rightness' and to strive for integrity and wholeness.[16]

Still with me? Good, and hang on – we are turning inwards now, because the next perspective on purpose builds on this developmental perspective, but

12 H Playfoot and R Hall, *Purpose in Practice – Clarity, Authenticity and the Spectre of Purpose Wash* (Claremont Communications, 2015).

13 M Porter and M Kramer, "Creating Shred Value: Redefining Capitalism and the Role of the Corporation in Society" (2011) *Harvard Business Review*.

14 Simon Sinek, *Start With Why* (Penguin, 2011). Sinek's model was originally conceived as a perspective on business development, but has much wider application.

15 Sinek's is ultimately a market-led perspective – an organisation 'needs' purpose and will derive value from it, if by having a purpose the organisation is better able to meet the expectations of its people, its customers and the markets in which it is doing business. This perspective basically takes the view that the system is shifting in favour of a more purpose-led perspective. An organisation at the sharp end of this movement can derive an advantage by meeting the expectations of the market better than its competitors can, but it cannot move unilaterally and independently of the system within which it is operating.

16 Frederic Laloux, *Reinventing Organizations* (Nelson Parker, 2014).

brings it back to the individual, and right into your brain. As discussed above, Daniel Cable identifies purpose as one of the triggers of engagement for people at work, because it activates the brain's 'seeking system'. In this thinking, purpose is only partially related to the nature of the work in question, encompassing, too, the sense of purpose that people might feel by virtue of the impact they have, the difference they can make, and the relationships and interactions they participate in. Finally there is a perspective on purpose which is primarily about individual wellbeing. This perspective says that a sense of purpose brings a sense of coherence and significance and thus improves our health and increases our life expectancy.[17] In a work context, it also increases our intrinsic motivation, enthusiasm and resilience.[18 19]

So far, so edifying, but where does all that leave us? Is this all theoretical nonsense? I don't think so. I think there is a compelling unifying narrative which runs through all of these different perspectives, which is both philosophically coherent and practically inspiring.

So – yes, an individual's purpose can theoretically be almost anything, but all the evidence suggests that it is commonly aspirational, and related to 'being part of something'.[20] The things that give us a sense of meaning and that activate the neurological conditions for engagement are not generally entirely self-seeking.[21] People like to galvanise around a common goal, or approach, or story that is bigger than themselves; this is an important aspect of wellbeing. This in turn is consistent with the perspective that it is both natural and advantageous for organisations to consider the 'inner rightness' of their activities and chimes with Sinek's theory that companies that 'start with why' do better. All of these theories then support and drive the long-termist and wider societal perspectives favoured by those who approach purpose from a 'new capitalist' or 'corporate responsibility' perspective.

And ta-dah! Now we are edging towards a workable definition of corporate purpose as something that is commonly understood but individually owned, and which has some bearing on our impact and relationships, individually and corporately. As Quinn and Thakor say[22] "... when an authentic purpose

---

17 PL Hill and NA Turiano, "Purpose in Life as a Predictor of Mortality Across Adulthood" (2014) 25(7) *Psychological Science* 1482–86.

18 Daniel M Cable, *Alive at Work: The Neuroscience of Helping Your People Love What They Do* (Harvard Business Review Press, 2018). But this is only true – all these benefits only prevail – if it is your own purpose: a purpose that you have bought into and feel, not something that you have taken on board cognitively because somebody in your organisation told you that a particular cause was particularly worthy and wrote a glossy paper about it.

19 This is reminiscent of the Japanese concept of *ikigai* – the notion that a person's unique purpose is found deep within them, at the intersection of their profession, their vocation, their passion and their mission – H Garcia, and F Miralles, *Ikigai: The Japanese Secret to a Long and Happy Life* (Penguin, 2016).

20 Connected Commons, "Network Investments that Create a Sense of Purpose in Your Work", *Connected Leadership*, www.connectedcommons.com.

21 Roy Baumeister, Kathleen Vohns, Jennifer Aaker and Emily Garbinsky, "Some Key Differences Between A Happy Life And A Meaningful Life" (2013) *Journal of Positive Psychology*.

22 Robert E Quinn and Anjan V Thakor, "Creating a Purpose Driven Organisation: How To Get Employees To Bring Their Smarts And Energy To Work" (July/August 2018) *Harvard Business Review* 78–85.

permeates business strategy and decision-making, the personal good and the collective good become one".

5. Harnessing the power of purpose

For myself, I am convinced by both the moral and commercial arguments which support the case for organisations discovering and committing to pursuing a purpose which is linked to an overtly good wider societal purpose, as the best means by which to drive long-term value. I like this quote from Punit Renjen, the Deloitte Global CEO:

> *Purpose answers the critical questions of who a business is and why it exists beyond making a profit ... But to be more than just words, purpose must guide behaviour, influence strategy, transcend leaders – and endure.*

But in a sense, the case I am making in this chapter for the importance and relevance of purpose is a more pragmatic one which says that whether or not you buy the notion that a purpose 'should' be any one thing or another, firms that truly have an authentic purpose[23] have an advantage in a number of respects – connecting with clients, attracting talent, building reputation, enhancing quality, fostering creativity[24] ... and in navigating and thriving throughout periods of change.

6. Discovering purpose

Clearly, though, it is futile for a leader to seek to simply decide upon and articulate a purpose at a firm-wide level and then instil it in others. Would that lawyers were that biddable! Rather, purpose is better understood as something that is already there, inside your firm and inside your people. Sacha Romanovitch, the former CEO of Grant Thornton, talks about 'discovering' an organisation's purpose, and compares it to Michelangelo's famous (perhaps apocryphal) explanation when asked how he went about creating his statue of David:[25] "I saw the angel in the marble, and carved until I set him free."

We need to think in terms of discovering purpose, rather than in terms of imposing it.[26] This is a careful, rigorous and iterative process. We all can – and do – generate our own unique narrative based on a given set of common facts.[27]

---

23 Purpose must be authentic in order to deliver the advantages noted, and only an authentic purpose is likely to be sustainable and viable within an organisation's wider societal and systemic context and to be 'useful' far beyond any particular project or target. That is to say, it will always be useful to have a purpose which inspires discretionary effort, encourages a longer-term view, helps with the balancing of competing priorities; it will always be advantageous – especially in the age of AI – to put human judgement and emotional conviction at the heart of your organisation.

24 For a further example, see the case study in relation to DTE Energy, as reported by Quinn and Thakor in the Harvard Business Review in July/August 2018 – Robert E Quinn and Anjan V Thakor, "Creating a Purpose Driven Organisation: How To Get Employees To Bring Their Smarts And Energy To Work" (July/August 2018) *Harvard Business Review* 78–85. And see also Daniel Coyne's observations in *The Culture Code*, in relation to the Meyer restaurant chain and in relation to Pixar: Daniel Coyne, *The Culture Code: The Secrets of Highly Successful Groups* (Penguin, 2018).

25 Sacha Romanovitch in conversation with Professor David Grayson, at Grant Thornton breakfast seminar, 27 March 2018.

The ultimate challenge for leaders and firms is to begin to curate, guide and weave these individual narratives together so that they form part of a wider, inclusive, firm-wide narrative that everyone can own and feel part of. This begins to explain the ineluctable link between purpose and story.

The nature of a purpose-led approach is that the work is ongoing – you need to hold the purpose front and centre and use it to aid focus and guide decision-making, even sometimes at short-term cost. Everyone in the firm needs to tell stories about it over and over again so that it sinks into the collective consciousness, gradually shifting the culture, changing thinking and performance, and allowing a new approach to processes and governance to evolve.

7. Once upon a time – the role of stories

In his brilliant book, *Be More Pirate,* Sam Coniff Allende sets out a model for change which has storytelling at its heart. Drawing on lessons from the 'Golden Age of Piracy', Coniff Allende explains how pirates "creatively weaponised" the art of storytelling in order to get attention and further pursue their purpose – skulls and crossbones and bleeding hearts on black flags, weaving fierce myths right into the heart of the establishment.

Now, lawyers are not pirates. But they are autonomous, independent thinkers. They like hard facts and have a profound integrity. They are cynical about obvious attempts to influence or coerce them to think x or to do y .... fine rhetoric gets marked-up in red pen, spin doctoring and flagrant attempts at bribery are just ignored. Stories, however – good stories – are different, and I found their impact to be transformational when they were used as part of the CMS merger process.

So, what is it about stories? What gives them their power? Three hundred years after the pirates, Daniel Coyle gives us an answer from neuroscience:[28]

> *We tend to use the word* story *casually, as if stories and narratives were ephemeral decorations for some unchanging underlying reality. The deeper neurological truth is that stories do not cloak reality but create it, triggering cascades of perception and motivation.*

So, the stories themselves become part of the action. Stories are not neutral then, and nor are they innocent. And yet, stories are also subtle. They are dynamic and spacious, and people – pirates and lawyers alike – can own them,

---

26 John Coleman, in his HBR article "You Don't Find Your Purpose – You Build It" takes issue with this idea of discovering purpose and argues that people need to create their purpose instead. To the extent that Coleman means that you should not sit around waiting for your purpose to descend suddenly upon you like a butterfly, I agree with him; I agree that you need to work to find your purpose, but I maintain that the work is more about unearthing than it is about creating. (John Coleman, "You Don't Find Your Purpose – You Build It" in *Harvard Business Review* (October 2017)).

27 K Fujita *et al*, "Construal Levels and Self Control" (2006) 90 *Journal of Personality and Social Psychology* 351–67.

28 Daniel Coyle, *The Culture Code: The Secrets Of Highly Successful Groups* (Penguin, 2018).

develop them, and make them their own. This makes them a respectful means of communication. They allow for the listener's intelligence and perspective, and leave space for interpretation and nuance.

One of the key differences between a series of facts of the sort that lawyers so love and a story is the addition of context, emotional content and sensory detail – what Aristotle called *pathos*.[29] We need to make a little room here for something both before and beyond the rational. In their capacity to influence, challenge and engage us, stories steer even the most logic-loving of us beyond the empirical and around our tendency towards confirmation bias[30] and engage with a different part of us.

Stories can paint a vision of the future. They can be about 'who we are', and can show us what we value. Stories also give context. They can help to explain strategies, and relative priorities. They can show us what matters, who matters and what success looks and feels like.

But stories, well chosen and well told, can also have a kick in them. They can call people out on their lack of alignment or commitment, or name an unresolved issue. Provided stories are authentic and honest they can disarm listeners and help to reframe challenges.

All of this means that stories have a degree of power. At times of change, if you have a good story and hold it high, and tell it well, you hold in your hands the power to pull people together for a common cause, and to help them navigate change.

8. What makes a good story?

At the end of the day a 'good story' is one that works – that engages you, or moves you, teaches you something, or makes you think differently.

All that said, there are stories and then there are stories, and so let's touch on a little bit of what we know about what makes a good story if your intent in the telling of the story is to drive or embed change. Good stories for these purposes address five areas:[31]

- They start by talking about how the world is changing – maybe there's a burning platform, or maybe there's a golden egg, or maybe both. At CMS, for example, the leadership team talked about changes in clients' needs and expectations, about the opportunities presented by technology and about shifts in the legal market.
- Then, good stories explain "what we're going to do about it" – we're going to create a distinctively different future-facing law firm ...

---

29 The very etymology of the word 'narrate' has tangled up in it two separate concepts – 'telling', and 'to know in a particular way'.

30 Our tendency to select only those facts that help us to confirm what we already think we know.

31 A Armenakis, S Harris and K Mossholder, "Creating Readiness for Organisational Change" (1993) 66(6) *Human Relations* 681–703.

- Why ... to better serve our clients ...
- How ...we're going to merge three great firms.
- Next, good stories emphasise commitment – in terms of allocation of time, resources, expertise and money, but also in terms of authentic and dedicated sleeves-up leadership from the top.
- Finally, good stories talk about why it is worth all the effort – not only for the firm, but also for its clients and people, and for society as a whole.

Law firm leaders have a role to play in both developing and telling the story, and as it puts on weight, it becomes your vision and strategy, and all the riper for the telling.

As it is communicated, the story continues to evolve and develop, and to plant seeds of other stories. This is the means by which your people become empowered – because they start to sense-make and then to tell their own stories and, in the very act of doing so, they contribute to, or even change, the overall story of the business.

9. Really human leaders

Of the three key components I outlined earlier in the chapter, we have talked about the really clear sense of purpose, and the compelling stories. Let's now consider what it means as a leader to deliver those two elements – and how and why it entails showing up as a real human being – whole-hearted, authentic and a little vulnerable.

In 2014, in partnership with Cranfield University's Doughty Centre for Corporate Responsibility and *The Financial Times*, Coca-Cola commissioned research into current and future business leaders' opinions about the relationship between profit and purpose – now, and in the future.[32] The results are striking. All current and future leaders who participated in the survey agreed that a purpose-led approach builds engagement, increases trust, fosters innovation and increases an organisation's relevance to future generations. Yet while nine out of 10 current CEOs believe that their organisation has a clear purpose, only two out of 10 future leaders agree, and 'management attitudes' is identified as one of the two biggest barriers to the successful adoption of a purpose-led approach.

That there is sometimes a gap between intention and perception, between ambition and execution, should come as no surprise – the demands on leaders today are huge, varied and complex, and coming at them at speed, and leaders may be ill-equipped to navigate their way through and set a clear path for

---

32 Cranfield School of Management & The Doughty Centre for Corporate Responsibility, commissioned by Coca-Cola Enterprises, *Combining Profit And Purpose: A New Dialogue On The Role Of Business In Society* (October 2014).

others. We need something different – an open, vulnerable, questing and questioning, creative form of leadership.

This is a high vision, a big ask, and not a little daunting. I have read enough management books in my time to know that this is where things can get a little dispiriting. There will follow a long list of the things that leaders should do, all of which I will heartily agree with and underline, and fully intend to implement … I might even fold down the corner of the page so that I can find the list again easily … and then real life comes bursting back in, and all of the pearls of wisdom I've underlined become just Yet One More Thing on my never-ending to-do list.

Instead, then, let's consider just three broad perspectives or areas that leaders may wish to focus on – without distilling anything down into lists, so you can put that pen away – by lingering a little longer on those three words – whole-heartedness, authenticity and vulnerability.

One of the things I loved about my role with CMS was that I was privileged to inhabit two worlds. As a former lawyer, I understand intimately how lawyers think and what is demanded of them in the environment they work in. I love their focus on quality, their intelligence and rigour, their ambition to deliver brilliantly for clients every time. But when I was a kid and involved in a youth theatre group, I was always happiest in a black T-shirt, organising props and costume changes in the wings, listening in on the sound deck, or perched on the lighting rig working the spotlight. The same has proven to be true in my career. I love being on the business side of the business, helping to make it happen.

As a result, during the early post-merger period, I felt immense empathy for everyone involved in every aspect of every challenge we found ourselves facing in those early weeks. I also felt immense responsibility. Up to a point, this was a completely healthy and actively desirable frame of mind for a change leader to be in – big change projects need empathic people who take responsibility! But on the CMS project, I fell for a short while into the trap that I have seen countless others fall into and positioned myself essentially as the gatekeeper between the two halves of the organisation on operational matters. "Talk to me," I basically said. "Talk to me, and I will get it sorted."

Of course, while this perhaps worked extremely well for the handful of people I was able to help personally, it was hardly a scalable or sustainable solution!

Everyone on the team had to work out how best to use our time and resources to help as many people as possible make a success of these early weeks, and it fast became clear to me that I needed a different mindset. To stay focused on the past rather than the future – should I have predicted this? should I have done more to prepare people? – kept me reactive and defensive. It also risked being too controlling, and so potentially disempowering for people around me. I was trying to make everything okay right now instead of letting people work their way into a better future.

That realisation was a mini-turning point for me. The facts had not changed, but I got back that scintilla of time between thought and action that is the aim of so much mindfulness practice. In that narrowest silver sliver, I rediscovered a degree of detachment, the capacity to prioritise, the power of choices and my sense of humour. I learned a huge amount by observing the behaviour of the senior leadership team and its impact on people across the firm. Around this time, amongst the core team there emerged a very fluid and informal sort of daily, sometimes hourly, priority setting, based simply on asking "What's best next?" and then doing that thing.

The senior leaders, each in their own way, clearly brought their entire selves to bear to tackle the challenges we were facing. Looking back, this obvious, authentic, humanity was a key part of the merger's ultimate success: yes, there were some challenges, but nobody could doubt that the leadership cared, and would show up time and again and get their hands dirty to fix things. This also served to ignite bravery and resourcefulness in others. There was a certainty, a sureness of purpose, a confidence, sometimes an almost childlike glee and curiosity that was compelling and infectious. This, for me, is what we mean when we talk about whole-hearted and authentic leadership.

But what about that altogether tricksier concept of vulnerability?

Letting go of the (false) certainty that a process-led approach to change confers, requires a degree of vulnerability. This is because it requires us to admit that we don't know the answer to everything.

In her 2012 book *Daring Greatly*,[33] Brené Brown references a compelling body of research on the role of vulnerability in leadership. Leaders who show vulnerability are perceived as courageous and can inspire others to follow suit. In addition, the sheer act of admitting to not having all the answers frees others up – gives them the space, opportunity and agency to create, take initiative, innovate, and experiment.

While we might understand this intellectually, it feels deeply uncomfortable. Perhaps particularly in professional services organisations, we still inhabit a paradigm which equates leadership with expertise, problem-solving, having all the best ideas, and being directive. What's more, if we are to retain ultimate responsibility as a leader – and I believe we should – then it feels much more comfortable to bear the weight of that responsibility if one also believes that one retains ultimate control. There is also a point around a leader's responsibility as the storyteller: at times of great uncertainty, we need to be able to look to our organisation and its leaders and to believe that they, at least, know where we are all going.

But we must not equate vulnerability with weakness, vagueness, or woolly

---

33 Brené Brown, *Daring Greatly – How the Courage to be Vulnerable Transforms the Way We Live, Love, Parent and Lead* (Penguin, 2012).

thinking. Unbounded, yes – a leader simply saying, "I don't know" could be weak. It could be indicative of a lack of direction, or even competence, and it could lead to uncertainty and a crisis of trust in the wider firm. That is absolutely not what I am advocating for here. But it is also abundantly clear from the business and political world around us, surely, that a point-blank refusal to engage with some vulnerability presents even greater threats to trust and good decision-making – namely blaming, avoiding the question, making excuses, or hubris.

By contrast, properly framed, the vulnerability of not-knowing can be a defining trait of the most transformational leadership. A 'good' vulnerable leader is not saying, "I don't know why ....", or "I don't know what's important", or "I don't know where we are headed" … Rather, a good leader is asking 'how' questions:

This is a new and complex challenge. I don't necessarily know how to solve it on my own. Given what we're about as a firm, and our values and strengths, I know there must be lots of options. What does the team think?

Whenever there is a leader who truly embraces this approach leading a change project, the impact is incredible. Their confidence in what they are doing and why, and their clear sense of where they are ultimately headed, never waivers – and that is apparent to those around them throughout, and confers confidence and reassurance. But such leaders, by also reaching out to their teams, are also able to generate more ideas, and better ideas, and implement them faster, and with a much greater level of engagement, than anything anyone would have been able to achieve alone.

In my experience, leaders who demonstrate some vulnerability in this way bring a multi-layered benefit to their organisation. First, and most obviously, they maximise the chances of finding a good solution to the particular problem in hand, by opening the floor to all of the talent, expertise and experience within the organisation. Much more importantly, they establish the conditions which will make the generation of new ideas and the successful resolution of future problems much more likely. They are role modelling the vulnerability and curiosity required to tackle complex issues. They are creating a space for others to step into and create and deliver. They are demonstrating a willingness to take risks and cultivating trust, while also being realistic. Create a context within which vulnerability can happen, and the potential prize is enormous – trust, empowered and engaged teams, creativity, initiative, innovation, action. Collective intelligence. The framework within which vulnerability can happen most safely – and with the best chance of delivering what it promises – is a framework of purpose and stories.

Law firm leaders, then – showing up as authentic, whole-hearted and vulnerable can bring purpose and stories right into the heart of their merger integration experience – bringing meaning to the work people do, helping them to feel valued, and rigging the environment for success – thinking about which of their rules, systems and processes truly support their business and which get in the way. They can think about what they measure and reward, what they celebrate, what stories they tell. They can think about how the physical environment is arranged to support belonging, how they structure teams, and how they cascade information throughout the organisation.

10. BECAUSE – the outcomes

I said at the start of the chapter that those firms who can shift their collective mindset around change, by virtue of being rooted in a clear purpose, with some compelling stories, and being led by whole-hearted, authentic and vulnerable leaders, will find themselves able to navigate the inevitable challenges that a period of merger integration will bring, and able to avail themselves of a number of opportunities, seven of which can be summarised in my BECAUSE model for merger integration and organisational change.[34] In closing, let's just touch briefly on what some of those challenges and opportunities look like:

10.1 Belonging

Engendering a deep sense of belonging is absolutely vital for individual wellbeing and corporate performance, particularly during periods of profound change, which can pose a threat to our sense of self and safety. Three aspects are in my experience particularly productive to focus on – building connectedness and relationships; creating an environment in terms of physical surroundings and daily routine in which people feel safe and authentic and can thrive; and building identity, for individuals, teams and the firm as a whole.

There are lots of practical things firms can do to tackle all three aspects, and the details will vary according to context – but at core, for all organisations, a clear sense of common purpose and some shared values are, I believe, vital. Stories are one of the most potent tools to help with building connectedness and identity in particular, because they engage people at the deeper emotional level at which issues of belonging and identity operate, and build a richer and more vibrant context for people to aspire to be part of.

10.2 Evolution

Strategy is dead! So says pretty much every business academic worth their salt. These days, it is all about VUCA – that is to say, our world is so volatile, uncertain, complex and ambiguous that it's a wonder we can put one foot in front of the other. The pace and nature of change in the legal market in particular is such that we have to be able to change direction on a hairpin.

---

34 The model is explained in full in my book: Jennifer Emery, *Leading for Organisational Change: Building Purpose, Motivation and Belonging* (Wiley, 2019).

That does not of course mean that every firm just wakes up and reinvents itself every morning. However unpredictable circumstances may feel on occasion we are none of us, really, just making things up as we go along. But how to strike that balance? How can a firm remain open to possibilities and awake and reactive, and yet crack on with intent, focus, and without mayhem? And why?

There are a number of advantages that a more evolutionary approach to strategy setting and prioritising can bring to a firm, particularly in the context of merger integration:

- the ability to move swiftly and to be decisive;
- the freedom to move in a manner which bests suits a particular complex context at any given particular time;
- the empowerment and increased engagement of everyone in the organisation; and
- better quality decisions being made by those best qualified to make them.

If that is the prize, how to get there? Organisations that are truly evolutionary in their outlook are strikingly focused on outcomes rather than means. They focus on the big picture. They favour values, deeply rooted and widely lived, over rules and policies. They are experimenters – they try new things and don't worry too much if some ideas don't work. There are, I think, three guiding principles or approaches which underpin these characteristics, namely the vulnerability in leaders that we explored above that enables them to seek out solutions; a posture of hope (self-belief and knowing you have options, basically), and a practice of pausing, listening and reflecting.

10.3 Confidence

The word 'confidence' itself comes from the Latin *con fides* – meaning with trust or with faith. In yourself, in others, in circumstances. By definition, confidence does not equate to certainty. It is about stepping into a gap; it is about throwing your hat in the ring.

Throughout the CMS merger, I watched the senior leaders role model and exude confidence in a number of ways. Being always available to listen to people – their concerns, ideas and opinions, both informally, and in thrice-weekly 'listening' coffee sessions. Without fail, those sessions would yield a new idea, which the leaders would then set in motion. I saw clarity and decisiveness in relation to the myriad of decisions, big and small, which came across the leadership team's desk – never flinching at the unexpected, dealing with politically fraught decisions around roles, conflicts, whatever, with clarity and astuteness, and always prioritising the person and the relationship at the heart of any issue. The leaders also retained a twinkle in their eye throughout the whole period, never forgetting to stay curious, play a little, enjoy the sheer privilege and challenge of what we were engaged in.

But confidence can be an elusive thing at the best of times. On top of this, periods of profound change present some particular challenges to our ability to feel confident and I watched this play out both for individuals and for the firm as a whole throughout the merger. In my experience, there is no single failsafe method for acquiring confidence. That said, over time, I have seen individuals benefit from focusing on four areas in particular, and it is interesting to think about how these areas also apply at a firm-wide level.

The four areas of focus then, are, first, reframing – speaking of opportunities and excitement, rather than threats and concerns, for example; secondly, very explicitly drawing on past experiences to build standing and reputation; thirdly, consciously staying rooted in one's own sense of purpose; and finally being prepared to stand up tall and take space.

10.4 Agility

There are some paradigm shifts in societal and business models and in the availability of information and technology which are driving organisations to become much more agile. When firms are changing anyway, post-merger, they should be looking to design-in as many aspects of agility as possible. Agility balances stability and dynamism – much like a gymnast's strong spine, and purpose and stories serve as both the strong spine and the enabler of dynamism in agile firms.

McKinsey identifies five defining features of the most agile organisations: they are purpose-led; they have dense networks; they have rapid decision and learning cycles and experiment; they have people models which support agility; and they have enabling technology as an integral part of how they do business. Law firm leaders can and should take practical steps to build in all of these. At least in the legal sector, and possibly for the majority of us, one of the hardest aspects of the features listed by McKinsey to develop is the willingness to experiment and take risks. Once again this requires us, as individuals and leaders, to address issues around fear and vulnerability.

10.5 Understanding

In order to understand why understanding matters, consider the mounting pile of carnage which develops when communication doesn't work well and understanding isn't present.

There's the frustration in the moment, there's inefficiency, which can lead to wasted effort, duplication, dropped balls, missed opportunities, or create unnecessary risks and lead to a drop in quality and to mistakes. You can miss out on the unknown unknowns – the good idea that never was because the two people who each held half of the idea could not communicate with each other.

Poor communication can actively drive a wedge between people – people can get overwhelmed by the sheer volume of information coming their way – which then leads to a risk that they will miss something important – and also means that people don't feel heard, understood or valued. This over time leads to people being disengaged, and a lack of cohesion in teams, and all of the above leads to untold destruction of value in a firm.

During periods of change, all of the above can be particularly acute for a number of reasons[35] and in every change project I have been involved in, communication has been a very significant issue. Communication is really hard to get right, not least because different stakeholders tend to want very different things. A sense of purpose and the ability to tell stories are absolutely fundamental to the development of understanding in firms.

Law firm leaders must remember that communication is at least as much about listening as it is about speaking, and should be mindful about what information is communicated, when, in what context, and by whom. They should also consider the purpose of a piece of communication itself – is its primary purpose to clarify and give information, or are you seeking to go deeper, create enlightenment, change hearts and minds? This deeper form of communication depends on establishing common ground and a common language, and on understanding and appreciating difference – again, all areas where purpose, stories and leadership are key.

10.6 Simplicity

Complexity seems to follow change around like an ambulance chaser. It is a scourge, and it slows firms down and saps goodwill. A purpose-led and story-driven approach can help firms to eschew unnecessary complexity – Netflix describes this as eliminating barnacles – and in this way to both increase efficiency, and achieve a sophisticated simplicity[36] that will better enable them to focus their intelligence, attention and energy on the fine details and nuances that truly matter.

There is, for example, simplicity of message – firms that are clear about their purpose can hook everything to that, and tell stories that all lead back to this one unifying factor. There is simplicity of information – people can be given relevant information in context, rather than just being deluged. There can be simplicity of decision-making and, in turn, simplicity of execution, because

---

35 People may lack familiarity with each other, and so we can't use all those shortcuts and awareness of one another's proclivities in order to add clarity to an unclear message. Levels of trust may be low and people may perceive a lack of transparency and fear that information is being kept from them. On the other hand, the sheer volume of information to be communicated is likely to be much greater than usual. Finally, an organisation may already be on the back foot in terms of rolling out unfamiliar systems and processes, or in terms of building engagement and cohesion, and so the impact of a wrong note in terms of communication has a much greater adverse effect.

36 H Garcia and F Miralles, *Ikigai: The Japanese Secret to a Long and Happy Life* (Penguin, 2016).

purpose and stories can build trust and ignite action. There is also then a resulting simplicity of structure and rules.

10.7 Energy

Energy encompasses the concept *du jour* of 'resilience' but it is bigger than this, and also includes inspiration, creativity, whole-heartedness and momentum. A prolonged period of profound change can become a perfect crucible in which to burn off energy and resilience, but it can also, done well, actively create energy.

Friedrich Nietzsche famously said: "He who has a why to live can bear almost any how."

More than 50 years later, we now have research to support the argument that a clear sense of purpose can increase resilience.[37]

At an organisational level, a recent research report by Tomorrow's Company in collaboration with Danone, which looked at the value of a purpose-driven approach across 20 global companies found that one of the key ways in which purpose generates value is by becoming a source of energy and commitment for people within the organisation.[38]

Paul Dolan in *Happiness by Design*[39] argues that purpose is in partnership with pleasure as two components of happiness. If people have a clear sense that their work is purposeful, they will to some extent trade a degree of pleasure in pursuit of the purpose. This is a better framing than 'delayed gratification', which implies that there's nothing in this for me, now. If I am feeling purposeful and engaged, that in itself is the 'something in it for me'.

One key role of stories in keeping us resilient and energising us is, once again, that they keep us connected to our purpose. Another role of stories in this context is that they help us to imagine a route through. By recalling times in our own lives where we have faced similar challenges, or by hearing others' stories, we can remember successes (and increase our dopamine), build our confidence, regain a sense of control and autonomy (and reduce cortisol), and be optimistic about the future. Homer already knew this: "Be strong, saith my heart. I am a soldier, I have seen worse than this."

---

37 BP Rutten *et al*, "Resilience in Mental Health: Linking psychological and neurobiological perspectives" (2003) 128(1) *Acta Psychiatrica Scandinavicam* 3–20.

38 Tomorrow's Company Report, with Danone, *The Courage Of Their Convictions: How Purposeful Companies Can Prosper In An Uncertain World* (Mark Goyder and Norman Pickavance, 2018).

39 Paul Dolan, *Happiness by Design* (Penguin, 2014).

Learning to lead: perspective on bridging the lawyer leadership gap

Scott A Westfahl
Harvard Law School

1. Introduction

In an increasingly dynamic, volatile and uncertain global economic environment, the corporate legal profession faces many challenges, threats and even opportunities. Many are surfacing out of new business models and legal regulatory frameworks, potentially disruptive technology and increased competition from multi-disciplinary business solutions providers (particularly the Big Four). A surprising and increasing number of new businesses and alternative legal services providers are working on disrupting the legal profession, primarily through technology and management systems designed to lower legal costs through efficiency and/or to improve legal outcomes through more deliberate and careful process engineering. Some alternative legal providers like Axiom or the growing Potomac Law Group in Washington, DC are experimenting with new human capital models to leverage the strengths of gig workers who prefer to offer legal services through flexible platforms rather than rigidly hierarchical, up-or-out law firm partnerships. The meteoric and global growth of the Corporate Legal Operations Consortium (CLOC) in the past four years signals the direct engagement of in-house legal departments, who are working around law firms and with legal tech companies to streamline the delivery of in-house legal services.

In the midst of all of this change and uncertainty, law firm leaders are called upon to design strategies, identify threats and opportunities, implement change, communicate with clarity and even prepare for effective generational succession. Shockingly, in the past five years innovation has become such a hot buzzword at law firms that it is now almost meaningless due to overuse and a failure to understand its import. Traditionally, a law firm leader's demand for innovation would sound something like, "We really need to be more innovative – what are all the other firms doing?!" Now, by contrast, we see firms naming partners to be 'heads of innovation' and even experimentation with design thinking-based approaches.

Yet even with all of this change, stress and pressure to innovate, most law firm leaders have had very little – if any – formal leadership training. Worse, many insist upon continuing to maintain full legal practices of their own even while assuming enormous leadership responsibilities. Leverage is difficult for them to find with respect to those leadership responsibilities because law firms chronically underinvest in leadership development. This chronic underinvestment threatens even large, profitable law firms and is compounded by the increasing amount of leadership turnover now occurring at many large firms. In the absence of effective leadership training and development, succession becomes a perilous journey and places firms at high risk.

Why do law firms invest very little in leadership development relative to any other type of professional services firm, such as accounting and consulting firms? First, there is the inertia of "it's not broken, so don't fix it". Many firms assume that if they choose people who are smart and have booming practices, those people will figure out how to become effective leaders. But does that not seem to be an extremely risky strategy, given the global size and scale many firms are now reaching?

Secondly, the flat structure of law firms and the need to create the illusion that all partners are equal owners of the business often stands in the way of specific leadership development initiatives. Wall Street, accounting and consulting firms have no qualms about identifying and offering leadership training for high potentials, but law firms particularly struggle with that concept. They have not achieved the organisational maturity necessary to accept that each partner brings unique strengths and cannot be expected to excel at every aspect of being a partner, including leadership. Nor have law firms found ways to hold leaders accountable to the same degree as consulting and accounting firms. The latter use 360-degree reviews, regular rotation of leaders and advanced governance structures to monitor, develop and refresh leaders. Some observe that lawyers have a greater need for autonomy and resist rules and procedures more than other professionals. If lawyers are indeed harder to manage as a result, it is not surprising that leadership as a concept is undervalued within legal organisations.

Perhaps the biggest reason for law firms' chronic underinvestment in leadership development is the difficulty of adapting a long-term investment perspective in a business where all profits are fully distributed each year, and the effective share price of a law firm is the amount of profit each partner thereby receives. The need to retain existing talent and compete in the lateral partner-hiring market seemingly justifies their short-term focus. Most firms fail to see that outlining a longer-term plan and investing in longer-term initiatives like leadership development will:

- cement loyalty;
- attract talent; and
- help hedge against total collapse due to ineffective leadership.

On an individual level, partners are in a bind. They face increasing pressure to bill hours and generate new business. There are little or no incentives or encouragement for them to build their leadership skills or volunteer for early leadership experiences. The leadership learning model is therefore high risk and almost entirely sink-or-swim. Yet, if asked, no lawyer would dispute that Michael Phelps did not become the greatest swimmer in world history by figuring it out on his own.

In the US, at least, the leadership gap in law firms would not be so great if US law schools, like their business school counterparts, invested in teaching law students how to collaborate, work in teams, manage people and projects, and think and act like leaders. It is stunning in some ways because the evidence is clear that lawyers often achieve positions of enormous leadership responsibility. Lawyers begin their professional careers at a significant disadvantage and it is hard to catch up, especially when you do not know what you do not know.

Another factor that impairs the ability of lawyers to catch up is that, early on in their careers, they need to focus most of their attention on building technical legal skills because they did not learn them in law school. The attention this requires crowds out the equally important building of professional skills such as leadership. As associates begin to delegate work and manage people and projects, their attention is not redirected. They continue to believe that technical expertise is paramount and fail to better balance their focus on learning how to lead as well as produce. The traditional law firm model of lawyer development is significantly out of alignment with market needs, as my colleague David Wilkins and I have extensively discussed. The lawyer development 'triangle' we suggest requires law schools, law firms and law departments to collaborate to provide lawyers, across the arc of their careers, with training, experiences, mentoring, coaching and resources to develop their legal technical skills; key leadership and professional skills; and effective professional networks.[1]

2. The origins of leadership style and behaviours

To frame a discussion of learning to lead, let us first consider the essence of leadership styles and behaviours. During the 2008 US presidential campaign, we saw two very different kinds of leaders vying for the Oval Office prize. During that election, it occurred to me that the significant contrasts between the leadership styles of Barack Obama and John McCain were similar to those I had seen first-hand somewhere before.

My father was a US Navy submarine captain during the Cold War. I grew up observing a leadership model that emphasised a quiet, calm, efficient, almost scientific, approach that also gave individual commanders a great deal of

1 See Scott A Westfahl and David B Wilkins, "The Leadership Imperative: A Collaborative Approach to Professional Development in the Global Age of More for Less" (2017) 69 *Stan L Rev* 1667.

latitude to deal with uncertainty and take calculated risks. Operating at depth with nuclear weapons and a nuclear reactor, submariners think through every move with great care.

My best friend's father graduated from the US Naval Academy a few years after my father did. Presumably, they had similar leadership training in that environment. But after graduation, their career paths and the environments in which they operated quickly diverged. Like John McCain, my best friend's father became an A-4 pilot and flew off carriers during multiple deployments to Vietnam. His job was to fly over enemy territory and destroy surface-to-air missile batteries so that they could not fire at the heavy bombers following behind his attack squadron. Essentially, he made himself a target and relied upon his skills and quick reactions to destroy the batteries before they shot him down. His leadership style came out of that experience. Under pressure and enemy fire, he needed to operate independently and take quick, unexpected and often radical action to survive.

See the contrast? One leader under extreme pressure (literally under 1,000 feet of water) requires cold, calm, steady decision-making and teamwork. Another leader when under fire must be the ultimate, unpredictable maverick – doing the unexpected to survive and defeat the enemy.

Flashback to 2008: President-to-be Obama campaigned with extreme care and discipline and refused to get drawn into emotional outbursts or trapped in extreme positions. Senator-candidate McCain, by contrast, kept making radical, unexpected moves, like suspending his campaign to deal with the financial crisis and later asking unknown Alaska Governor, Sarah Palin, to serve as his running mate. Ultimately, the nation decided that in the time of financial crisis and after years of surprises and extreme reactions – including the decision to invade Iraq – a steadier, calmer hand was right for the times.

How is this relevant to learning to lead? First, any approach to learning to lead must start with the understanding that there is no one 'right' leadership style. Different leadership styles are appropriate for different contexts, and leaders adapt to face the challenges they meet. Secondly, how leaders develop their leadership style is also a matter of context. The environment in which leaders learn and grow as young professionals shapes their concepts of leadership. So do the role models they observe and the training they are given, if any. As they first ascend to leadership roles, people attempt consciously or unconsciously to develop their own leadership style out of all these kinds of factors. How they behave as leaders when faced with specific challenges will depend upon their evolving leadership styles.

3. Learning to lead: the process

The purpose of this chapter is to show that learning to lead can and should be a conscious, thoughtful and deliberate process and should include a range of tools that can help people learn. Research has shown that learning for adults happens 10% by training, 20% by observation and 70% by experience and experimentation – the hands-on component.[2] For law firm lawyers, there are significant deficiencies in the way they learn in all three of these dimensions.

4. Executive education helps lawyers catch up

Let us start at the top of the pyramid. Unfortunately, neither law schools nor the continuing legal education world have meaningfully embraced the teaching of leadership to lawyers, though the recent organisation of a new leadership section of the American Associate of Law Schools is a very welcome step forward. We have moved beyond the notion that law schools' only responsibility is to teach students to think like lawyers. We need to continue to gain momentum by encouraging the law schools that are embracing the notion that leadership is a practical skill which they should teach. In the US and around the world, training for experienced lawyers almost exclusively focuses on deepening substantive and technical legal expertise. In the US, formal training for experienced lawyers originated principally from the desire of the bar, which is self-regulated, to protect itself from consumer complaints about lawyers. The many states that have adopted continuing legal education requirements have only in recent years begun to give credit for law practice management-focused courses. More broadly around the world, there is growing interest in teaching lawyers to be leaders, as witnessed by the increasing number of firms participating in leadership programmes at various universities and working with universities to design custom leadership programmes for their partners.

4.1 The executive education model

The good news is that a new model has emerged. Businesses around the world have long invested in executive education for corporate leaders. As executives approach new levels of responsibility, they attend intense, case-focused training programmes to accelerate their leadership readiness and capabilities. Executive education programmes for lawyers are now emerging that achieve the same effects and offer hope for a highly efficient way to help lawyers and legal organisations quickly rectify their chronic underinvestment in leadership development.

How does the model work? It started in the 1940s with partnerships between businesses and top academic institutions, which worked together to design highly immersive, relatively short-burst programmes to focus on key leadership challenges. The idea was to provide just-in-time, contextual learning to support

---

2 Michael M Lombardo and Robert W Eichinger, *The Career Architect Development Planner*, 1st edn (Minneapolis, Lominger, 1996).

executives across the arcs of their careers. Case studies of real leadership situations quickly became a core element of the executive education model. These cases provide the all-important context that is critical to cementing learning and ensuring its relevance.

Cases are also particularly effective because participants are more likely to remember the lessons from an executive education programme if the lessons are taught through the power of a story, which helps to embed learning in long-term memory. This happens through participants' natural inclination to pay more attention to a story than a lecture, and the deeper engagement that happens when participants grapple with the elements of the story and test them against their own and others' experiences. Research consistently shows that both attention and engagement correlate highly with encoding in long-term memory, and that emotion also plays a key role. When leadership cases are well written and well taught, participants debate vigorously about controversial people and situations and are thus more likely to remember and try to apply critical lessons drawn from the cases. Simulation cases are often even more effective, as participants are challenged to work in teams to solve difficult problems, which helps them to explore and learn about team dynamics, decision-making and leadership.[3]

Another critical component of executive education is the selection of the participant group. Contextual learning requires that participants have a baseline level of shared experiences, responsibilities and perspectives. Thus, most executive education programmes try to organise courses by peer groups, with enough diversity to provide rigorous classroom dialogue but not so much as to risk disengagement among participants who feel the programme may be at the wrong level for them. In the end, these peer groups of participants learn as much from each other as from faculty. They form close bonds even in a short programme. This strengthens their professional networks and within a law firm can greatly increase trust among partners. They achieve a much stronger appreciation of each other's abilities and perspectives through class debates and exercises focused on the challenges they face in the real world.

The intense nature of executive education often surprises lawyers, who expect to be able to attend a programme, passively listen for a week and walk away with an idea or two and a couple of new contacts. When they realise on the first day that the classroom is a forum for discussion and debate and they

3 As one example, we have developed a new simulation for law firm leaders based upon the 'adaptive leadership' model pioneered by Harvard Kennedy School of Government Professor Ron Haifetz. In the simulation, teams of four to six law firm leaders are challenged to form their own law firm. Then, as the executive committee of their firm, participant teams must meet to debate and make a collective decision in three very difficult scenarios that present 'adaptive' problems for which there is no available technical solution. Through experiential learning and practice, participants learn to recognise 'adaptive' problems and work to create a deliberative decision-making environment that fully considers the implications of a tough decision for all key stakeholders and for the organisation's core values.

are required fully to engage, they typically do so enthusiastically. One small trick that faculty often use on the first day is to refer and ask questions about very obscure details of a case – this signals to participants that they must do their homework and come to class very familiar with the cases assigned!

4.2 The focus: what does executive education for lawyers require?

(a) *Taking perspective*

One of the hardest things for lawyers to do in the world of the billable hour is to step back in order to gain perspective on where they are in their careers. Indeed, one of the most tragic consequences of the task-driven, time-is-money approach to the practice of law is that lawyers sometimes lose all sense of their strengths and their goals. They lose touch with their broader networks and when suddenly faced with a career crisis (eg, a recession hits or they lose a major client), they have a difficult time thinking through what to do next. Career counsellors describe the phenomenon of lawyers writing résumés with expectations that the only thing they are qualified to do is exactly what they have been doing, even if that work is not available. Often lawyers lack perspective on their strengths and abilities, have lost focus on longer-term goals and have neglected the connections and contacts that are most likely to provide them with their next opportunities.

Through its intense, focused nature, executive education helps lawyers gain critical perspective, usually at key career transition points like moving into more senior leadership roles. Executive education programmes for lawyers often start with a case that describes the many challenges and responsibilities that participants face in their roles. The 'producer-manager dilemma' that participants all face comes to light and often provokes emotional, cathartic reactions. They have not previously taken the time to understand that their professional lives are often vastly more complicated than those of their business leader clients because, unlike business leaders, lawyers in leadership roles are required to manage and lead the business of their practices and firms while also doing real legal work and serving and developing clients. CEOs have the luxury of managing and leading without having to produce in the traditional sense. Opening lawyers' eyes to the reality of the producer-manager dilemma sets the tone and dramatically increases participants' buy-in to the executive education model. They feel understood and begin to engage.

(b) *Unpacking leadership*

In some ways the word 'leadership' is a foreign concept to lawyers. It is not part of their traditional training and, unlike other professional services firms, law firms rarely use the word 'leader' to describe anyone but people in top management roles. When I first started to use the word 'leadership' in building a competency model for law firm associates, more than one sceptical partner loudly raised objections. They insisted that associates needed to focus exclusively on developing technical legal skills and any effort to build their leadership skills or their professional networks would be distracting to that purpose.

The good news is that the increasingly competitive market for legal services is generating much more interest in unpacking what leadership means in a law firm and how it can provide competitive advantage. Of most interest are the following key areas:

- Leading people and teams (eg, motivating professionals; providing feedback and having important conversations; understanding critical elements of team dynamics and effective team process; and aligning talent development systems with firm culture and strategy).
- Client leadership (eg, building client relationships; enhancing client communication to have more influence and impact with clients; innovating new models of client service; and comparing client service models from around the world).
- Sector leadership (understanding how to drive collaboration, gain buy-in for sector initiatives and understand the competitive forces that are shaping clients' industries, in order to be able to help clients 'see around the corner' with respect to the legal implications of those dynamic forces); and
- Firm leadership (eg, understanding what strategy is and is not; understanding business unit versus corporate strategy; learning how to drive strategic planning and implementation; understanding practice segmentation and its implications; leading change and aligning organisations to achieve strategic goals; learning how to recognise 'adaptive' versus 'technical' problems and creating an environment where firms can adapt in situations where their core values are tested; and, increasingly, learning how to drive innovation through design thinking-based approaches).

Interactive case discussions and simulations provide context, and faculty will facilitate this in a dynamic way that allows them to introduce leadership concepts and frameworks – and language – that participants can apply in their day-to-day jobs when they return to their firms.

For example, law firm leaders often struggle with holding their fellow partners accountable and having direct, honest conversations with them. Mid- and senior-level associates who supervise junior lawyers often neglect their responsibility to give hard feedback, both directly to the junior associates and in writing on their annual review forms.

One of the most popular cases I have seen used in executive education programmes illustrates the importance of having timely, important conversations about performance, in order to avoid the need for very difficult conversations later on. Participants are introduced to a classic model for having such conversations and role play and practise its application. Through the power of story (the case), they are much more likely to remember the key learning point. Through the power of practise (the role play), they are more likely to be effective at managing such situations in the future.

Another example relates to the need for law firm leaders to understand key principles of strategy. Many fail to see that growth in and of itself is not a strategy, and that the key to avoiding race-to-the-bottom, price-based competition is to create significant differentiation in the market. Traditional business schools' strategy cases and new ones that have been developed about law firms help participants in executive education to ground their decision-making in fundamental, reliable principles.

(c) Introducing core business skills to lawyers

Executive education in the business world has always focused on introducing and reinforcing core business skills. Beyond leadership, such skills include, for example, finance, valuation, accounting and marketing – all skills to which many lawyers have had little or no academic exposure. Thus, a critical element of executive education for lawyers needs to be an interdisciplinary approach to such concepts, so that lawyers can learn in context how to apply core business skills. Asking law firm leaders to obtain MBAs, by contrast, is impractical and marginally not likely to be worth the effort. Learning to lead requires the building of broader business skills – but in a way that is directly applicable and relevant to the challenges faced by law firm leaders. Some US-based firms are now experimenting with mini-MBA type programmes for new associates; others are considering the example of Milbank, the New York-based law firm that sends all of its mid- and senior-level associates to Harvard Law School for a series of week-long business and leadership skills programmes over a three to four-year cycle.

(d) Applying relevant research

Executive education for lawyers needs to be research-based. Lawyers are inherently sceptical of theories and anecdotal evidence and are the world's most skilful debunkers of hypotheses. They have earned their standing by challenging assumptions, so executive education programmes that shortcut the empirical knowledge will suffer.

As a result, it is highly advantageous to locate executive education within leading academic institutions rather than consulting firms or other independent centres. Academic-based research is rigorous, peer-reviewed and arguably much less tainted by profit motives. Within a university, executive education programmes can also introduce broader, more interdisciplinary research and learning (eg, leading academic experts on core business skills, the psychology of influence and the global economy all contribute to Harvard Law School executive education teaching).

Also, people and outside organisations much more readily share data and perspectives with academic researchers, who are not viewed as competitors. This allows for much greater development of relevant cases that touch upon current 'hot-button' issues that participants are facing.

4.3 Providing learning experiences that are truly differentiated

Executive education for lawyers helps them learn to lead more effectively because of the differentiated way the learning occurs. Lawyers typically learn through self-study, straight lectures, 'talking head' panels, or (from law school) intimidating Socratic dialogue. The executive education model provides an interactive, collaborative approach that often surprises participants. The idea that you build upon others' ideas rather than tear them down law school-style is in itself a key differentiator.

4.4 Achieving an organisation's particular goals through custom programmes

One form of executive education – a custom rather than open enrolment programme – is often used to help an organisation address its own particular goals. For example, a law firm might partner with an academic institution to create a custom programme focused on the teaching of strategy frameworks in order to help the firm's emerging leaders to develop and more effectively execute the law firm's strategy. Custom programmes can combine a mix of standard and customised cases and can be taught in a tailored way to match a firm's specific challenges. A firm's leaders can also become involved in designing and even co-teaching particular sessions, to provide additional context and grounding in the firm's goals for the programme. The core elements of the executive education model greatly enhance learning and can significantly deepen relationships, trust and collaboration among peers within the same firm.

5. Thoughts on observation, experience and experimentation

As noted above, adult learning theory suggests that, beyond training, it is critical to provide opportunities for people to observe and also to practise the application of what they are learning. As far behind as legal organisations are in training lawyers to be leaders, they lag even further behind in providing most lawyers with structured opportunities to observe, experience and experiment with leadership.

5.1 Watch and learn

With respect to observation, corporations routinely establish high-potential programmes through which up-and-coming people are allowed to shadow and learn from senior executives. By contrast, law firms usually isolate leaders and very few allow associates anywhere near discussions about, for example, firm strategy, finances or plans to innovate. A few firms like Latham & Watkins have figured out that including associates on key committees like the partner election committee helps prepare them for the senior leadership positions they may someday hold.

In an analytical study I once conducted with Indiana University Law School Professor, William Henderson, we learned that judgement was the competency most highly correlated with distinctive success as a senior associate at a major law firm. That begs two questions: how do you hire for judgement and how do you accelerate the teaching of it? Our best answer to the latter question was to provide early opportunities for associates to shadow and observe how successful senior leaders exercise judgement.

London law firms anecdotally report that their now fading tradition of having article clerks sit at desks within senior partners' offices provides the clerks with a much better sense of how partners make important judgement calls. Law firms would do well to consider this lesson and to deliberately structure these kinds of shadowing opportunities.

5.2 Learn by doing – earlier

As a final suggestion for helping lawyers learn to lead, law firms should consider the leadership rotation principles long employed by corporations, consulting firms and even the military. At major consulting firms, consultants who are given leadership roles have an expectation that they will typically undertake those roles for four to six years. Leadership positions deliberately rotate and younger partners are given significant opportunities as a result. Further, because there is a culture of leadership rotation, it is much easier to convince a leader to step aside for the next person, as being replaced is not stigmatised. Also, consulting firms typically provide associates with direct opportunities early on to lead initiatives (eg, office hiring or running business unit retreats). Day to day, their engagement managers, who are three to five-year associates, run client matters. The firms encourage associates to take ownership of their careers, seek leadership opportunities and find their passion.

Law firms could emulate this model by providing opportunities for associates and younger partners to lead internal initiatives such as:

- efforts to understand, explore and experiment with new technologies, such as artificial intelligence and blockchain;
- design-thinking based hackathons to pilot new approaches to challenging client or internal problems;

- office or business unit hiring;
- retreat planning; and/or
- market- and sector-facing knowledge development efforts.

Firms spend a tremendous amount of time and money hiring terrific talent but then do not challenge them to learn to be leaders. Worse, firm governance structures do not usually include term limits and leaders are often chosen through politically charged processes rather than with a deliberate eye towards succession planning. In the US, this has also resulted in disappointing numbers of women and minority lawyers being appointed to law firm leadership positions (as low as their numbers are in terms of equity partnerships, their leadership position numbers are much worse, as the MCCA/Vault annual reports on law firm diversity show). Since new research in the corporate world continues to prove that diverse leadership teams correlate very positively with higher returns on equity and organisational performance, law firms should take heed and re-examine how they pick and rotate their leaders.[4]

6. Conclusion

The lawyer leadership gap is real and critical, particularly as the markets for clients and talent become increasingly competitive. To address this gap, law firms should:

- consider significantly increasing their commitment to formal programmes aimed at developing lawyers' leadership skills, including executive education programmes; and
- thoughtfully design and construct opportunities for younger lawyers to observe leaders in action and build leadership skills at an earlier age.

Such efforts will help current leaders to increase their leadership skills and knowledge and to develop the next generation of outstanding law firm leaders.

4 See, eg, Thomas Barta, Markus Kleiner and Tilo Neumann, "Is There a Payoff from Top-team Diversity?" (April 2012) *McKinsey Quarterly*; and Anita Woolley and Thomas Malone, "What Makes A Team Smarter? More Women" (June 2011) *Harvard Business Review*.

How to hire leaders who thrive in their roles – both partners and business professionals

Heidi K Gardner
Harvard Law School

1. Introduction

Law firms' war for talent is rooted in their war for clients. Increasingly, sophisticated clients are demanding much more from their law firms, including cross-disciplinary problem-solving that draws on expertise in law, business, technology and strategy. One-dimensional legal problems have swelled into multi-faceted business problems that span departments, disciplines and geographies. As one general counsel put it, "I don't have legal problems. I have 'problem' problems."

Moreover, regulatory changes have opened the door to increased competition from new players in the legal arena. The focus on quality metrics and output-based performance measures is upending traditional ways of measuring work. Clients are demanding diverse teams because they know that diversity promotes innovation and superior quality. Technology is driving down costs and creating both opportunities and threats for many kinds of legal working. As a result, law firms are facing the urgent question of how to adapt to a globalised legal marketplace in the midst of disruption and reinvention.

For law firms, hiring great lawyers isn't enough. Strategically minded firms are also seeking strong business professionals: leaders who focus on the successful operation of the firm in core functions such as marketing, finance, IT and human resources. Talented business executives streamline processes to enable lawyers focus on the 'bread and butter' of the firm. The best business professionals are therefore just as critical to firm profitability and success as their legal counterparts.

For new laterally hired partners and business professionals, a firm's collaborative prowess determines how easily they will be integrated and how quickly – and whether – they will thrive. Collaboration helps bring lateral hires up to speed with a firm's culture, allows them to get to know their colleagues (and vice versa) and, most importantly, builds trust between lateral hires, their peers and new clients. As our prior research uncovered, two kinds of trust are essential foundations for collaboration: belief in others' technical abilities (ie, competence trust) and belief in their intentions and integrity (ie, character trust).[1] The trick, of course, is making sure that your firm is set up to foster this kind of lateral-incumbent collaboration.

Years of empirical and qualitative research show how cross-departmental, smart collaboration is one of the essential elements for increasing the odds that a lateral hire will be successful and productive in their new firm. Supported by my extensive empirical research at Harvard University, this chapter will outline how firms can foster collaboration among newly hired partners, business professionals and their peers by using specific systems in the pre-hire, recruiting and onboarding phases. Doing so will increase their chances of making lateral hiring more successful within this ever-changing legal landscape.

2. Speed is key

We can now demonstrate empirically that smart collaboration is essential to ensuring that lateral hires can become successful and productive, post-move. For more than a decade, I have been studying issues related to leadership, teamwork and talent optimisation in professional service firms. During my time on the faculty at Harvard Business School and now at Harvard Law School, I have amassed a database comprising millions of data records across multiple law firms, including a decade's worth of their timesheet, personnel and financial records. Together with my research team, we combine statistical analyses with insights from hundreds of in-depth interviews with lawyers and other professionals, law firm leaders and clients. Recently with my colleague Anusia Gillespie, we have deepened the research focus and produced the special report, "Smart Collaboration for Lateral Hiring: Successful Strategies to Recruit and Integrate Lateral Hires in Law Firms."

Figure 1: Collaboration and lateral hires: two paths

1 Heidi K Gardner, *Smart Collaboration: How Professionals and Their Firms Succeed by Breaking Down Silos* (Harvard Business Review Press, 2017) 79–81.

Our analyses show that collaboration has to happen quickly – if laterally hired partners are to be successful at their new firm, they must be sufficiently integrated with incumbent partners and clients within the first 18 months, if not sooner. Specifically, two things both need to happen in that short time – laterals need to have had the opportunity to work on at least a couple of the firm's incumbent clients (on pitches, if not actual projects), and they need a couple of long-term partners to help on the client work they generate (either clients they imported or new clients). If either is missing, new hires are at a higher risk of leaving; if neither happens, they are very likely to leave the firm by their three-year anniversary, as illustrated in Figure 1.

We believe that the same truths apply to business professionals: early opportunities to engage in initiatives with their colleagues (both peers and partners) make laterally hired business professionals more likely to be productive and to remain with the firm. As one chief marketing officer said about laterally hired professionals in her firm, "We have to hit the ground running – not just fast, but toward the absolute right goals, and in the way that jives with the firm's culture. We make sure that new [non fee-earning] employees at all ranks have at least two substantive, team-based projects starting Week 1 at the firm. For chief-level business professionals, at least one of those projects involves direct work with partners, ideally on client-related matters. The few times those projects failed to materialise, the employee failed to get properly stuck in and ultimately left defeated. Those mistakes were ours, and we learned from them."

3. Critical action steps to improve lateral hiring

Our research uncovered that firms need to recalibrate how resources and time are spent on preparing to hire, recruiting, and integrating lateral hires.

Figure 2: Resource allocation by phase of hiring: current v ideal

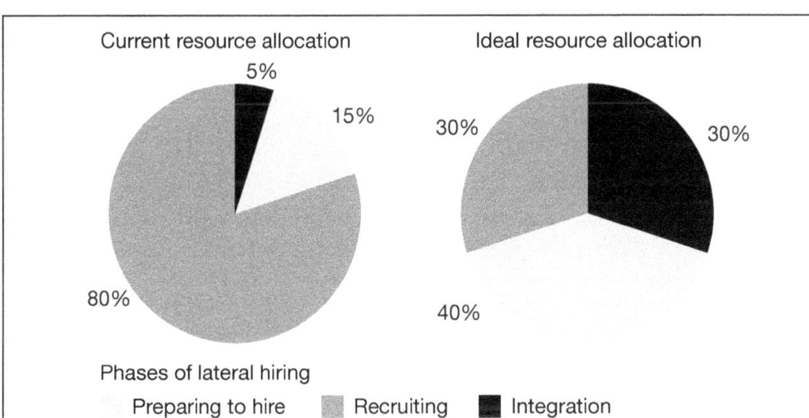

Many firms are not only failing to hire candidates with collaborative skillsets and experiences, but also misallocate their resources, as shown in Figure 2. Of the three phases of the process – preparation, recruiting and interviewing and integration – our studies show that firms currently spend far too much time on the middle step (screening and wooing candidates), and barely any on the others. To make lateral hiring a success, firms need to spread their efforts more evenly across the three phases.

The following sections lay out the steps required for each stage, and then highlight a few key best practices where firms can make the biggest impact when it comes to hiring the right kind of leaders – that is both partners and high-ranking business professionals.

Table 1: Stage 1 – preparing to hire

Stage 1: Preparing to hire (ideally, 40% of resources)
• Connect your talent plan to the firm's strategic plan. • Update analysis of future needs. • Define the expertise needed and think creatively about who is best placed to meet objectives. • Consider internal 'laterals' before looking for external candidates. • Create a data-driven business plan. • Run analyses to track pockets of 'churn and burn'. • Define the role and articulate the required capabilities. • Develop the talent pool. • Allocate the support necessary for success.

3.1 Define the expertise needed and think creatively about who is best placed to meet objectives

Firms need to have the right people in the right positions performing the right functions, and in this market that means addressing the right questions, such as the following:

- What function do we need to meet our objectives?
- How do we position that function within the firm?
- How is the role we are hiring for essential to the success of the function?
- What are the skills and expertise needed to succeed in that position?
- Do those include being a lawyer?

Perhaps the expertise needed for a professional position does include being a trained lawyer. But the flipside is also true: perhaps the firm thinks it needs to hire a lawyer when in fact a highly skilled businessperson in the technology sector, for instance, would better align with the position objectives. Taking that one step further, when your firm embraces collaboration among its lawyers and other professionals, that allows you to embrace even more complex client needs.

3.2 Create a data-driven business plan

Strategic considerations and financial models should answer the threshold question of whether the firm should hire. Factors such as expanding business opportunities, new offices in specific geographic markets, partner or staff turnover and newly developed (or growing) practice or sector-focused groups should be considered. Analyse current capacity and utilisation to reveal whether the emerging market needs can be covered by an existing internal resource.

If a lateral is indeed the best option, then objectively gauge your firm's readiness to absorb the lateral. Has that office, practice or department just hired a cohort of other laterals who are consuming all the integration attention and energy? If a leader is to be hired from outside, is the practice group appropriately leveraged and will he or she have adequate associate support? Your ability to answer these questions ties directly to your ability to help a newly hired lateral succeed.

The analysis must not stop at high-level strategic considerations, however. You need a robust, data-based analysis that forms the business case for each lateral hire. Many firms believe that they already have such a system in place, but most of the plans we have reviewed are more about arguments than analyses – which is unsurprising, given that they were written by lawyers who had been neither supplied with data nor trained to perform quantitative analyses. Instead, engage your financial and business development experts to collect and dissect both internal and market data to calculate anticipated return on investment (ROI) for each proposed candidate.

If your firm decides that a lateral hire is the best option based on convincing evidence and a sound strategic plan, then you should produce a business plan toward that end. The plan should include firm- or client-specific objectives with a named individual responsible to see it through to completion. This plan should be developed for business professionals as well as attorneys. Accountability is critical.

3.3 Define the role and articulate the required capabilities

Many firms need to improve the level of accountability they build into the hiring process, which requires actions in the preparation stage. It is hard later to measure the ROI on a new hire if you are not clear on what he or she was supposed to do in the first place. This phenomenon is true for partners, but is particularly pronounced for lateral business professionals.

With respect to partners, the hiring partner should have a clear view on what role the lateral candidate will play based on the business plan supporting the decision to hire. The role could be to build business in a specific industry sector or contribute a needed kind of expertise to a particular client team. The firm should define the capabilities required to perform the role, including technical expertise, how well the person works on and contributes to teams, and leadership and management skills. What we see, however, is that even when firms set forth these sorts of aspirations in a business plan, they fail to define the capabilities required. Instead, they default to hiring the candidate who promises to import the largest book of business to the firm.

When it comes to business professionals, firms need to gain clarity and consensus about what are a new joiner's responsibilities. For example, a challenge often arises with the CMO position. A firm will often believe this role is needed; but what exactly is that need? Is it for someone who will lead a sales team, optimise operations or run communications? If you hire a high-level marketing person, offering a high salary and promising a strategic role for what really turns out to be a grinding operations position, then you have a problem. The new hire will uncover the 'bait and switch', however unintentional, and will lose trust and any loyalty to the firm. In this instance, not only does the need remain unfulfilled, but you have thrown money at the problem in an unproductive and time-consuming process while the competition is getting ahead.

3.4 Allocate the support necessary for success

Firm support is critical for lateral hires and you need to start lining it up at this stage, long before you begin the actual recruiting process. The type of support required will differ with each hire; firms should undergo a thorough review of the business plan for the newcomer in order to match the objectives with the support offered. An explicit conversation about resource allocation aligns expectations, ensures leaders' commitment and sets the stage for later holding people accountable for achieving a sufficient ROI. The types of resources required may be financial, cultural or internal, such as support staff, technology or even office location. For example, a partner who moves to a larger law firm with the goal of broadening his or her practice geographically should have robust travel support, including a designated budget, internal administrative help and introductions to key partners and clients in targeted locations. Further, the firm should consider whether lateral lawyers are being hired to explore new territory or exploit the firm's existing capacities. Again, the business plan is essential for making resource allocations that are both strategic and perceived as fair.

For business professionals, the type of support required tends to be more complex. What support does a C-level business executive need in a law firm? First and foremost: respect. Lawyers – who likely do not have the expertise of a chief financial officer or other executive – must work to understand the expertise that the business professional is bringing to the table. Two implications arise in this regard. First, although business professionals – unlike lawyers – do not have a licensing requirement to perform their work, their expertise is no less valuable to the firm. Secondly, although it is client-facing lawyers who typically get credit for generating revenue, their success in terms of both quality and volume often depends on expertise from business professionals.

Correcting these misconceptions is an important first step to adequately valuing business professionals and having the conversations necessary to determine and allocate the right resources – including reporting lines, financial allocations, support staff, internal networks and cultural support – upon hiring. Firm leaders must set the tone and embrace the value of their business professionals; otherwise, they are setting them up for failure.

Although law firms today typically spend their greatest effort on the recruiting stage, our research has uncovered numerous ways to improve the process so that you reap the highest returns on that effort. The steps we recommend in this next section draw on both social science research and best practices from professional service firms to help guide you in optimising your recruiting and interviewing stage.

Table 2: Stage 2 – recruiting and interviewing

Stage 2: Recruiting and interviewing (ideally, 30% of resources)
• Search for capabilities over credentials. • Evaluate candidates across four key capabilities. • Identify and train people to conduct behavioural-based interviews. • Determine key qualifications and assign scores to each. • Use the interview data to debrief and make decisions. • Close the deal.

3.5 Evaluate candidates across key capabilities

Hiring is greatly improved when organisations perform multiple interviews to triangulate on the attributes defined in stage one as imperative for the role. As other chapters in this book focus on assessing and developing leadership competencies (see the "Leading lawyers in a VUCA world" chapter by Gardner, Normand-Hochman and Richard), this chapter examines collaborative capacity (ability to develop, work with, and leverage networks) because collaboration is critical to their ability to integrate into their new firm, and cultural role fit.

3.6 Collaborative capacity

Something required of all candidates – from partners to business professionals and associates – in today's competitive environment is 'collaborative capacity'.[2] This refers to a candidate's suitability to become the kind of contributor who can truly leverage your firm's full set of expertise in order to solve both the firm's and its clients' most complex, high-value problems.

Table 3 lists additional key competencies associated with strong collaborators, with sample prompts that interviewers can use to probe.

Table 3: Key collaborative competencies to test with candidates

Key collaborative competencies	Sample interview prompts to elicit example
• Adaptability • Conflict management • Initiative and follow-through • Integrity • Learning motivation/curiosity • Listening and probing • Networking • Perseverance • Persuasiveness (leading without authority) • Political sensitivity	• Tell me about a situation when you teamed up with colleagues to solve a really tough client problem. • Follow-on: How did you find the right experts? How did you know they were capable? How did you convince them to join the effort? What role did you play after the team was formed? • Describe a time when you needed a colleague's input on client work, but that person did not respond to requests. What did you do? • Give me an example of a time when you uncovered an opportunity to serve a client with a multi-practice team. What ultimately happened? What role did you play in helping to build a committed and accountable team? How did the client respond? • How do you handle a situation when a colleague underperforms or does not meet expectations?

2 Heidi K Gardner, *Smart Collaboration: How Professionals and Their Firms Succeed by Breaking Down Silos* (Harvard Business Review Press, 2017) 53–55.

Next, tackle collaboration head-on with the candidate. How can you directly assess a candidate's actual collaborative capabilities? Our advice is to get the issue on the table well in advance of the interview. If you are using a search firm, make sure it is extremely well briefed on your demands for collaboration and is prepared to pre-screen candidates for this quality. Candidates turned off by this will rule themselves out.

It is worth emphasising that collaborative capacity is an equally important trait among business professionals. In today's environment, COOs of law firms need also to be leaders in human resources, business development and other C-level functions. These executives need to have a deep appreciation and understanding of everyone who is sitting at the proverbial table, as these central functions now collaborate with each other to drive revenue opportunities. While this was unheard of pre-recession, that is no longer the case. The C-level mandate is no longer just about support; it is about actually driving a delivery system to clients.

3.7 Cultural role and fit, and the diversity caveat

Turnover as a result of poor culture fit can cost an organisation between 50% and 60% of the person's annual salary.[3]

Evaluators implicitly gravitate towards and explicitly fight for candidates with whom they feel an emotional spark of commonality. Professor Lauren Rivera's research of elite professional service firms shows that cultural reproduction in elite professional service firms produces new hire classes that mirror "firms' existing employees in cultural signals and lifestyle markers".[4] Cultural cohesion is the glue that can hold firms together through good times and bad; but an obvious implication of placing significant weight on similarities is the potential for hiring a demographically homogenous workforce. In Rivera's research, interviewers favoured extracurricular activities associated with the white upper-middle class that were acquired through intense, prolonged investment of material resources and time not only by job applicants, but also by their parents.[5] Further, she found that: "Given that less affluent students are more likely than upper-middle-class students to believe that achievement in the classroom rather than on the field or in the concert hall matters most for future success and focus their energies accordingly the types of cultural similarities valued in elite firms' hiring processes had the potential to create inequalities in access to elite jobs based on parental socioeconomic status."[6]

Even firms which espoused a commitment to diversity still used a process that had a disproportionately negative effect on socioeconomically diverse

3 https://hbr.org/2015/07/recruiting-for-cultural-fit.
4 Lauren Rivera, *Hiring As Cultural Matching* 1017.
5 *ibid*, 1017–18.
6 *ibid*.

candidates. Firms that devoted significant resources to increasing diversity still held the belief that achieving a baseline of cultural similarity represented recruitment success.[7] In essence, these firms sought surface-level diversity, but still prized deep-level (ie, cultural) homogeneity in new hires.[8] This is not the type of diversity that produces the variety of ideas, perspectives and attitudes that lead to superior team performance; it only serves to produce a population of people who may not look the same.

In addition to assessing for cultural fit, firms must have candid conversations about the role responsibilities – both good and bad. Every job has its challenges. Think of interview conversations and the process leading up to hire as creating what organisational behaviour expert Denise Rousseau has coined the "psychological contract".[9] This contract governs expectations in the reciprocal obligation between the firm and the new hire. In having honest conversations with candidates about the position's opportunities and potential difficulties, the firm develops an authentic relationship that will inspire loyalty once the candidate joins the firm, and avoids the risks of new hires feeling that they have experienced a 'bait and switch'. Firms that provide a realistic job preview also help candidates to opt out if they realise that it is not a good role fit. It is cheaper and more reliable for candidates to opt out of the process early than to proceed when they are ultimately a bad fit for the job, and this self-selection will result in a hire who is ultimately a superior fit.

Firms that analyse their own cultures, pinpoint desirable attributes of existing players and hire for those attributes will best assimilate and retain talent. That edge is a true competitive advantage in today's hot labour market. In addition to the lateral hire's ability to 'hit the ground running' and higher likelihood of staying with the firm with proper integration, successful integration colours the lateral's perception and therefore experience of the firm and can influence team performance.

Table 4: Stage 3 – integration

Stage 3: Integration (ideally, 30% of resources)
• Make laterals' experience meaningful from day one and start even before they officially join. • Acquaint with the culture and shape processes around new hires' strengths. • Assign a peer mentor. • Assist new joiners in building their networks. • Hold new joiners, the hiring partner and peers accountable for success. • Continuously audit and revamp the lateral integration process.

3.8 Hold new joiners, the hiring partner and peers accountable for success

As discussed in Stage 1, creating an agreed-upon business plan with projected ROIs is critical because without a concrete plan, it is impossible to hold anyone accountable for results (see section 3.2). Law firms are notoriously bad at holding their lawyers and professionals directly accountable. Instead, firms tend to rely on a vague notion of reputational accountability – that is, people will perform to maintain their reputations, even if no one is monitoring them.

For example, a practice leader who advocates for and successfully brings a new partner on board is typically not directly accountable for that new partner's performance. Aside from reputation for making a good hire, the only way the practice leader is held accountable is indirectly through compensation. The rationale is that if the lateral partner performs poorly and the practice area suffers as a result, the practice leader's compensation will also dip, since it is tied to overall performance. While this general accountability provides an incentive for the practice leader to ensure his or her practice's performance, it does not necessarily incentivise the practice leader to hold the new partner accountable for the business and development plans created at the outset of the hire. Nor does it force the practice leader to alter his or her behaviour. Instead of engaging the new lateral to pursue a new client opportunity, for example, the practice leader may turn to a longstanding partner who's a 'known entity' and seen as less risky. Without someone at the firm who is directly accountable for following up on the promises of a newcomer, these types of issues will snowball, with the likely result of a premature departure of what was once a promising – and expensive – lateral hire.

The business plan and accountability issues are even more pronounced for lateral business professionals. Our research interviewees consistently noted that if a business case was created for the lateral business professional, it was generally not revisited for accountability purposes. Instead, it went in a file and stayed there. As an executive at one large international firm described: "We certainly don't do the same level of involvement [for executive hires] that we would for a lateral partner. I mean, it's surprising, but true. And I think it's just managed a little bit differently. We tend to work through a process of the various chief officers recruiting different people at either the director level or associate director level and going through their review, and then other chiefs will be involved in kind of vetting that person. But it's just not as rigorous in my view as it would be, say, for a lateral partner."

Allowing such ambiguity with respect to performance objectives is a recipe for frustration and limited success. Consider using outside consultants to help

---

7 *ibid*, 1009.

8 *ibid*.

9 Denise M Rousseau, "Psychological and Implied Contracts in Organizations" (1989) 2(2) *Employee Responsibilities and Rights Journal*.

define these measures. To improve lateral success and hold stakeholders accountable, firms must do the following:

- Make it clear to hiring groups that their ability to hire future laterals will depend on how successfully they integrate each newcomer. You might not be able to measure immediate financial results, but you can track activity. For example, how many partners have used the newcomer's expertise to develop joint pitches or to create new IP such as white papers? When partners do create these opportunities, celebrate them across the firm. Recognition for good behaviour not only encourages more partners to engage in it, but also helps to spread the newcomer's reputation as a collaborative, value-adding asset within the firm.
- Set expectations that the integration process will be three to four years, and create goals for what is expected to happen in each of those years.
- Check in with the lateral hire with respect to the hire's business plan, individual development plan and other agreed-upon metrics at three-month, six-month, nine-month and one-year intervals to identify and remedy issues before they escalate.

Most law firms need to become far better at setting and communicating specific objectives. For example, at the three, six and nine-month check-ins, and later in reviews, there is often no clarity around, "I need you to do A, B and C" or "I expect you to do X, Y and Z". Instead, the language is qualified or hedged – there are no bright lines. Interviewees suggest this practice is in place to provide the law firm with as much wiggle room as possible, possibly for fear of future lawsuits. We believe this is one area where law firms would do well to take a bit more 'risk', and clearly delineate and communicate objectives and expectations to employees and hold them accountable for the same.

3.9 Post-hire mentoring and accountability

Most firms already have a nominal 'buddy system' for incoming hires, but far too few of those programmes actually work. To create the highest chances of a lateral hire being successfully integrated, you need to take some specific steps to ensure that mentoring happens (in multiple directions, as discussed below), and that all parties are held accountable for delivering post-hire collaboration within the first 12 months:

- Work with laterals as soon as they join to develop a strategic client service plan, which identifies specific opportunities for them to involve incumbent partners. Leaders should facilitate those introductions, and make it clear to incumbents that they are expected to participate.
- Assign a peer mentor for new hires to help them learn the firm's culture-insider knowledge, such as people who serve as 'honest brokers' in the firm to help connect partners with client or other work. Ideally, this

mentor will be someone whom the new hire met and connected with during the recruiting process so that they have already established a level of interpersonal trust.

- Gain commitment from a few specific people in the hiring group (practice, office, or ideally, both) who are responsible for introducing the newcomer to several predetermined accounts or other kinds of strategic contacts, as outlined in the pre-hire business plan. And require them to report on progress – to you, or at least their practice leader (whose feet you then hold to the fire), not to a functionary in HR. Again, the key here is specificity and accountability.
- Use competency grids to assess the collaborative and mentoring abilities of both the newly hired partner and those in the surrounding practice. (If you do not have these tools, your professional development staff need to source or create them.)
- Provide a budget for laterals to visit colleagues, even for exploratory conversations, and set the expectation that they will use the full budget (appropriately) within the first six to eight months. Expect laterals to report back to you with opportunities they have uncovered, and when, how, and with whom they are taking action.
- Hold formal internal roadshows for laterals to present their client work to offices, practice groups and sectors. Make sure the local leader has spoken with the lateral ahead of time to suggest specific people or account opportunities that the lateral can reference during their presentation, and to ensure that the highest-potential collaborators attend the roadshow.
- Make it clear to hiring groups that their ability to hire future laterals will depend on how successfully they integrate each newcomer. You might not be able to measure immediate financial results, but you can track activity – how many partners have used the newcomer's expertise to develop joint pitches or to create new IP such as white papers? When partners do create these opportunities, celebrate them across the firm. Recognition for good behaviour not only encourages more partners to engage in it, but also helps spread the newcomer's reputation as a collaborative, value-adding asset within the firm.

At the end of this rather long list, it is probably worth putting in a plug for good citizenship within your firm. Good citizens in the senior ranks of your firm typically are willing to contribute – their time, contacts and knowledge – generously, without calculating direct returns. They act with faith that building up their colleagues' capabilities is the right thing to do and trust that they may ultimately benefit from this in an indirect way. They do not keep score or mentally track reciprocity. Leaders need to recognise these citizens for the tremendous value they bring.

Central to all the techniques cited above for setting the stage for post-hire collaboration is culture. Our research shows that culture – more than processes – enables, encourages or inhibits collaboration; processes merely reflect culture – whether it is flourishing or stunted. As you venture into this new, complicated and rewarding realm, watch for signs of cultural chafing, and attend to what needs to be fixed.

4. Conclusion

In today's competitive marketplace, your firm's ability to attract, integrate and ultimately retain partners and business professionals is critical. Smart collaboration is not optional – it is a business imperative for the strategic growth, profitability and sustainability of a firm. Collaboration done 'right' requires strong leadership, sustained efforts and deep commitment from your partners and business professionals at all levels to collaborate with the newcomers. The money and energy your firm puts into fostering smart collaboration – including the recruitment and retention of key laterals – will pay you back many times over.

About the authors

Mariano Batalla
Partner, Batalla
mbatalla@batalla.com

Mariano Batalla is a partner in the corporate/M&A practice of Batalla in Costa Rica. He has been responsible for leading overall firm strategy, talent management and business development. He received his law degree *summa cum laude* from the University of Costa Rica and undertook his graduate studies in business administration and professional service firms at Harvard University and Tufts Fletcher School.

Mr Batalla has specialised in corporate and compliance matters, cross-border Central American M&A transactions and financing and development of large-scale real estate projects. Drawing on his business acumen and expertise, Mariano has advised professional services firms in strategy, positioning, talent management and pricing matters.

He is an officer of the Law Firm Management Committee of the International Bar Association, a visiting professor of service design and entrepreneurship at INCAE Business School and an adjunct professor of entrepreneurship at University of Costa Rica Business School. Mariano is also a founding member of the World Economic Forum's Global Shapers chapter in Costa Rica and a former instructor of innovation and entrepreneurship at Harvard University.

Alexis Caught
Partner, Strategy Four
Alexis@StrategyFour.com

Alexis Caught is the co-author of the Harvard Law School Case Study on Business Development Skills for Partners (*Chasing Growth at Sasker Devereaux*, HLS 15-12) and of the book *Natural Networking.*

After qualifying in media law and communications, Mr Caught joined a leading strategy consulting firm to focus on consumer insight and corporate strategy. Here, his interest in qualitative research was born and honed – leading to working across Europe, Russia and Asia to study and understand peoples' behaviours, motivations and habits.

On his return to the UK he joined the Møller Professional Service Firms Group based at Churchill College, University of Cambridge, before moving in-house with a client to concentrate on their European marketing activities.

Upon returning to Strategy Four and Møller, Mr Caught has concentrated largely on research and consulting on generational leadership in professional service firms.

Kevin Doolan
Partner, Møller Institute
Kevin.Doolan@MollerInstitute.com

Kevin Doolan spent more than 25 years as a law firm partner, the last ten of these as part of the management team with a focus on business development. In 2013 he left to join academia and created the Harvard Law School Case Study on Pricing Professional Services with Professor George Triantis at Stanford Law School (HLS 13-17). Mr Doolan divides his time between teaching and consulting and is guest faculty for both IE Law School in Madrid and Harvard Law School where he teaches pricing and business development on their Accelerated Leadership Program.

Mr Doolan is a partner at The Møller Institute, based at Churchill College, University of Cambridge and is the author of *The Financial Times Guide to Mastering Services Pricing*, published by Pearson.

In his consulting work Mr Doolan advises professional services firms in North America and Europe on leadership, pricing, business development and that tricky task of working successfully across different generations in the workplace.

Susan Saltonstall Duncan
President, RainMaking Oasis LLC
sduncan@rainmakingoasis.com

Susan Duncan began working with law firms in 1980 and has provided management consulting services to more than 150 law firms, other professional service organisations, associations and nearly 1,000 individual professionals. Her consulting firm works with firms, practice groups and individual professionals on firm and practice/sector strategy, business and client development, succession planning, feedback and needs assessment interviews, lateral integration strategies, firm values, visions and culture and innovation.

Ms Duncan is a thought leader on law firm management, innovation, business development and succession planning. She regularly publishes a bi-weekly blog called "InFocus – Insights on Legal Practice, Leadership and Talent" and has published numerous chapters in books and articles in legal publications.

Ms Duncan also served in in-house roles including director of professional development, director of business development and as chief strategy officer for a Global 25 law firm. She was inducted as a Fellow in the College of Law Practice Management (COLPM) and into the Legal Marketing Association's Hall of Fame. She has been widely published in legal publications, is regularly quoted in the press and speaks for national and international associations.

Jenni Emery
Global people and culture leader, Arup
jenni.emery@arup.com

Jenni Emery is a world leading expert in people, culture and change. She is the global people and culture leader at Arup, the leading design and engineering consultancy, and author of *Leading for Organisational Change: Building Purpose, Motivation and Belonging* (Wiley, 2019).

A lawyer and executive coach by background, Ms Emery has spent 20 years designing and delivering strategy, managing change and unlocking potential across the world's largest law firms and other professional service firms. She particularly loves to work in the context of transformational change and unites fierce intellect, big heart, and sleeves-up pragmatism to deliver lasting results. She led the three-way merger of CMS, Nabarro and Olswang in 2017.

Ms Emery is passionate about the power of purpose, storytelling and wholehearted leadership to transform business, communities and society.

Ms Emery is a trustee of Spurgeons Children's Charity and a non-executive adviser to start-ups in the legal sector.

Laura Empson
Professor in the management of professional service firms, Cass Business School
Laura.Empson.1@city.ac.uk

Professor Laura Empson is director of Cass Business School's Centre for Professional Service Firms, and senior research fellow at Harvard Law School's Center on the Legal Profession.

She has dedicated the past 25 years to researching professionals and the professions. Her research into professional service firms, funded by a series of prestigious government grants, encompasses themes as diverse as: leadership and governance; organisational, cultural and identity change; professionalisation of management; mergers and acquisitions; knowledge management; professional careers and social mobility and partner evaluation and reward systems.

Professor Empson is committed to translating her academic research for a practitioner audience. Her latest book is *Leading Professionals: Power, Politics, and Prima Donnas* (Oxford University Press, 2017) and her most recent *Harvard Business Review* magazine article is "How to lead fellow rainmakers" (March 2019). Her BBC documentary "Insecure Overachievers" was broadcast in September 2018.

From 2013 to 2016 she was an independent non-executive of KPMG LLP (becoming INE chair in 2015). She acts as an adviser to many of the world's leading law, accounting, investment banking, actuarial and management consulting firms, and is a regular speaker at partner conferences.

Professor Empson was previously associate professor at the University of Oxford. Before becoming an academic, she worked as an investment banker and strategy consultant.

She has a PhD and MBA from London Business School. Visit www.lauraempson.com.

Deborah B Farone
CEO, strategic marketing adviser, Farone Advisors LLC
deborahfarone@gmail.com

Deborah Farone is an adviser to law and other professional service firms on business strategy and targeted marketing and is a speaker at professional forums and retreats. She has served as chief marketing officer at two of the world's most successful law firms, Cravath, Swaine & Moore LLP and Debevoise & Plimpton LLP. At both firms, she built and led their marketing communications and business development departments. She has also held positions as a marketing specialist at two global advisory firms, Willis Towers Watson and Ketchum.

Ms Farone is the author of *Best Practices in Law Firm Business Development and Marketing* (PLI, 2019), a book based on more than 60 interviews with leading law firm leaders and marketers, general counsel, and innovators in the profession. The book has been called a unique resource for law firm leaders, practising attorneys, legal marketers, consultants and educators who want to uncover the best marketing practices in the legal profession.

Ms Farone is also past president of the Legal Marketing Association's New York

Chapter and was recently honoured with LMA New York's Legacy Award, in recognition of making "a distinguishable mark on the chapter and the profession".

Jaime Fernández Madero
Founder, Fernández Madero Consulting
jfm@fmaderoconsulting.com

Jaime Fernández Madero is a consultant in strategy and management law firms in Latin America. He is the founder of Fernández Madero Consulting (FMC), associated with Hildebrandt Consulting. Mr Fernández Madero was one of the founders of Bruchou, Fernández Madero & Lombardi, one of the leading law firms in Argentina.

Mr Fernández Madero provides advice to law firms on a variety of matters including strategy, management, leadership and governance and talent. He is the author of *Organizando Firmas de Servicios Profesionales. El caso de los Abogados*, published in 2012 by Thomson Reuters La Ley.

Mr Fernández Madero is a visiting professor at Management de Firmas Legales en Latinoamérica, organised by the IE Law Executive Education programme, and director of Universidad Di Tella, Argentina, for the Management de Estudios Jurídicos programme.

Heidi K Gardner
Distinguished fellow, Harvard Law School
hgardner@law.harvard.edu

Heidi K Gardner, PhD, is a distinguished fellow at Harvard Law School's Center on the Legal Profession and faculty chair of the school's Accelerated Leadership Program. Previously she was a professor at Harvard Business School. Dr Gardner's book *Smart Collaboration: How Professionals and Their Firms Succeed by Breaking Down Silos* was published in 2017 by Harvard Business Press, and became a *Washington Post* bestseller.

Named by Thinkers 50 as a Next Generation Business Guru, Dr Gardner recently co-founded the research and advisory firm Gardner & Co (www.GardnerandCo.co).

Dr Gardner has authored more than 70 books, chapters, case studies and articles. She is a regular contributor to *Harvard Business Review*. Her research received the Academy of Management's prize for Outstanding Practical Implications for Management.

Dr Gardner has lived and worked on four continents, including as a Fulbright Fellow, and for McKinsey & Co and Procter & Gamble. She earned her BA in Japanese from the University of Pennsylvania, a master's degree from the London School of Economics and a second master's and PhD from London Business School.

Herminia Ibarra
Professor of organisational behaviour, London Business School
hibarra@london.edu

Herminia Ibarra is the Charles Handy professor of organisational behaviour at London Business School. Prior to joining LBS, she served on the INSEAD and Harvard Business School faculties.

An authority on leadership and career development, Thinkers 50 ranks Ms Ibarra among the top management thinkers in the world. She is a member of the World Economic Forum's Expert Network, a judge for the *Financial Times*/McKinsey Business Book of the Year Award, and one of Apolitica's 100 most influential people in gender policy. She was the 2018 recipient of the Academy of Management's Scholar-Practitioner Award for the contributions of her scholarly research to management practice.

Ms Ibarra is the author of best-selling books including *Act Like a Leader, Think Like a Leader* and *Working Identity: Unconventional Strategies for Reinventing Your Career*. She writes regularly in the Harvard Business Review and leading academic journals as well as business publications including the *Financial Times, Wall Street Journal*, and *New York Times*. Ms Ibarra speaks internationally on leadership and organisational transformation.

A native of Cuba, Ms Ibarra received her MA and PhD from Yale University, where she was a national science fellow.

Mark Mortensen
Associate professor, Area Chair INSEAD
mark.mortensen@insead.edu

Mark Mortensen is an associate professor of organisational behaviour, based in Fontainebleau France. He holds both a PhD and MS from Stanford University, as well as a BA from Colby College. His research focuses on the changing nature of collaboration, with a particular emphasis on global/virtual work and dynamic and overlapping teams. He publishes his work in a range of academic, professional, and popular press outlets and his contributions have been recognised through academic awards as well as leadership and editorial board positions. He teaches in many custom and open-enrolment executive programmes, the MBA core, and the doctoral programme. He also consults widely on team dynamics, global work, power and networks, and related topics. Prior to joining INSEAD, Professor Mortensen was on the faculty at the MIT-Sloan School of Management and McGill University School of Management.

Rebecca Newton
Organisational psychologist, London School of Economics and Political Science;
CoachAdviser
rebecca@coachadviser.com

Rebecca Newton is an organisational psychologist and senior visiting fellow at the London School of Economics and Political Science in the department of management. Dr Newton has spent 20 years advising clients and teaching on leadership, change and management practice. Her doctoral research was in the psychology of change leadership in law firms. She was a visiting fellow in the psychology department at Harvard University, and has taught executive education for LSE, University of Cambridge and on the Accelerated Leadership Program at Harvard Law School. Dr Newton serves on the editorial board of the *Journal of Change Management*, is a regular keynote speaker, contributor to the *Harvard Business Review*, and is the author of *Authentic Gravitas: Who Stands Out and Why*.

Dr Newton is the CEO of CoachAdviser, a coaching and consulting practice based in London, working with clients globally on leadership, professional and team development, collaboration, organisational culture and change.

Rebecca Normand-Hochman
Leadership consultant and coach, Institute of Legal Talent & Leadership
r.normand-hochman@
legaltalentandleadership.org

Rebecca Normand-Hochman is a leadership consultant and coach who brings research-based people management strategies to the legal sector. Since 2010, she has been working with leaders and partners of international law firms across Europe to help them build and implement refined talent and leadership approaches and develop effective personal leadership styles.

Through her consulting and coaching work, Ms Normand-Hochman has done hundreds of psychometric assessments to measure the competencies, motivations and needs that lawyers have in the various stages of their development in over 40 areas (client relationships, ability to manage stress and pressure, to influence others, to lead teams, etc).

In parallel, Ms Normand-Hochman is the founder and a director of the Institute of Legal Talent & Leadership which helps legal organisations and individual lawyers implement talent and leadership best practices for themselves and their teams. Through the institute, she researches, consults and writes with a number of other experts in the field of leadership in the law. She is an officer of the International Bar Association's Law Firm Management Committee and is the editor of four books published by Globe Law and Business in partnership with the International Bar Association.

Larry Richard
Founder and principal consultant,
LawyerBrain LLC
drlarryrichard@lawyerbrain.com

Dr Larry Richard is the founder and CEO of LawyerBrain LLC (www.lawyerbrain.com), a consulting firm that serves premier law firms and corporate legal departments in the areas of leadership, change management, talent selection and development, feedback, motivation and lawyer resilience and well-being.

Dr Richard is recognised as the leading expert on the psychology of lawyer behaviour. A graduate of the University of Pennsylvania Law School, he was a litigator for 10 years before earning his PhD in psychology from Temple University. Since then, he has gathered and analysed personality data on thousands of lawyers, and consulted with hundreds of legal providers on a wide range of complex issues.

Known for his ability to distil cutting edge scientific principles into actionable recommendations for improving lawyer performance, Dr Richard is a frequent presenter at professional conferences, and a sought-after keynote speaker.

Scott A Westfahl
Professor of practice, director of Harvard Law School Executive Education
swestfahl@law.harvard.edu

Scott Westfahl is a professor of practice and the director of Harvard Law School Executive Education. Within the law school's JD curriculum, he teaches courses on leadership and innovation. In his executive education role, he oversees the law school's global leadership programmes for law firm leaders, general counsel and other lawyer-leaders. He also collaborates with HLS colleagues and other Harvard faculties to design and teach custom programmes for law firms, law departments and other legal-related organisations. He focuses his executive education teaching and writing on leadership and teams, innovation, the motivation and development of professionals and organisational alignment from an innovation, talent development and diversity and inclusion perspective. Prior to joining the HLS faculty in 2013, Professor Westfahl practised law and led talent development within large law firms and also led professional development for McKinsey's Washington DC office. He graduated from Harvard Law School in 1988.

Peter Zeughauser
Chair, Zeughauser Group
zeughauser@consultzg.com

Peter Zeughauser is chair of Zeughauser Group, a legal consultancy. He has served as lead adviser on over 25 mergers and acquisitions for market leading international, national, regional and boutique law firms, including the largest ever transatlantic law firm industry merger, two of the three 2018 transatlantic combinations, the first alliance combination between an Am Law 100 firm and a PRC law firm (2005) and most of the strategic PRC–US law firm alliance combinations that followed, including alliances under the Shanghai Free Trade Zone regulations, which were modelled on the pioneering 2005 alliance combination. In his role as a trusted merger adviser to law firm leaders, clients have noted Mr Zeughauser's skills at partnership consensus building, identification, assessment and building value propositions for merger opportunities, facilitating bilateral discussions and analysis of data exchanges and negotiations, and integration of partnership structures, capital requirements and accounts, compensation and systems and other key terms.

Kent Zimmermann
Principal, Zeughauser Group
zimmermann@consultzg.com

Kent Zimmermann is a principal with Zeughauser Group. He is one of the leading strategy advisers to law firms in the US. Last year, he advised on each of the three largest law firm mergers to close worldwide. He is currently advising multiple firms on active merger discussions, and he is also advising three Am Law 25 firms on firm-wide strategy.

A former general counsel and chief executive officer, Mr Zimmermann counsels and provides insights to industry leaders on the challenges and opportunities they face as a result of the segmentation, specialisation, consolidation, and globalisation of the legal services market. As part of this work, he routinely conducts one-on-one interviews with chief legal officers, managing directors and business unit heads at market leading Fortune 500 and global companies.

Mr Zimmermann is valued for his sophisticated understanding of the evolving legal market and inside knowledge of the strategies and best practices of high-performing law firms.

Modern Legal Practice

Globe Law and Business

Modern Legal Practice
Business • Strategy • Leadership

Editorial
Robert McKay

Us Too? Bullying and sexual harassment in the global legal profession
Kieran Pender

The lawyer sandwich – a lot of baloney and a little pickle ... tenaciously entrenched on a slab of sourdough
Agnes Foy

Culture eats strategy for breakfast
Darryl Cooke

Leadership in law firms – indulgence or necessity?
Christopher Saul

Learning to lead
Monica Burch

How partners can develop the leadership qualities your firm needs
Rebecca Normand-Hochman

How leadership challenges evolve over the career of a lawyer
Christopher Bockmann

Flexibility: the new business imperative in law firms
Manar Morales

Strategy and why it is important
Nicholas Luckman

A competent legal procurement team is worth their weight in gold – insights from the 2019 Legal Procurement Survey
Dr Silvia Hodges Silverstein and Rebecca Bell

Legal touch: the secrets of staying top-of-mind
Itzik Amiel

Book Review
Lynne's Laws of Leadership – 20 Big Lessons for Leading a Small Law Firm
By Lynne Burdon
Review by Robert McKay

Globe Law and Business

July 2019 • www.globelawandbusiness.com

Subscribe today and as a new subscriber receive:

- Your first issue free of charge
- 20% discount on your first year's subscription

Publication dates:
Quarterly
Hard copy ISSN:
2398 - 5410
Hardcopy only:
£295 per annum
Discounted price:
£236 per annum

Go to **http://modernlegalpracticeoffer.globelawandbusiness.com** for full details and subscription offer.

About Globe Law and Business

Globe Law and Business was established in 2005, and from the very beginning, we set out to create law books which are sufficiently high level to be of real use to the experienced professional, yet still accessible and easy to navigate. Most of our authors are drawn from Magic Circle and other top commercial firms, both in the UK and internationally.

Our titles are carefully produced, with the utmost attention paid to editorial, design and production processes. We hope this results in high-quality books which are easy to read, and a pleasure to own. All our new books are also available as ebooks, which are compatible with most desktop, laptop and tablet devices.

We have recently expanded our portfolio to include a new range of journals, Special Reports and Good Practice Guides, available both digitally and in hard copy format, and produced to the same high standards as our books.

We'd very much like to hear from you with your thoughts and ideas for improving what we offer. Please do feel free to email me on sian@globelawandbusiness.com with your views.

Sian O'Neill
Managing director
Globe Law and Business

www.globelawandbusiness.com

New Special Report

Globe Law and Business

For full details, go to
www.globelawandbusiness.com/PFL

New Good Practice Guide

Globe Law and Business

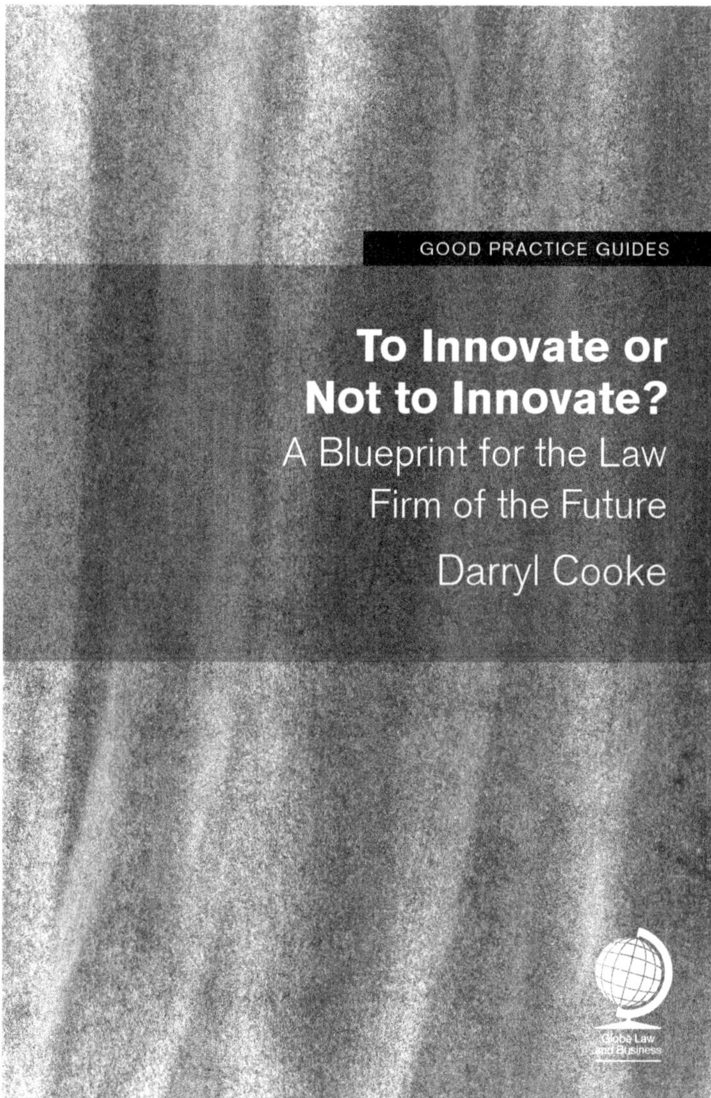

"Cooke rightly concludes that the management of law firms is "an awesome responsibility" because management decisions don't just impact those who work at the firm – those decisions also impact their families and friends. Sprinkled throughout the stories, discussions and facts supporting why and how firms can evolve, are many insightful (and for law firms, revolutionary) Cooke-isms."

Mitchell Kowalski
Strategic Advisor on Legal Operations and Author

For full details, go to
www.globelawandbusiness.com/inn

New Special Report

Globe Law and Business

"Eminently readable and based on long experience, this special report is applicable to – and certainly useful for – any lawyer in any stage of a legal career, from early days to pre-retirement."

Phillip Taylor MBE and Elizabeth Robson Taylor
Richmond Chambers

For full details, go to
www.globelawandbusiness.com/LAW

www.ingramcontent.com/pod-product-compliance
Ingram Content Group UK Ltd.
Pitfield, Milton Keynes, MK11 3LW, UK
UKHW062251150926
8656IPUK00007B/39

9 781787 422865